Early Encounters—Native Americans and Europeans in New England

Early Encounters—Native Americans and Europeans in New England

From the Papers of W. Sears Nickerson

Delores Bird Carpenter

Michigan State University Press
East Lansing
1994

All Michigan State University Press books are produced on paper which meets the requirements of American National Standard of Information Sciences— Permanence of paper for printed materials ANSI Z39.48-1984.

Michigan State University Press
East Lansing, Michigan 48823-5202

02 01 00 99 98 97 96 95 94 1 2 3 4 5 6 7 8 9

Library of Congress Cataloging-in-Publication Data

Nickerson, Warren Sears, 1881-1966
    Early Encounters—Native Americans and Europeans in New England : from the papers of W. Sears Nickerson / [edited by] Delores Bird Carpenter.
        p.   cm.
    Includes bibliographical references and index.
    ISBN 0-87013-351-9 (alk. paper)
        1. Indians of North America—New England—First contact with Europeans.
    2. Indians of North America—New England—History. 3. New England—
    History—Colonial Period, ca. 1600-1775.
    I Carpenter, Delores Bird. II. Title.
    E78.N5N53   1994
    974'.01—dc20   94-19500
                                                                      CIP

To thank Nick who understands why
and
To honor my Cherokee heritage

Contents

Life and Legend on Cape Cod

Native American History and Genealogy

Illustrations

Acknowledgments

It is with sincere appreciation that I acknowledge the many people who assisted in the research and preparation of this manuscript. I thank Charlotte Price, the curator of the William Brewster Nickerson Memorial Room at Cape Cod Community College, for calling my attention to the few pieces by W. Sears Nickerson in the Memorial Room. I am grateful to the daughters of W. Sears Nickerson for permitting me to prepare this publication based on their father's papers. I am especially grateful to his daughter, Jean C. Primavera, who shared with me her memories of her father and who followed through on my many requests. Mark Hertig, Museum Curator of the Archives of the Cape Cod National Seashore, South Wellfleet, Massachusetts, which houses most of the Nickerson material, gave total support to this project and was very tolerant of my many interruptions into his routine schedule. Thomas R. Doyle and Michael Whatley, also at the Cape Cod National Seashore, were likewise very helpful. I thank Elizabeth A. Little, editor of the *Bulletin of the Massachusetts Archaeological Society*, for giving me permission to reprint the two articles by Nickerson that appeared in the *Bulletin* and for introducing me to Great Moose (Russell H. Gardner) who sent me copies of his correspondence from Nickerson. Brian Cullity, Curator of the Art Museum at Heritage Plantation in Sandwich, Massachusetts, contributed the photo of the painting of "The Wading Place Bridge," which is used by permission of The Cape Cod Five Cents Savings Bank. Doug Flynn loaned me his collection of books on Native Americans and early settlers. David Still contributed to the formation of the title.

I gratefully acknowledge the host of librarians who helped along the way. I can always count on the staff at the library at Cape Cod Community College: Greg Masterson, the director; Adrienne Latimer,

Jeanmarie Fraser, Nancy Kiehnle, Patricia Fisher, and Mary Sicchio, reference librarians; and Kathleen Kersey in inter-library loan. Alexa Crane, reference librarian at the Sturgis Library in Barnstable, Massachusetts, which has the Stanley Smith Collection, was very helpful. Other librarians whom I wish to acknowledge are the following: Gregory H. Laing, Haverhill Public Library; Florence Fitts, Falmouth Historical Society; Dottie Hanson, Yarmouthport Public Library; Patrick Flynn, Virginia Smith, and Catherine Craven, Massachusetts Historical Society; Ernestine Gray, Mashpee Archives; Mary Reynolds, Fall River Public Library; Lee Regan, Plymouth Public Library; Randall Mason, Sturgis Library; Paul Cyr and Tina Furtado of the Special Collections at the New Bedford Free Public Library; Jennie Rathbun and Roger Stoddard at the Houghton Library; and Jane Fiske at the New England Historical Genealogical Society.

Gretchen Widegren, Graphics Technician at Cape Cod Community College, took many of the photographs, including those courtesy of the Cape Cod National Seashore.

A number of people helped with entering primary material into the computer, with photocopying, or with proofreading. I thank Connie Connell for typing some of the pieces. I am indebted to Connie Connell and Kathleen Malenky Bent for indexing and to George Daniel Bent, Jr., six weeks old, who permitted his mother to work at this task. The following Project Forward students under the supervision of Delynda Walker entered some of the primary material into the computer: Elizabeth Tazewell, Anusha Piyasena, Eric Wexler, and Allen Northcutt. I thank Manuel Silveira, Carol Call, and Dick Northrop for photocopying; Dick, who heads Cape Cod Community College's Copy Center, on several occasions dropped whatever he was doing to fill my requests. I am grateful to Frederic Keith Carpenter and to Keith William Bull who helped with proofreading. Also, Frederic Carpenter introduced me to Sandra Rodrigues.

Sandra Rodrigues, a historian with special interest in European expansion, Canadian and French exploration, and the Plymouth Colony, entered the project as I just passed the half-way mark. She served as a researcher, doing much of my "footwork," locating sources for articles where no citations were made, looking up primary sources that were cited, and checking the accuracy of the text against these sources, always furnishing me a photocopy or the text, itself, for my verification. She grouped the works for the table of contents and wrote most of the first draft of pages 8-16 of the introduction which placed Nickerson's accounts in historical context. Not only did she enable me to finish the project sooner but she also gave me new insights into the material.

I thank Dean Hosni Nabi, Associate Dean Bruce Bell, and Dr. Lore Loftfield DeBower for granting me release time to finish this book.

I cannot imagine doing the project without the help of E. Carleton Nickerson, President Emeritus of Cape Cod Community College and nephew to W. Sears Nickerson. Nick's contributions to this book, which were almost daily, were so consistent, so numerous, so varied in nature, and so broad in scope that it would be impossible to list them all. He was my cheerleader all the way.

I am grateful to Fred C. Bohm, Director of the Michigan State University Press, who made many suggestions, especially toward the improvement of the introduction, and to Julie L. Loehr, Editor in Chief, and Kristine M. Blakeslee of the MSU Press for their roles in editing and production. I would also like to thank Michael Brooks, who designed the cover and the text, and Jane Latham for all her work behind the scenes at the Press.

Introduction

Columbus: The First Encounter

In 1986 D. W. Meinig[1] called attention to the dual meaning of the word "encounter." "In the benign sense, it means 'to meet unexpectedly.' But in its root sense, it means 'to meet in conflict.'"[2] W. Sears Nickerson through his historically-based accounts of first encounters between Native Americans and Europeans in New England encompasses both these meanings, whereas the current revisionist views of Columbus, the man credited with *the* first encounter, have stressed the root meaning. Since there is a tendency (however illogical) either to credit or to blame all that has taken place since 1492 on Columbus's landing and since all other landings have shared many similarities and have bred parallel consequences, it is helpful to compare and contrast subsequent contacts with that most celebrated (albeit notorious) model. The plethora of books on the subject of Columbus in the wake of the Quincentenary speaks to our need to once and for all "set" history straight on the matter. As the numerous writers have no doubt realized, this is no easy task.

There are many difficulties in obtaining a fair historical reading of Columbus's explorations. Surviving accounts are often difficult to assess after the passage of time. Columbus was secretive and could be vague, contradictory, and self-serving in what he wrote. His elevation to heroic stature has further distorted the history. The Columbian Quincentennial saga is incomplete because that is the nature of history. "All works of history . . . are interim reports. . . . History is not only what happened long ago but it is also the perception by succeeding generations of those events and those people."[3] It is this organic aspect of history that was experienced in the Quincentenary.

1

The world was changing . . . and so was Columbus's reputation in history. World war and relentless strife, tyranny and greed, widespread poverty amid plenty, and economic expansion that ravages nature without necessarily satisfying basic human needs—modern life was making disbelievers of many who once worshipped at the altar of progress. If they now doubted progress, they also came to question Columbus, who had been the icon of progress. . . . The Columbus of 1992 is the postcolonial and demythologized Columbus. He has been stripped of the symbolic cloak of optimism and exposed as a human being whose flaws were many and of reverberating consequence. The imagery imposed on him is now more apt to be that of pessimism concerning the human condition. Another Columbus for another age.[4]

It is generally agreed that Columbus was motivated by wealth, fame, and hereditary titles.[5] A religious desire to provide riches for crusades in conquest of Jerusalem is also evident.[6] Also, using the Aristotelian doctrine of natural slavery, Columbus sought to increase the monetary benefits of his voyages by enslaving the native populations.[7] His exploitative attitude was fixed at the outset,[8] as was also noted by John Noble Wilford in *The Mysterious History of Columbus*, who wrote, "Not for anthropology had he sailed across the ocean, and increasingly his journal entries reflected an interest less in the people as they were than in what they and their land could mean for Spain."[9]

In judging Columbus, one should be reminded that "'Uncritical adulation and (equally uncritical) lambasting . . . are both unhistorical, in the sense that they select from the often cloudy record of Columbus's actual motives and deeds what suits the researcher's Twentieth Century purposes. That sort of history caricatures the complexity of human reality by turning Columbus into either a bloody ogre or a plaster saint.'"[10] Perhaps, the best assessment of Columbus is that "he was a consummate mariner . . . but his skill and fortune deserted him on land."[11]

No doubt of greater significance than the issue of "ogre" or "saint" is that "Today the world is even more closely linked than it became in October 1492. This, then, may be the most significant result of Columbus's voyages—not that he discovered 'a new world' but rather that, from his time on, two 'old worlds' merged into one. In this new world we must learn the intricacies of living interrelated lives."[12]

Indisputably, the arrival of Columbus produced a clash of cultures further hampered by death by disease, by cultural oppression, by disrespect for native culture or traditions, by colonization, by violent usurpation of native lands, and by brutalization of native inhabitants.[13]

The subsequent explorers of occupied shores, with goals as varied as those of Columbus, invariably encountered vast cultural differences.

Anthony Pagden observed, "the traveller, the discoverer, the settler, the immigrant, the missionary and the colonist: all such people came to America with battered ambitions, different expectations and different objectives. But if they were at all sensitive, they all in time came to see that, culturally at least, incommensurability was inescapable." They wanted to transform unfamiliar cultures of which they had no prior understanding, into something recognizably like their own.[14]

Atrocities

Verbal communications between Europeans and Indians collapsed on fundamental cultural and philosophical differences.[15] With these cultural clashes, the resulting atrocities and the pattern of revenge or retaliation were set in motion. With Columbus, the tenor of his milieu is often recalled to show how ingrained violence was.

What Huizinga calls "the violent tenor of life" in the fifteenth century was so pervasive—death was so daily, brutality so commonplace, destruction of the animate and inanimate so customary—that it is shocking even in our own age of mass destruction. . . . At the simplest level there was the violence of everyday life. . . . At another level there was the sanctioned violence of local authorities whose punishments were meted out on a daily basis on the scaffolds of the public squares in almost every town and city. . . . On a higher level still, there was the Church-sponsored violence known as the Inquisition . . . under whose jurisdiction countless millions were imprisoned, by whose decree countless hundreds of thousands were killed. . . . Then, finally, there is the violence of nation-states such as Spain, just then forming in Europe, and the principalities, duchies, margravates, republics, seigneuries, dominions, earldoms, and noble factions and royal families of all sorts, each one struggling to determine which should dominate in that formation and how wide its scope should be. To them, deadly violence was nothing less than the daily stuff of politics.[16]

People of such background made contacts with natives (who had their own violent confrontations with other native groups and their own methods for meting out justice within their own groups) which initially were friendly. Such honeymoons were short-lived as some incident invariably happened, potentially having its roots in cultural ignorance, no doubt oftentimes rooted in insensitive natures with possibly evil motives. This set up a never-ending chain of retaliations. The eye for an eye theology of revenge became a vicious cycle. Only a few of many examples will suffice to illustrate this pattern.[17]

Las Casas described an incident in 1502 in the time of Nicolés de Ovando. The Spaniards then enjoyed friendly relations with Indians on Saona Island, near Santo Domingo, and frequently visited them to get Cassava bread. On one visit, tranquillity was shattered when a dog, for a laugh, was told to attack the chief, whereupon the dog, tearing the chief's intestines out, killed him. Revenge followed, as was often the case, on those who had nothing to do with the incident.[18]

In New England, it should have been no surprise when natives met their unfamiliar visitors with hostilities. In 1602, when Bartholomew Gosnold came into Elisabeths Isle on Buzzard's Bay, some natives helped the English dig sassafras and feasted with them, yet within less than two weeks four natives attacked two crewmen. Perhaps the natives' change in attitude had something to do with Gosnold's stealing a canoe that four men had abandoned in fear. Or perhaps they resented Gosnold's group being amused at their response to hot mustard which they could have thought to be poison. In 1603, English sailors on a voyage under Martin Pring were digging sassafras at a barricaded post on the tip of Cape Cod when Pring's party stole a large birch bark canoe and released, when they tired of the natives' eager company, their two great mastiffs. Such friendly beginnings often ended in tragedy.[19]

Therefore,

what the Pilgrims called "The First Encounter" was not, except for them. Fresh from European ports, the Pilgrims could not know that the natives who received them so ungraciously were not acting out of some atavistic racial hatred or primitive xenophobia but from a well-founded sense of revenge for injuries inflicted by earlier European visitors. By 1607 or 1620, when most textbooks before the '70's began the American story, many of the native peoples of the Atlantic seaboard had experienced fifty or a hundred years of contact with European ships, men, and erst-while colonies. Predictably, many of those contacts ended in suspicion, fear, and conflict.[20]

Nickerson's account of "The First Encounter" is a classic example of this animosity. The Native Americans made a surprise attack on the Pilgrims as they were breaking camp, though this should have been expected based on the behavior of the Pilgrims on two previous explorations when they took a kettle, all the ears of corn they found, and as much loose corn as they could carry. Later, they returned to "Cornhill" and found the rest of the corn which they had buried and took it as well. They also dug into some graves, suspecting from the beginning that they were graves.

Nickerson's story "First Blood: The Death of the Carpenter of St. Malo" relates the death of a white man in a skirmish over a kettle. This account, however, has a positive note in that the problem was not with the group of friendly Nawsets who had previously greeted them, and Champlain, Captain in Ordinary to the King and Royal Geographer, believed the Nawset Sachem when he said that his men had not killed the carpenter; therefore, Champlain released his hostage who proved to be a friendly Nawset.

Nickerson's "The Fight at Fortune—Champlain at Stage Harbor" is quite another story. After several friendly encounters with the native population, the tide turns, this time over the issue of a hatchet. A series of retaliatory horrors follow.

Nowhere is the retaliation cycle more vividly illustrated than in Nickerson's account of "Mary Corliss Neff" where grisly details of the massacre by the Native Americans under French leadership is followed by paralleled horrors perpetrated primarily on native children by two white mothers and a young lad.

Isolation Versus Technology

Since American Indians developed their ways of life in very nearly complete isolation, the growth of their civilizations was hampered and their defenses against the major Old World diseases, especially smallpox, were weakened.[21] "Spanish military technology—ships that used sails as well as oars, arquebuses, cannon, metal armor and swords—was formidable. Effective, too, were their four-footed compatriots—the mastiffs and the horses."[22]

Other explorers had similar technological advantages. "The ships coming to the Americas carried soldiers, merchants and missionaries. The missionaries' role of pacifying and evangelizing the indigenous peoples in the Americas was indispensable. With this process completed, the seizure of the land and mineral wealth was made easier."[23] The church legitimized racism. Words like "heathen" and "pagan" made it acceptable to cast aside legal and ethical norms in dealing with native people. Such a usage of the church continued into Nickerson's life, as is evidenced by a letter to Nickerson from Warren K. Moorehead about the Tercentenary in Boston in 1930. Moorehead, who was in charge of the Stone Age village to be managed by descendants of the New England Indians wrote, "I would prefer to have Penobscot and Passamaquoddy Indians because an assistant to the priest who has them in charge could come down and maintain discipline."

Cultural Clashes

Nickerson, at least, made a Herculean effort to use his imagination in depicting native people, especially in his works "The Old Sagamore—Mattaquason of Monomoyick," "Micah Rafe—Indian Man: Last Full Blood on Lower Cape Cod," and "The Praying Indians of Lower Cape Cod." James Axtell understood that "Imagination is the key to moral understanding. . . . But Europeans, even those who moved to the new worlds, remained incapable of recognizing 'the others' they met as both *different* from and *equal* to themselves."[24]

The fact that these encounters took place on the Indians' turf forced them into a primarily defensive mode. "To counter this offensive, the natives resorted to five basic strategies, which were not always sequential or mutually exclusive: initially, they tried to *incorporate* the newcomers; when that failed, they tried at various times to *beat* them, to *join* them, to *copy* enough of their ways to beat them at their own game, and to *avoid* them altogether."[25] Nickerson writes about these different strategies. "The *Sparrow Hawk*" is an example of incorporation of Governor Bradford and his men. The stories of "Micah Rafe" and "The Old Sagamore" are of efforts to beat, to join, and especially to copy enough of the white men's ways to best them at their own game.

When two cultures encounter, usually both are changed. Acculturation in New England was the result of the specific plans of one people to change the other. According to James Axtell, "'The Indian, in their [New England settlers'] lights, was immoral, pagan, and barbarous. So, characteristically, they tried to remake him in their own image through the time-honored but formal institutions of English education—the church, the school, and the college.'"[26] On the other hand, Europeans did not always encounter the native population from such a self-acknowledged position of superiority. The western frontier is an example of settlers adopting native ways for survival, meaning a steady movement away from the influence of Europe.

Mutual Exploration

Too often, in cataloging all the negatives of Columbus's "discovery" of the Americas, we forget that "the process of exploration has itself typically been multiracial and multicultural."[27] "First Blood: The Death of the Carpenter of St. Malo," "The *Sparrow Hawk*," "Exploit of a Cape Cod Indian at Louisbourg," and "The Praying Indians of Lower Cape Cod" show mutuality of exploration and acculturation. James Axtell explains that, with good reason, the theme of the Columbian Quincentenary was the *mutuality* of discovery and acculturation during five-hundred years of ongoing "encounter." He points out that the theme of the Quadricentenary in 1892 was far different.

> In Spain and the United States particularly, the dominant cause of celebration (not mere commemoration or reflection) was the progress of Western technology, Christian religion, and democratic institutions over the Western Hemisphere, particularly among the "benighted" and "primitive" peoples Columbus "discovered" (as if they were lost). . . . Unacknowledged were the cataclysmic ravages of disease, warfare, injustice, and dispossession that were the major (but not only) legacy of that encounter. No accounting was made of the frightful human toll of history, the incalculable costs of "progress," "civilizations," and "empire."[28]

Among those who between the 1892 Quadricentenary and the Quincentenary in 1992 endeavored to tell anew the history of a few of these encounters was W. Sears Nickerson, a man who in many ways had turned his back on the 1892 perspectives and reached forward through his imagination of the "otherness" of "others" toward 1992 in surprising ways.

Content of Nickerson's Research

In the pages of this book, the reader will find incidents of first encounters that span the coming of the Vikings circa 982, the arrival of the French in 1605, the settling of the English in 1620, and the subsequent wars among the French, the English, and the Native Americans from 1690-1745. These incidents include the first conflicts at Nawset Harbor, at Stage Harbor, and at First Encounter Beach, their cooperation at Louisbourg, and the effect of the Praying Indians in preventing attacks on settlers. Yet, there is also the horror of the attacks on the early settlers and the equally appalling counter attacks, especially those of two white women, Mary Corliss Neff and Hannah Duston. W. Sears Nickerson's research has covered the entire range of the human predicament: birth, love, ecstasy, tragedy, and death. Moreover, one will read a reflective exploration, not enjoyed by the early Europeans, of the lives, legends, histories, and genealogies of some of the Native Americans who were all but annihilated by the unrelenting certainty with which the Europeans tackled the task of subduing the wilderness and its inhabitants.

One problem faced in addressing the Nickerson papers is reconciling this variety within his work. While the parts can clearly be grouped under larger themes, the wide range makes it necessary to give each some historical context, however superficial, in order to make more visible the common thread within the works themselves and their natural link with the progression of both Nickerson's roots and his research.

The Vikings

Long before the arrival of W. Sears Nickerson's ancestors on the *Mayflower*, the coast of North America was visited by Vikings and by French explorers. Nickerson describes the experiences of these earliest visitors in several of his writings, and his descriptions reflect the state of historical discussion of the earlier twentieth century. In "The Wineland of Leif the Lucky," Nickerson relates a composite story of Viking sagas from original sources. In this work, Nickerson tries to prove that Leif's predecessor, Biarni, landed at Cape Cod. In trying to prove his point, Nickerson uses his own knowledge of sailing and navigation in an attempt to pinpoint Biarni's sailing distance. However, Nickerson fails to realize that modern notions of time, distance, navigation, and technology cannot be applied to sailing during the tenth century.[29] Therefore, it should be noted that Nickerson's claim is based on speculation, rather than solid evidence.

The French

Nickerson also relates several stories of first encounters between North Americans and the French. The early history of the French in North America was a troubled one and inevitably involved conflict with the English and several Indian tribes. Something must be said about French exploration in the early seventeenth century as it relates to both "First Blood: The Death of the Carpenter of St. Malo" and "The Fight at Fortune—Champlain at Stage Harbor." French fishermen had spied the coast of North America long before Champlain did. Early exploration throughout the sixteenth century was financed by the French for political and economic reasons. The French were struggling to maintain the balance of power in Europe. Like other European monarchies, the French were also looking for riches and a quick route to the trading wealth of the Far East. Among the explorers for France were Giovanni da Verrazzano who explored the North American coast, discovering New York and Narragansett Bays, and Jacques Cartier who discovered the St. Lawrence River.

In "First Blood," an account of the earliest authentic record of the killing of a white man by a Cape Cod Indian, Nickerson identifies the man who was killed as the title character. While Nickerson fails to document where he located this piece of information, it is a good possibility that this claim is correct. St. Malo was an important French port, famous for its capable sailors, including Cartier.[30] It is quite possible that the man Nickerson writes about was indeed a carpenter from St. Malo.

It is interesting to note that Nickerson chose to write about violent confrontations between the French and the natives. The two above-mentioned articles may lead one to believe that the French had only poor relations with Native Americans during the early period of exploration and settlement. However, this was simply not the case. While the French had their share of problems with some of the tribes (notably the Iroquois), they were also able to ally with others further to the north. In addition, the French had to maintain friendly relations with at least some of the tribes if they hoped to profit from the fur trade. In this lucrative enterprise, Native Americans acted as middle men; therefore, good relations were necessary to keep it going.

Nickerson deals mainly with French exploration rather than colonization. The French established a settlement at Port Royal in 1605, but the first permanent settlement was at Quebec in 1608. Champlain was instrumental to French settlement as well as exploration. Even today we are indebted to Champlain for his written accounts as well as his maps. He was also a key player in forging the alliance with the northern Indian tribes.

The motivation behind French exploration and settlement was mainly economic. In this respect New France was successful, as the fur trade brought great wealth to France. However, the nature of the fur trade was not conducive to French settlement, since the lifestyle of fur traders was nomadic. These traders had to travel great distances to barter and trade furs. This activity led to the establishment of distant trading outposts deep in what is now the continental United States. In the French mercantile system, colonization was always secondary to the fur trade and the money it brought in. Throughout the period from discovery and well into the eighteenth century, the French viewed New France as a place to make money, not as a potential new home. Settlement was a consideration but not a priority.

The Arrival of the English

Before getting too far into the story of New France, it is necessary to introduce another player in this drama—the English—especially since five of Nickerson's articles deal with passengers of the *Mayflower*. The story of the Pilgrims is one that most Americans have heard. As children, we are taught that the Pilgrims came to this country for religious freedom. We also are told that once they arrived on the shores of North America, the Pilgrims got along so well with the Indians they encountered that the two groups shared the first Thanksgiving together. As Nickerson pointed out, these accounts are inaccurate. As children we never hear how the passengers of the *Mayflower* took all the corn and beans that they found in an Indian village, purposing to pay the Indians if they should meet them again.[31] The fact that they did so six months later must have been little solace to the Native Americans who had lost their food supply and the seed to plant the next year's crop. In retrospect, it is not surprising that the new inhabitants soon met with hostility.

Religion was unquestionably a factor in the Pilgrims' search for a new home. Some of the Pilgrims were Separatists from various parts of England who chose to organize a religion outside of the established church. Persecution of Separatists was merciless throughout the country. As a result, religious freedom was the motivating factor behind the Separatists' move to Holland in 1608.

William Bradford wrote about the reasons for the Separatists' move to North America. The first reason he cited was economic. As immigrants, the English could only get low-paying, menial jobs that allowed them a low standard of living in the united provinces. The Separatists faced difficult times in Holland and felt that they could not endure such hardships much longer. Life in Holland was so bad that Bradford wrote, "yea, some preferred & chose ye prisons in England rather than this libertie in Holland, with these afflictions."[32] It was the hope of Bradford and his fellow Separatists to find "a place wher they might have libertie and live comfortably."[33]

Bradford stated that the move to America was also inspired by the Separatists' children. The Separatists were bothered by the "evil examples" their children were exposed to. They were upset over the "great licentiousnes of youth in yt countrie" to which many of the children had succumbed.[34] Some of the younger Separatists were leaving the fold and adopting lifestyles "tending to dissolutnes & the danger of their soules."[35] It must be kept in mind that the Separatists were conservative Puritan extremists. Other religious groups of the day would not have been so incensed over this supposed corruption. For example, the Separatists were appalled by the "feasting" of the Dutch after church on Sundays. Therefore, in order to better protect the souls of their children, the Separatists decided to move.

Another reason Bradford gave for emigrating to America is seldom mentioned. Bradford wrote that the Separatists had a desire to spread their religion. "Lastly, (and which was not least,) a great hope & inward zeall they had of laying some good foundation, or at least to make some way therunto, for ye propagating & advancing of ye gospell of ye kingdom of Christ in those remote parts of ye world."[36]

Bradford never explicitly stated that the Separatists were leaving Holland for religious freedom. Religious freedom was a necessary consideration when choosing a place to relocate, but it was not a reason to leave. It is highly doubtful that the Separatists would have left Holland solely for religious freedom unless their safety was threatened.[37]

It also must be noted, as Nickerson points out, that the Separatists were not in favor of religious toleration. They wanted the freedom to practice their own religion, but they were not at all tolerant of other beliefs. This is quite evident in their condemnation of the Dutch and in their persecution of Quakers in the New World. At the time that the Pilgrims made their voyage, Europe was involved in its last great religious war, the Thirty Years War (1618-1648). The idea of religious toleration was still not widely accepted. Most who participated in the wars of religion believed that eventually one religion, their religion, would defeat all others and restore Christian unity; the Separatists were no exception.

Not all of the people who came to America on the *Mayflower* were Separatists, and not all of the Separatists made the journey from Holland. Many remained in Holland for the rest of their lives.

The Landing

The debate has not been resolved as to why the *Mayflower* landed at Cape Cod and later Plymouth rather than Virginia as originally intended and stated in the charter. Some say that it was by accident or due to fault on the part of the ship's captain, Christopher Jones.[38] Still others say that the shift to a different site was a deliberate move to steer clear of the Anglican Church in Virginia and avoid further persecution.[39]

The Pilgrims were "permitted" to settle in North America by a series of patents, granted first from the Virginia Company and later from the Council of New England. They were financed by a group in England called the Adventurers. As a result of this financial arrangement, the Pilgrims established a communal system by which they abided until 1627. During this time no individual could own land or personal property. The colonists found this situation unsatisfactory, and, in 1627, they secured the right to own land and work for personal gain.[40] After this time, the colonists began to govern themselves in a more democratic way. The Governor of Plymouth and his assistants were chosen by free men. In 1636, a body of laws was codified.[41] Plymouth colony was short-lived, however, as on 7 October 1691, it was incorporated into the Massachusetts Bay Colony.

Native Inhabitants

Long before any of these settlers arrived in North America, there were numerous native groups inhabiting the land. In the New England area, several key groups must be mentioned. The Nawsets occupied Cape Cod; the Wampanoag and Pokanoket lived in the Plymouth area, and the Massachusetts lived around Boston. The Nipmuck lived in the area that is now western Massachusetts. Rhode Island was occupied by the Narragansett and the Nehantic. The Pequot, Mohegan, and Nehantic lived in what is now eastern Connecticut. These territories were fairly well-defined since the indigenous population of this area was not nomadic. Each group had its share of rivals and enemies, and the arrival of the French explorers and the English settlers changed the balance of military power among the native peoples of the region.

When western Europeans came face to face with the long-established cultures of New England, conflict was inevitable. And whereas the French and the English could not get along in the Old World, they likewise did not get along in the New World. Although conflict was inevitable, war was not constant. Some of the tribes coexisted peacefully with the French and the English. In fact, when the time came to choose sides in a conflict, Native Americans often allied with either the French or the English so as to gain an upper hand against their own tribal enemies.

Nickerson writes about many encounters between the natives and the Europeans. Most of the incidents about which he writes involve conflict and violence. They were narrow in their focus, so it is important to place them in a proper historical setting. For example, the kidnapping of Mary Corliss Neff and Hannah Duston occurred during a time of war in the colonies when such incidents were not uncommon.[42] Since they are isolated in focus, the implications of such stories can lose significance if one is not aware of the broader context of the specific incident.

Accounts of violent encounters such as "First Blood: The Death of the Carpenter of St. Malo" and "The First Encounter" cannot be fully analyzed without engaging in a great deal of speculation about the state of mind of the Native Americans, none of whom left written records of these incidents. The reader must ask what motivated such aggression. On the surface, it looks as though Native Americans were at fault. However, since there are no native sources to describe these encounters, we must read between the lines of written sources such as Champlain and Bradford. We cannot ignore the fact that these accounts are likely to be biased in many ways. Such a statement is not made to slight Champlain, Bradford, or any of the others who left us their invaluable accounts. However, in our efforts to reexamine history in a context relevant to our own time, we cannot ignore the fact that the only extant sources were written by European men who saw themselves as superior to the native "savages." It is not likely that, in the event of conflict with the natives, that these authors would be willing to admit that Europeans were aggressors or that they provoked a fight. It is possible that writers like

Champlain and Bradford may well have omitted facts that would show the Europeans in a negative light. This is not to say that they lied (although that, too, is possible); rather they may have skewed or omitted facts. They also may have been unaware of what actions were deemed offensive by the natives. For all of these reasons, we must keep in mind that our primary sources are likely biased. If the natives had written accounts of the exact same incidents, it is probable that they would differ significantly from those written by Europeans.

Other encounters fit more easily into an overall historical sketch. The French and the English had both friends and enemies among the various Indian tribes. Overall, the French had a better relationship with them than the English did. The main problem the French had with the natives was their continuing conflict with the Iroquois. Early in the history of New France, Champlain allied the French with various Indian tribes such as the Huron and the Algonquin.[43] This early alliance was mainly established for commercial reasons—to further the fur trade. It ultimately led to conflict with the enemy of these tribes, the Iroquois. In addition, the Iroquois later allied with the English, which only worsened the French situation.

With the notable exception of the Iroquois, the French had a relatively good relationship with groups in New France. One of the main reasons the French had better relationships with Native Americans than did the English was due to the economic bases of the respective societies. Those who settled New England were not only trying to make money but also were looking for a place to live.[44] If one doubts the desire of the English for land, then one need look no further than the Pequot War of 1637 to find proof of this desire. Problems started when settlers from Massachusetts Bay Colony began to establish settlements in what is now Connecticut. They had no legal right, either from the English or from the natives who lived there, to begin this expansion.[45] The rate of settlement grew without apparent order for about four years. The result was a series of violent exchanges between the Pequot, the Niantics, and the European settlers. The colonists viewed the war as a struggle between Good (themselves) and Evil (the Indians). The decisive end to the conflict came with an attack on the Pequot village at the mouth of the Mystic River. This Pequot settlement consisted of 300-700 people. This surprise attack, which took place when the majority of the men were away from the village, was a brutal massacre that brought an end to the once great strength of the Pequot. The few who were not slaughtered during the attack were either killed later or were enslaved. The Treaty of Hartford in 1638 dissolved the Pequot Nation.[46]

Although Nickerson makes no mention of this war, it is important to mention it here because it set a precedent for all future relations between

European colonists and Native Americans in New England and elsewhere. In this case, settlers of Massachusetts Bay, Plymouth, and Connecticut were able to put aside their religious differences and unite to defeat a common enemy. Indians for many reasons did not do this. The Narragansett sided with the English against the Pequot, thus aiding in the destruction of their old enemy, the Pequot Nation. It was not until later, when the Narragansetts themselves were threatened, that they realized the necessity of Indian unity for strength. Ironically, it was the Narragansett who later led the pan-Indian movement to defend the Indians against the English threat.[47]

The French and Indian Wars

Nickerson wrote about the exploits of several people during the French and Indian wars. These wars were, in fact, a series of conflicts that corresponded to larger conflicts on the European continent. The first of these wars was known as King William's War in the colonies and as the War of the League of Augsburg in Europe (1688-1697).[48] The colonies were soon drawn into the conflict. The French, the English, and the Indians, notably the Iroquois, were all involved in the hostilities. The Iroquois were trying to stop French expansion south of the Great Lakes and also wanting to divert the center of the fur trade from Montreal to Albany and hence from France to England. Once the French and English went to war in Europe, war naturally broke out in the colonies.

It was during this war that the events inspiring stories about Mary Corliss Neff and Mary Smith took place. King William's war was not characterized by campaigns and organized battles; the hallmark of this conflict was guerrilla warfare. The French and their allies on one side and the English and the Iroquois on the other engaged in a series of raids, surprise attacks, and border skirmishes in New England, New York, and New France. The two sides did not face each other on an open battlefield as was the practice in Europe. Surprise attacks were made against defenseless towns whose inhabitants had done nothing to provoke them. Innocent people on both sides were massacred or taken prisoner. One of these random attacks was at Oyster River in 1694.

The main reason Oyster River was singled out for an attack was because the French and their Indian allies were running out of supplies; naturally they decided to take them from the nearest English settlement.[49] One hundred and four people were killed at Oyster River on 18 July 1694, and twenty-seven others were taken prisoner.[50] Of these twenty-seven prisoners, Nickerson wrote about the captive Mary Smith.[51]

Queen Anne's War

Another conflict that served as a backdrop for a Nickerson story was Queen Anne's War (1702-1713), which in Europe was called the War of the Spanish Succession.[52] It was during this war that the adventure of Elizabeth Vickery occurred.

Not surprisingly, another European war had spread to the American colonies. Almost immediately French Canadians resumed border warfare and attacks that they had engaged in during King William's War. New England was once again the primary target. Elizabeth Vickery was one of the people caught in the middle during a French raid on a Cape Cod trading sloop on which she was traveling to Boston to buy her wedding attire.[53]

This transatlantic war ended in 1713 with the Peace of Utrecht. It is difficult to say who won. It is probably better to describe it as a stalemate. A Bourbon was placed on the throne of Spain, but the French were forced to make concessions in the colonies. The French lost Hudson's Bay, Newfoundland, and Acadia "according to its ancient limits."[54] The French were also forced to recognize English authority over the Iroquois.[55] Peace lasted in both Europe and the colonies for more than twenty-five years after this war.

The War of Austrian Succession

The War of Austrian Succession broke out in Europe in 1740. In the colonies, this was known as King George's War, and hostilities did not begin until 1744 when France declared war on England. This conflict began in Europe when Maria Theresa ascended the throne of Austria. Although her claim was legitimate since she was the daughter of the previous ruler, other European nations, discounting a woman's claim to the throne, saw this as an opportunity to attack Austria. With only England and Holland as her major allies, Maria Theresa had to fight to keep her throne.

Maria Theresa's plight was probably of little interest to the colonists or the Indians. Their main concern was that France and England were at war again and it was time to choose sides. The most famous incident in this struggle was the taking of the French fortress at Louisbourg, an important naval base on Cape Breton Island. This was also basically the headquarters for French privateers who attacked ships from New England. When the New Englanders saw their chance to attack Louisbourg, they took it. Nickerson describes the actions of an Indian from Cape Cod during the taking of the Grand Battery at Louisbourg in "Exploit of a Cape Cod Indian at Louisbourg—1745."

The capture of Louisbourg was a short-lived victory. When France and England sat down at the peace table in 1748 to iron out the details of the Treaty of Aix-la-Chapelle, it was decided that Louisbourg would be returned to France. In relation to the colonies, the treaty basically involved the return of pre-war colonial boundaries for France and England. Maria Theresa kept her throne, but the English lost Louisbourg.

The French and Indian War

The last in this series of colonial wars was known simply as the French and Indian War (1754-1763). The European counterpart to this war was the Seven Years War. Unlike the earlier struggles, this one began in America. The Treaty of Aix-la-Chapelle had done nothing to resolve land disputes between France and England in America. The bone of contention was the possession of the Ohio Valley. The English colonists were moving into this region and competing fiercely with the French in the fur trade. England also wanted to acquire additional land for settlement of its growing population. The French believed the Ohio Valley was theirs and that the English had to be expelled in order to protect the fur trade.

This dispute became the last great conflict involving the French, the English, and the Indians in the American colonies. Not surprisingly, given English expansion most Indians chose to side with the French. They understood that the English wanted their land more than they wanted to trade. As we all know, the English won the war. The French forces were seriously divided between the Canadian faction and the French faction that came from Europe. Even worse, the command was divided as well. In the end, France lost almost all of its American possessions, and the Indians would eventually suffer the same fate.

W. Sears Nickerson

Sometimes Fate follows a peculiar path in selecting the chroniclers of her history. An uneducated seaman turned undertaker, confined by his heart trouble, seems an unlikely candidate to become a historian. Yet, the *New Bedford Standard Times* in June 1957 reported that an Ormond Beach, Florida man, who had documentary proof that nine of his ancestors were aboard the original *Mayflower* when it made its historic voyage, was keeping a daily progress chart on the then current ocean crossing of *Mayflower II*, the replica of the ship which brought 120 Pilgrims to America in 1620.

"They were a tough bunch," W. Sears Nickerson said with a faint smile. "And if you want to know what a Pilgrim looked like, take a look at me." We did. We saw a tall man with gray hair and searching eyes that seem to scan all horizons. His slender figure and erect carriage make it hard to believe he's 77. And for a brief moment, we saw a Pilgrim standing barefoot on the *Mayflower's* deck clad only in a short sleeved shirt and walking shorts, which were Nickerson's attire during the interview.

It may seem astonishing that a descendant of passengers on the *Mayflower* would seek to become a member of an Indian tribe. Yet, Nickerson, a man of contrasts who understood both cultures, wrote Supreme Chief Sachem Ousa Mekin in 1928, asking him about becoming a member of the tribe.[56] Mekin responded,

as for becoming a Member of the tribe, that is problematical just now. Though you could join the National Algonquin Indian Council[57] as an Associate member or tribal if you know you are an Indian, and the Tribe you belong to.

Earlier in the letter Mekin wrote, "You may have Indian blood in you. Would be glad to know it, or to help you if I can." He gave Nickerson the secretary's address to write, adding,

You might mention my name as I am Chairman of the Com. on applications for Membership and will be pleased to recommend you for Membership. You will then be in line for further action later on in our Cape Tribes, for unless we should adopt you into one of the Tribes, *you can't join*. Old Customs die hard and that was our way.

This dichotomy grew out of the outward facts of Nickerson's life, that is his personal route with Fate, and out of his devotion to his origins on Pleasant Bay (The Bay), his probing of its mysteries, romanticizing their possibilities, and his subsequent reliving of them through his self-spun dramas based on careful research of a people exterminated by his ancestors when they settled the new land.

Birth

The outward facts of Nickerson's life are simple. He was born Warren Sears Nickerson in East Harwich, Massachusetts, 5 December 1880, the youngest in a family of nine boys and three girls.[58] He wrote,

My father Warren Jensen Nickerson, married Mary Atkins of Chatham, who was the daughter of a deep-water sea captain, Captain Joshua Atkins.[59] They set up housekeeping in the old Enos Rogers house northwest across the swamp from grandfather Nickerson's. Father was a district schoolmaster in those days, "boardin'" "'round" with the parents of his pupils in proportion to the number of children they had in school. He taught everything from the ABCs to Navigation, but it was not long before the hungry mouths of his own growing brood outdistanced the meager salary of a country school teacher. He turned to the sea for a living as most Cape Codders were doing at that period and finally joined the cod-fishing fleet which harbored in The Bay. In later years he pioneered in the newly developed cranberry culture and made that his sole occupation. . . . The house where mother and father lived and where I was born is now (1949) owned by a Mr. Hubbard and is only a short distance from my Nick-Shack. It was built in 1807 during the `Embargo' and the wide boards for its floors and panelling were run in through the blockade. . . .[60]

Early Memories

Early memories of New England life were important to Nickerson. Among his earliest recollections were watching the great ocean going vessels pass by the back of the Cape and looking for the fishing boats coming in around Great Point. Sometimes he would see the *Cynosure* or the *Louie & Rosie,* commanded by his brother Josh, or the *Abel W. Parker* or the *Charles H. Sprague,* of which another brother Oscar[61] was skipper. "Then we at home would dip our flag to say "Hello" and "All's well", while they in turn would signal back to us with the ship's ensign. It was no uncommon thing in those days to count fifty to one hundred sail off the Back Side [of Cape Cod] at one time."[62] It was a red letter day when his mother let the youngsters stay up to carry hot coffee down to the Bay shore when the boat-fishermen were late.[63] His sister Geneva, a writer herself, wrote to him, recalling their childhood: "I thought of the days when we cavorted over the hills sending forth wild war whoops, then flinging ourselves flat on the ground where the one bedraggled rooster's feather sticking in our hair mingled with the waving, sweet fern leaves." As a young man on many a dewy morning on Baker's Tarkil Meadow, Nickerson poled the salt hay with his father. Poling hay meant carrying it in little stacks on two horizontal ten-foot poles with a person on each end between the poles. Haying time to "the medders" was a heyday. Well-heeled with scythes, whetstones, and good old Jamaica rum, the mowers went down The Bay on the first of the ebb, ran their scow aground on the salt marsh, and mowed around her until the turn of the tide.[64]

Pleasant Bay

Since Pleasant Bay is central to much of his writing, being both source and inspiration for much of his work, it is important to note Nickerson's observations about that body of water:

> From the front door of my Nick-Shack I can overlook the whole length and breadth of The Bay. From there I see the mid-summer sun break up out of the eastern rim of the Atlantic and peer in through The Narrows as through an open window, to waken its sleeping waters. At sundown I watch the smoky sou'wester roll its blanket of fog down out of the Head of The Bay to put its waves to sleep again. And through the stillness of the night there comes up to me the soft lullaby of the incoming tide on its sandy shore.[65]

The waters of the Pleasant Bay and those of Nauset Harbor (formerly spelled Nawset) are the only area estuaries emptying directly into the Atlantic. The Bay's basin is actually a kettle hole left from the last ice age. The name Pleasant Bay does not seem to have come into general use until sometime in the eighteenth century. It was Monomoyick to the Indians, which probably meant Great Bay in their language. The Indians pronounced it Mono-mo-yick—the last syllable ending in a k—and the white men who visited while it was still Indian land and heard this name from the Native Americans tried their best to convey this sound in writing about it. Captain Thomas Dermer, the first white man of record to enter The Bay, spelled it "Manamock" in his letters in 1619. When the Pilgrims came down to Nawset from Plymouth in 1621 to take off the lost Billington boy,[66] they tell us of an Indian from "Manamoyacke" whom they met there, and the following year Governor Bradford himself led a corn-buying expedition right into "Manamoyake Bay." In 1626, Bradford again headed a relief party to the aid of the distressed crew and passengers of the *Sparrow Hawk*, shipwrecked "right before Manamoyack Bay." In later years, the Indian word was corrupted into Monomoit and finally into Monomoy (not to be confused with the current day Monomoy Point). Today the name Monomoyick is as completely lost to Pleasant Bay as the Native Americans to which it once belonged. Later, area residents adopted the literal English translation of the Indian word, calling it The Great Bay until it became Pleasant Bay.[67]

> From my front door I can also see the hills over The Bay under the lee of which my immigrant ancestor built his pioneer cabin. He was the first white man to settle in the Land of Monomoyicks. His house stood at the head of Ryder's Cove in Chathamport next door to the wigwam of the

Old Sagamore from whom he bought his land [in 1656]. Here they grew old together, the white man and the red, good neighbors always.[68]

Almost every foot of land from the West Shore of The Bay around Great Point and so on down the harbor to the Bars can trace its title to the deeds from the Monomoyick Sachems to William Nickerson and his children. . . . From that day to this, for nearly three hundred years and through ten consecutive generations straight down to me, the children and children's children of the Immigrant and his wife Anne have lived, loved, and with one exception been buried in the lands bordering The Bay.[69]

Nickerson at Sea

Leaving The Bay and the Orleans High School after the tenth grade, Nickerson sailed the Seven Seas for almost twenty years and touched at most of the world's major ports in the days of the square-rigger. Once he was a sailor on a Vanderbilt yacht. That was when one was considered a seafarer only after surviving a six-month apprenticeship on a windjammer's rolling deck; if a novice's stomach survived salt pork and hardtack for half a year, he could call himself a sailor. One time, when he was rounding the Cape on a sailing ship homeward bound for Boston, Nickerson recalled probably one of his most poignant memories from those days: "We cleared Chatham Bars, headed north up the beach, and as we opened out by Strong Island I took my spyglass and shinned up to the mizzen cross-trees. There, across The Bay, framed in the doorway of our old home with the morning sun striking full upon her, was my mother. She has been dead these fifty years but that picture is as plain in my memory today as if it were yesterday."[70] Another time in his seagoing days, while on the beach looking for a ship, Nickerson roomed at a boarding house run by a fortune teller. To stretch out her budget, she held seances on the side, and to help out Nickerson's finances, she gave him a job pulling the strings behind the scenes for her table tippings and used his voice to provide the answers from her spirit friends.

Marriage

After his years as a sailor, Nickerson returned to Harwich to become a steeplejack. He chose that occupation and followed it a couple of years because it was the nearest thing to shinnying up a mast. He decided that when people reach their thirties their ideas should become more settled. He married Donna May Corliss (1893-1973), a young woman from Wolfeboro, New Hampshire, on 1 September 1918. She had been the brightest in her class in Brewster Free Academy and had attended Mount Holyoke on a four-year scholarship to study to become a secondary teacher in Latin and English. She had a temperament different from Nickerson's. She was straight-laced, private; he was emotional, a romantic who cried at movies and was a great lover of Nelson Eddy. He was a people watcher and loved to meet people from whom he could learn. Although he was not a deeply religious man in the traditional sense, he was fond of hymns. He enjoyed getting together with his siblings. He was a stern father, more like a grandfather, not affectionate, but proud of his children. He was also a handyman who could fix anything he put his mind to. He was thought not to be sophisticated in the ways of business as he was "on the margin" borrowing for stock and was caught in the crash of 1929; he later told his daughter, Jean, "never invest in stock." Despite his unfortunate business ventures, Nickerson remained a conservative Yankee. This inherent frugality was exemplified by his attitude toward paper; he wrote on all kinds of used papers—letters he received or, a favorite, the back of the absentee bulletins that daily came to his wife's classroom. If he made a mistake while writing a letter on clean paper, he just turned the paper around and started over.

The Nickerson household was a peaceful one. Nickerson greatly admired his wife's college education; in turn, she was supportive of his writing. Nickerson told one potential publisher, "I will have my wife go over the text and correct my slips in punctuation, paragraphing, as well as general grammatical errors. She is a Mt. Holyoke graduate and a language teacher, while I got my A.B. as able seaman in a school where a split main-topsail was of much more concern than a split infinitive." They had three children: Mary, Jean, and Dorothy.[71] Nickerson had also had two children with his first wife, Imogene Howes Small: Mary and Elizabeth.[72]

Careers

After his brief career as a steeplejack, Nickerson next turned to what he thought would be his life's profession. He took a course at the Massachusetts School of Embalming. He then built a successful undertaking business in Harwich; he took great pride in his work, receiving great satisfaction in making someone look good in death. Nickerson also became involved in community service, serving on his hometown Board of Selectmen (city council). In addition, he was treasurer of the Cape Cod Chamber of Commerce, a director of the Cape Cod Trust Co., and he took part in many local Masonic, civil, and religious affairs. He said one reason for his success at the polls as a Harwich Town official was because half of the voters were named Nickerson. "So how could I be defeated on election day?" Much later, when the Nickerson Family Association started, Nickerson was in demand to speak at the July Brooks Park, Harwich Center annual meetings of 200 members.

Shortly before 1930, Nickerson had a heart attack, and it was then that the doctor told him he would have to move to a warmer climate, to relieve the strain cold weather placed on his heart. Nickerson liquidated the family's Harwich interests and moved first to 11 Framar Lane, Wellesley Hills, Massachusetts, for a drier climate and also thinking the girls could go to Wellesley College. From there he moved his family to Daytona Beach, making what he called a last ditch stand against possible adversity.

The need for leading a quiet life inspired Nickerson to open a gift shop in 1932. "This venture," says Nickerson, "survived wars, blackouts, depressions, and hurricanes and was one of the few to remain so long in the Main St. section" of the city.[73] He went into retirement 30 September 1952, at age 72.

Research and Writing

With much time on his hands after his heart attack, W. Sears Nickerson took up as hobbies the study of genealogy and research into the history of Indians in New England. From this interest in his own genealogy, which was readily traced back to the *Mayflower,* coupled with his sea-going knowledge, he wrote a book published in 1931 by Houghton Mifflin Company entitled *Land Ho!—1620: A Seaman's Story of the Mayflower Her Construction, Her Navigation and Her First Landfall.* Seven hundred and fifty copies were printed. Years later, in 1957, Nickerson received recognition for his research with the production of a medal, designed and cast by sculptor Berthold Nebel for the Cape Cod Pilgrim Memorial Association, to commemorate the arrival of *Mayflower II* in Provincetown Harbor. Of the one hundred medals struck, Nickerson received one with a presentation letter which included the following: "Some of our Directors, who have read your book "Land Ho" refer to it as the most authentic, interesting and best written book on the voyage of the Pilgrims and their life."[74] Nickerson later said of the book: "If I were to ever write it over I could condense it a great deal and give it better continuity. However, I was bed-ridden at the time, and it took me back aboard ship where I could forget my own troubles in trying to solve those of the *Mayflower.*" He tried to get the *Reader's Digest* to publish a paper on the first New England Town Meeting, condensed from *Land Ho!—1620,* which was referred to by him as a collector's item. Nickerson also told them, "so little of an authentic nature concerning the *Mayflower* and her passengers ever reaches the public eye." As to the paper's accuracy, Nickerson referred the editors to Samuel Eliot Morison of Harvard University[75] and Harry F. Sherman of the General Society of *Mayflower* Descendants, both of whom were familiar with his work. He added that he still held a certificate of seamanship for square-rigged ships.

In addition to writings that resulted from his personal genealogical research, Nickerson's extensive study of Native American genealogy and culture made him an unquestioned authority of the Lower Cape Indians. A Thanksgiving Day 1954 letter to his nephew Josh,[76] who was trying to get the Chatham Historical Society to publish Nickerson's papers on the Lower Cape Cod Indians, best describes his work.

I use the term "Lower Cape" to signify the terrain from Bass River to Provincetown. I have identified about thirteen hundred Indians by name in this territory, assembled them into families where possible, and grouped the families into the three Tribes into which they seem naturally to fall, namely The Monomoyicks, The Nawsets, and The Sauquatuckets. What I have learned about each individual is authenticated by references to old deeds, documents, court records, military lists, and the like. Taken as a whole, my Papers give a complete picture of Indian Life on the Lower Cape from the landing of the first white man until the last half-breed Indian hit the final trail to Mashpee or Gay Head.

The border lines between these three Tribes were not marked by definite maps and bounds, as you, of course, know. Nevertheless, they followed well known and distinguishing landmarks. Roughly, the bounds of the Monomoyick Tribal Lands, beginning at Allen's Harbor in Harwich Port, followed the sea around Monomoy Point and up the Back Side to Pochet. Pochet Highlands, as its name implies, was the dividing line between the Monomoyicks and the Nawsets, "poshe" according to the Natick Indian Dictionary meaning literally "it halves or divides." From here the line ran to Town Cove and out through Boat Meadow to the North Shore, where it followed the coast to Nameskaket. From there it turned inland again through Cliff Pond to Long Pond and Grassy Pond and so back to Allen's Harbor. Everything north of the Pochet-Great Meadow boundary was part of the Nawset Sachemry, while west of the Nameskaket-Long Pond line the Sauquatucket lands stretched up to Bass River, the Hokanom Marshes, and Nobscusset.

After the death or disappearance of Sachem Aspinet of the Nawsets in the abortive Indian plot of 1623 to wipe out the white colonists, Mattaquason, who was about the only Indian sachem between Boston and Provincetown not implicated in the plot, became the dominant leader of the Lower Cape Tribes. On the confirmation deed of the

Nawset Purchase, signed by all the "Ancient Indians," his name alone
was honored by the title "Sagamore." The disintegration of the Nawsets
and Sauquatuckets as tribal entities was swift and complete, and
Mattaquason gave their dwindling ranks a sanctuary out of his Tribal
Lands in what we know today as South Orleans. Here they hung on for a
while and became known as the Potanumicut Tribe. . . .

Mattaquason became known as The Old Sagamore, and my notes give
a completely documented history of him and his family from the time of
his birth, circa 1600, down to the death of his great great granddaughter
Hosey Ralph in 1800. She was the last of his blood-kin to live and die on
the ancestral Tribal Lands, as well as the last full-blooded Indian woman
on Lower Cape Cod. She was born, lived, died, and was buried within a
stone's throw of your [Josh's] house in East Harwich. This two hundred
year period covers the whole story of the Monomoyicks after the landing
of the white men.

I have my notes grouped under three covers. "Group I, The
Monomoyicks," made up of about one hundred and fifty single-spaced,
typewritten sheets . . . containing about sixty-four thousand words and
listing the names of some two hundred and seventy Monomoyick
Indians. These are assembled into families as far as possible; the information on each individual is documented by reference notes at the bottom
of each page, and each volume is indexed.

"Group 2, The Nawsets," contains about two hundred sixty-seven
sheets, one hundred and twelve thousand, five hundred and seventy-five
words, and the names of seven hundred sixty-five Nawset Indians,
arranged, documented, and indexed as above.

"Group 3, The Sauquatuckets," contains about seventy sheets,
twenty-nine thousand, eight hundred and fifty words, and the names of
two hundred and seventy Sauquatucket Indians, arranged, documented,
and indexed in the same manner.

This sums up to approximately four hundred and eighty-seven sheets,
two hundred and six thousand, four hundred and twenty-five words,
including a general introduction, explanatory maps and indices, and covers the lives of one thousand, three hundred and five Lower Cape Cod
Indians.[77]

Publishing Efforts

Nickerson devoted much of his life to finding a publisher and a depository for his Native American research. The Peabody Museum of
Archeology and Ethnology, Harvard University, currently has two

papers: "Micah Rafe," and "The Old Sagamore." Nickerson was trying to place the papers there 22 July 1942 when he referred the director to Henry Crocker Kittredge of St. Paul's School, Concord, New Hampshire, author of several books on Cape Cod history, for validation of Nickerson's knowledge on the subject. Donald Scott, the director, warned on 30 July 1942, that they were without funds to purchase such material. On 16 October 1942, Scott wrote that he and Dr. Brew were very much interested in what Nickerson had in his possession.[78]

In 1945 Nickerson tried to attract the interest of the New England Historic Genealogical Society. On 8 February 1945, the editor of their *Register*, William Carroll Hill, wrote,

> May I say that our library would be very glad to have for its permanent files and for preservation such Indian genealogical records as you would care to send us.
>
> While the Register custom does not permit of the printing of a genealogical record of Indian tribes, as such, it seems to me that a general story, dealing with the genealogical aspects of the Cape Indians would be most fascinating and interesting to our readers. By way of illustration there might be brought out in it some of the outstanding Red Men who dealt with the Pilgrims and something about their families.

He referred to it as a novelty. In a letter dated 18 May 1945, Hill declined to publish Nickerson's articles, saying the society was deluged with genealogical matter relating to the early New England families of English descent; he did, however, offer the society as a depository for Nickerson's data.[79]

Nickerson also wrote Stephen T. Riley, librarian of the Massachusetts Historical Society,

> I am presenting this copy of my story of "The Old Sagamore, Mattaquason of Monomoyick" to the Massachusetts Historical Society as a small thank offering for the many bits of bygone lore in its Collection which have been helpful to me.
>
> As you will see, this is not the product of a trained genealogist or historian. It does seem to me, however, that it would be too bad to just throw aside all this authenticated material, representing as it does years of tracking down the records of the old Indians of Lower Cape Cod, simply because it is the result of a layman's hobby and presented in unscientific language.
>
> I know it is of but slight interest to the general public whether Mattaquason was an Indian sagamore or an Indian dog, but I trust you can find room for it somewhere in your Collection where it will

be preserved and perhaps help some one else who may be interested in this particular subject.

On 23 September 1953, Riley requested to see a copy, but today there is nothing at the Massachusetts Historical Society by W. Sears Nickerson.

Nickerson's nephew, Joshua Nickerson, worked very hard for several years trying to help his uncle achieve publication. Among Josh's many efforts were contacts with Alice Guild, president of the Chatham Historical Society; Karl Murchison of Provincetown, who was editor of several journals in the field of psychology; Douglas S. Byers, Director of the Robert S. Peabody Foundation for Archaeology; Ted Weeks, editor of the *Atlantic Monthly*; and Charles Seymour, a long-time summer resident of Chatham, who was president emeritus of Yale University.

On 22 January 1956, Nickerson, perhaps embarrassed at the fruitless labor on his behalf, wrote to Josh, "But I had a good time writing them, and the time spent on them was a life saver for me. What I would really like to do is to have all my completed papers published under one cover, perhaps titled 'My Cape Cod Scrap Book,' or something like that. But I believe a publishing house would require an advance fee. I appreciate very much the good try you have made in my behalf and am sorry I cannot write in the frothy, catchy manner which sells regardless of whether or not the text facts are correct. I have to stick to the straight, narrative style and have my statements documented which means little to most people."

Massachusetts Archaeological Society

Nickerson, following his own leads, was finally able to find a publisher for two of his articles with the Massachusetts Archaeological Society. He wrote defensively in February 1957: "I have had some rather raw deals from be-lettered people who got hold of other Indian material of mine, gleaned from it what they could use and then returned it with a notation that it was of little value—forgetting to erase their cribbing pencil check marks. I am no trained researcher, but I have accumulated a large amount of documented material on the historical background of the Lower Cape Cod Indians which so far as I know cannot be found in any published work. All I ask is that I be given credit for the pioneering work I have done."

Understandably timid in the face of the possibility that they might consider his material, he wrote on 3 April 1957, to Maurice Robbins, the Director,

I was one of a family of twelve children and to keep the wolf from the door started going to sea when about fifteen years old. That about ended my "book larnin'," and the rest of my education was mostly picked up out of the dictionary and on shipboard in different parts of the world. I got a lot of geography free, but the only letters it added to my name were A. B.—Able Seaman—earned the hard way in the fo'c'sle of old time, deep water square-riggers. Those don't get you far among Indian scholars.

My grandfather gave me a good start in Indian lore when I was a lad. . . . I never lost my interest in things Indian and always looked forward to the day when I might have time to go to the records and verify some of the things I carried in my head. That time never came until I had come ashore and turned landlubber and then only because I wound up practically incapacitated physically by coronary trouble. It was then I took up the Indian trail in earnest to help me to forget the pain and to keep me from going nuts.

In the meantime I have collected genealogical items on hundreds of the Lower Cape Indians and thereby picked up quite a bit of their history since the coming of the white man. But I am still nothing but a ham operator; I do not speak the language of you trained specialists although I can understand yours; I do not even know the proper form for attaching reference notes to my papers.

. . . I feel it would be a waste of time and energy for me to cross swords with such recognized authorities as Mr. Speck.[80] You know, the High Church used to burn sailors at the stake for suggesting that the earth was round, and while I am familiar with his conclusions, he and I do not see the Cape Cod Indian world alike.

Robbins wrote Nickerson 21 April 1957,

You should not depreciate your abilities as a writer, the papers you sent along are excellently written, indeed, they could be published with a minimum of editing I assure you. Most important they are largely new information resulting from your own research, well documented, and excellently organized. These should by all means be published as the information they contain should be available to scholars. I knew Frank Speck very well (he is now deceased) and I know that he was not at all satisfied with his Cape Cod work. Were he alive he would be the first to welcome new information which would correct and amplify his brief study of the Cape Indians. If such material is not available in print the writers will do just as I did and copy Speck. We are all of us very glad when someone like yourself speaks up to correct us.

Speck did his best work among the Indians of Maine and his book called "Penobscot Man" is probably the best available on the Indians of that area. However, when he tried to work in Massachusetts and on the

Cape he did not fare as well. However as his is about the only modern work on that area it is largely used, as in the case of my paper. I wish you would allow me to send your manuscript to our Editor, Mr. Leaman F. Hallet, for publication in our Bulletin. We have a circulation of about 600 and cover the entire country. About seventy-five of the larger institutions of learning are among our subscribers.

On 5 May 1957, Nickerson replied,

Nevertheless I still can't shake that mean little inferiority complex which I am sure every self-educated person feels when he comes in contact with specially trained scholars. [Setting aside most of his insecurity and modesty, he continued,] I had never even considered the possibility that any Society such as yours would think it worth bothering with. Would it be copyrighted if you publish it, and would I get my copy back intact? It is the only good one I have. And would it be considered in any way unethical for me to continue sending in short sketches on this and related subjects to such local newspapers as the little *Cape Codder*, as I now do from time to time?

In the meantime, Josh was "checking out" the Massachusetts Archaeological Society. The middle of May, Josh quoted Douglas Byers:

"Indeed I do know about the Massachusetts Archaeological Society, having been one of those who assisted at the accouchement. It is [a] bunch of amateurs, some of whom consider themselves archaeologists, but most of whom are passively interested in 'Indians.' They have more than 500 members, but no spare money in the till. All their cash goes to publishing their quarterly Bulletin, except for a small bit used to run the Society, and some which they contribute to keep a rather nice museum going in Attleboro.

"Robbins was president for a time, then editor, and has been active for many years; however, he is no longer editor. That post is now filled by Leaman F. Hallett, 31 West Street, Mansfield, Massachusetts. He is a stockbroker by trade, but from the point of view of intimate knowledge of the Indians of New England, not only as individuals but also as regards their habits and history, is probably more well informed than anyone in New England since Gookin, who was the Indian agent in 1670 or thereabout."

Nickerson and Robbins continued to correspond. On 7 June 1957, Maurice Robbins wrote him explaining that he would receive five complimentary copies of the *Bulletin* in which any article written by him appeared.

June 13, Nickerson responded from Ormond Beach Florida where he had retired: "I like to take along my irreplaceable papers on my Indians and my ancestors for safe keeping and companionship unless I am sure they are in good hands. I will leave it to you to change any glaring errors in the format of my documentations which you think would knock some scholar's eye out. My reference notes are, as you might say, strictly hand made. And perhaps it might be well if you would preface it with a brief explanation that it was written by an old deep-water A. B. with an archaeological itch, who, from sheer force of circumstances, was forced to be satisfied with digging genealogical information out of the old records from his chair and couch."

With apparently nothing happening in the summer, on 6 October 1957, despite what appears to have been sufficient exposure to the fortunes of a would-be author, Nickerson, still a neophyte, wrote Robbins,

I understand perfectly, of course, that some of your valued members and readers on learning this Paper was the work of an untrained and self-educated researcher would blandly indicate that the subject matter was of little value, after they had cribbed from it free of charge whatever was new to them. This would be no new experience to me.

This Paper, however, representing many happy hours spent in the accumulation and compiling of the documented facts, is very precious to me . . . I am conceited enough to believe that no one, layman or professional, has ever done this before.

Since it has now been nearly four months since I mailed it to you, I am led to the conclusion that it was not worth the price of a two cent postal card in acknowledgment and, therefore, request that it be mailed back to me without delay.

Robbins responded coolly on 14 October 1957, "According to my file I acknowledged receipt of your manuscript under date of June 21, 1956. In this letter, of which I have a copy, I expressed my thanks for permission to publish and said that I had given the ms. to our new editor Mr. Leaman F. Hallet (West Street, Mansfield, Mass.) who had also read and agreed to publish the paper. I think that Mr. Hallet is too ethical to use any of your material without publishing and acknowledging the source of his information."

The *Bulletin of the Massachusetts Archaeological Society, Inc.* published "The Old Sagamore" in July 1958 and "Micah Rafe" in January 1961.

Interest in Native American History

It is not surprising that Nickerson in his confinement would have turned to the hobby of his own genealogical research. The fruits of those efforts could readily lead to his work on the *Mayflower*. What is less apparent is an explanation for his intense pursuit of Native American history. Almost a decade *before* his heart attack, the seeds for this work were clearly planted in a letter he wrote to himself 22 May 1921. This was inspired by a visit to the site where a new golf course was being laid near the Head of the Bay on the Chatham side of the Chatham Country Club to see the remains of two Indians found resting feet to feet, which were dug up while workmen were excavating for Bunker 16.

> Over them was growing an almost impenetrable thicket of dog briars, high blue berry bushes, & gray berried junipers. The gentleman who kindly showed me the exact spot where they were found, remarked that this was the hardest piece of ground to clear on the whole Links—and well it might be. As long as the Indians lived, this spot of ground would have been held too sacred to plant corn on, and it is highly probable that my ancestor, William Nickerson, who purchased all this land where the Links now are of Old Chief Mattaquason & his tribe—(possibly of these very Indians whose moldering skulls I held in my hands today—I who am eleventh in direct line of descent from this same William) would have respected the graves of the natives with whom he lived so amicably & his children after him until their last resting places were forgotten in the passing of time. So this hallowed spot came down to the present day untouched & undesecrated.
>
> It seemed to bring old William Nickerson & Chief Mattaquason a little nearer out of the forgotten past as I stood on this lonely spot, less than a quarter of a mile from the site where William raised his house-tree, and looked into the voiceless mouth & empty eye sockets of this relic of a human being who once was one of the tribe over which Mattaquason ruled & roamed a free man over these same hills which soon will be turned over to the golfer & clubman. . . .
>
> Just over the hill from these graves a clear, cold spring bubbles up through the white sand, and back of it on the slope of the hill, and surrounding it, is one of the deepest deposits of Indian shells known to these parts. Here their village clustered from great antiquity. On the high ground back of it is one of the finest out-looks to sea of any place here abouts, and no vessel passing north or south could skirt Chatham Bars without being seen from this village. Every voyager from Lief the lucky down to Gosnold, Champlain, Captain John Smith, & even the

Mayflower as she turned back from the dangerous shoals off Monomoyick must have been seen by every [warrior, woman,] and papoose.

Did these sightless eyes view for the first time the square sails & bluff bows of these advance guards of the fair-faced race who as yet had only crossed the Indian's vision but who was destined soon to push him off into eternity & run the plough share over the hearthstones & graves of their fathers?

Did they behold with wonder the bold Norse Thorvald as he was laid to rest in the sands of some headland with an arrow wound in his armpit, or were they peering across the Harbor when the fated Sparrowhawk struck on the Bar & her shipwrecked company were succored by the Indians & taken safely to Plymouth?

Or perhaps they looked out from among the leaves of the primeval forest & watched with suspicion the first white settler as he broke trail through the unmapped wilderness to raise his log cabin just over the hill from their village.

Perhaps these skeletons bore the bodies of a man who knew the visage & voice of this pioneer Nickerson, & learned to respect and trust him because he purchased his land of the Indians by deed & payment negotiated with them rather than with the English King who claimed their lands but in no title ever vested by purchase.

I wonder if they ever talked with Gov. Bradford & his interpreter Squanto when in 1623 they came into the Bay to buy corn & beans of the natives? Squanto was taken sick while here on this trip with the Governor & was buried somewhere around the shores of Pleasant Bay & who knows but that one of these might be all that remains of Squanto, himself. . . .

Pax Vobiscum (Peace Be with you)

The entire story was there in 1921, waiting for an opportunity to become a "speaking leaf."

Colleagues

Nickerson did not work in a void on Native American history and culture. He drew on the work of many people. Others gave him both material and emotional support. Self-educated archaeologists were common in the early twentieth century. Cleon Crowell and Stanley W. Smith were unquestionably Nickerson's most notable contacts. Crowell had a rare collection of all kinds of Indian artifacts from Eastham, Chatham, Harwich, and Brewster.[81] Nickerson, himself, became a collector of arrowheads, always poking with his cane in search of one. His correspondence with his friend, Stanley Smith, a collector of documents, was heaviest in the 1930s.

There were others: Frank Smith, Howard Torrey, and John H. Paine were partners in excavations. Gilbert R. Payson of Orleans wrote to Nickerson on 11 March 1933 telling him to feel free to "prowl" in his south lot, next to the shell heap, and to make himself at home in his "wigwam." Payson, a collector of arrowheads, discussed Indian names at length. He wrote that he had interviewed old gunners and haymakers' descendants concerning place names. He added, "I can easily understand your feeling about that white arrowhead on Strong Island, even though an `Outlander.' As I said with reference to the axe which sat on top of a wall, like a chipmunk, waiting for you and only you to see it, you must be guided by the spirit of some old Sachem, who likes the cut of your jib. I got a big kick out of finding the axe under Joe Sparrow's hen-house, but nothing like that, nor so romantic." This mixture of Native American and maritime terminology, no doubt, suggests the tenor of Nickerson's conversations with his associates. Depicting perhaps the competition as well as possible good humor among them, Payson concludes his letter with a post script. "Stanley Sandheap[82] Smith is too credulous. He believes all the yarns that his piratical and otherwise immoral neighbors tell him. It is a well known fact that no inhabitant of South Orleans has ever *bought* oars or rowlocks. They have given him the wrong medicine on Money Head and now on Monument Plains. Will have to advise him to stick to his documents."

In October 1928, Nickerson started a correspondence and working relationship with Warren K. Moorehead, Director of Department of American Archaeology at Phillips Academy, Andover, Massachusetts. On the 11th, Moorehead wrote from a stereotypical viewpoint with overtones of racial prejudice,

> There is to be in Boston, as you know, the Tercentenary in 1930. I am in charge of the stone age village to be erected and manned by descendants of the New England Indians. I called a meeting last May at Providence, saw numbers of New England Indians assembled at the Brockton fair, also have been at Oldtown, Maine, etc.
>
> You might be able to advise us with reference to any persons who are dark enough to be descendants of Indians, and who live in southern Massachusetts or Rhode Island. Frankly, I am disappointed with the result of my personal interviews. I don't think the modern Indians know much of anything about the past, and most of them are distinctly part negro. Dr. Speck tells me there are a few very dark and almost Indian types around Gay Head. I found a few at both

Oldtown (Penobscot) and Calais (Passamaquoddy). A man named Wixon, who claims to represent the Cape Cod Indians appeared at the Providence hearing. One or two of his people were rather dark, most of them did not look very Indian to me. There were also several others persons who claimed to be in the show business, and who came in "wild West" costumes. I told all these people if they took part they would have to put on the original New England costumes, be under my supervision and live in a stone age village. The sideshow element would be eliminated.

It seems that we are having more trouble over this small Indian village than the larger, more important and expensive factors of the celebration. The Penobscots and Cape Cod Indians are not even friendly. The Passamaquoddies do not think much of the Rhode Island Indians. Each community seems to want to man the village with their own people, therefore I have told these Indians that we are representing all New England. We are not confining our village to Narragansetts, Pequots, Podunks, Penobscots or any other band. Personally I would rather bring down Ojibwa, who are Algonkin,—the same as our Indians—only speaking a different dialect, because they are dark, are still aboriginal, know how to sing the old songs and put on interesting old entertainments. This solution however might not be approved by the authorities for the reason that the Ojibwa do not live in New England.

The people who are to inhabit the village will be under strict control. I would prefer to have Penobscot and Passamaquoddy Indians because an assistant to the priest who has them in charge could come down and maintain discipline.

If you know numbers of people who look like Indians, with not much negro type, I will be glad to have their names and interview them later. If I can find anything concerning the archaeology of the Cape shall be glad to send you the information.

We do not have Nickerson's response, but Moorehead on 31 October 1928, wrote, "I thank you very much for your good letter. It is one of the most satisfactory, if not the most, I ever saw."

Their correspondence continues into 1932. Nickerson sought information concerning hidden children, pottery, etc. It is not clear how much Nickerson helped Moorehead with his village as Moorehead's letters spoke only of all the many problems related to his project and always with a parallel attitude about all of his brethren, regardless of race. It is clear that Nickerson met with the Governor and Company of Massachusetts Bay regarding the celebration. Also, Nickerson met with

Moorehead at the Bellevue Hotel, Beacon Hill, on the 16th of November 1928, for lunch. Moorehead was very critical of the state on the matter, saying,

> What New England needs is team play and unity. These elderly gentlemen who form that Company don't seem to have the faintest conception as to how celebrations are conducted. They should rest assured that nobody would squander money with reference to the Colonial village. We did not hear the end of the meeting and nobody wrote me what occurred, but it is just such speeches as were made by Winthrop, the Hudson Bay doctor (was he a Cabot?) Professor Hart, who is almost in his dotage, and others that would affect a Legislature to act adversely. No wonder New England is slipping. They have a great opportunity to `get back on the map' in 1930, and if they would lay aside Beacon Hill dignity for a little while and get down to brass tacks, team play and the spirit of the great Middle West, they would win out. What possessed several of them to argue the details of an Indian village? If they can't trust the man in charge, get someone else!

Among other colleagues was Russell H. Gardner (Great Moose), a Wampanoag historian of some thirty-five years, who corresponded with Sears in the early 1960s. Sears said that he would have to leave to Gardner the task of working on the Indians of the Upper Cape.

Editorial Problems and Practice

It should be apparent by now the tremendous task facing anyone attempting to prepare Nickerson's works for publication. The varied nature of the subject matter and the very uneven quality of the different pieces made it absolutely necessary to create a separate editorial practice for each selection. For clarity, the editorial practice of each article is stated in a short introduction. Only the two published articles are reproduced exactly as they appeared in print. Some pieces have been edited by making minor revisions; others were shaped by combining several drafts; still others required extensive rewriting, even the addition of new material. At all points, including the letters by Nickerson quoted in the introduction, I have freely and silently corrected errors of all kinds, especially in spelling and punctuation. Nickerson in a "Finale" to his Indian genealogy spoke of some of his problems which became my problems:

If within my power, I have gone personally to the original sources myself, and for these I can vouch. Chief among these has been the superb Collection of deeds and documents which were signed by the Indians themselves in person or by mark, which my good friend Stanley W. Smith, Esq., has always so generously placed at my disposal. Published items in the *Mayflower Descendant* and in Smith's *History of Chatham* can be depended upon to be as nearly correct as is humanly possible.

On the other hand, quotations from the Massachusetts Superior Court of Judicature files must be taken with the mental reservations that after all they are subject to the frailties of the particular Clerk who happened to make them, although in the main dependable when decipherable.

Such publications as Freeman's *Cape Cod,* Swift's *Old Yarmouth,* Otis's *Old Barnstable Families* I have been obliged to more or less take at their face value. Paine's *History of Harwich,* while a gold mine of invaluable information, is almost painfully lacking as to the sources of that information. While too much credit cannot be given to the author for preserving to posterity such an amount of local historical material which otherwise would have been wholly lost, I have found it necessary in a number of cases to correct dates given in the text when compared with original sources.

Another source of error is from the unstandardized system of spelling used in the early records and documents. Often a given name may be found with as many as three different spellings all in the same sentence and by the same author. Add to this the attempts of several different scribes to spell a jaw-breaking Indian name as it sounded to them, and you have a conglomeration which would tax the talents of a mind reader.[83]

When Nickerson, himself, left sources for *his* work, I tried to check them. There was occasionally an insurmountable hurdle. Among the many references to the Smith Collection Barnstable, sixteen could not be located. Often, Nickerson left no sources, and I was forced to track down probable ones.

Nickerson did not date his articles, but most were probably written from the late 1920s through the 1950s. Many of Nickerson's ideas were already firmly established by 1921. (See pages 30-31 for Nickerson's 22 May 1921 letter to himself.) His most comprehensive work, *Land Ho!— 1620* was published in 1931. Leisure granted by ill health suggests composition was accomplished during his confinement. Nickerson tried to deposit the papers on Micah Rafe and the Old Sagamore in the Peabody Museum of Archeology and Ethnology, Harvard University in 1942. His contributions to a local newspaper, the *Cape Codder*, were published in the 1950s.

Yet another problem emerged from Nickerson's language. Consideration of the usage of the word "Indian" seems a minor point in light of such diction as "brave" and "squaw" and so many references to "blood" as it took on color, hence metaphoric auras. The same semantic noise exists with his usage of "Negro." I have frankly counted on Nickerson's love of all that is Native American becoming apparent to readers, who will also hopefully have an understanding of the attitudes current in Nickerson's day. A certain amount of historical tolerance is in order. However, the problem of language *was* brought to Nickerson's attention as early as 1928 when Supreme Chief Sachem Ousa Mekin wrote Nickerson addressing him as "My Dear Friend & Brother" and thanking him for his "speaking leaf."

> Many many thanks for your very kind remarks anent the Indians—so called—. Firstly we are not Indians. Only since Columbus named—or mis-named us Indian—are we so called. We are, or were, simply, Abnaki, Tarratine, Wampanoag—Penobscot or Mashpee—or Narragansett, or Pequot, or Sioux—or Cherokee—or—whatever our aboriginal name happened to be—I presume that you know all this.

Conclusion

The reader cannot presume that Nickerson knew "all this," but the reader hopefully will sense that Nickerson, in his self-educated way, tried, sometimes successfully, perhaps best in "The Wading Place Path," "Pompmo and the Legend of Paw Waw Pond," "Old Maushope's Smoke," "The Old Sagamore," and "Micah Rafe" to be intellectually bifocal, approximating an ethnohistorian, who tries to view intercultural encounters from both or all sides, using evidence generated by one culture to understand the other. The major subject of study is "otherness," the often ineluctable differences perceived in one group by another.[84]

Perhaps, Nickerson would have shared Sale's opinion that there was salvation to be found in the New World but that it was not in exploitation, colonization, settlement, progress, power or technics, or in towering cities; rather salvation was "there especially in the Indian consciousness, in what Calvin Martin has termed 'the biological outlook on life.'"[85] Perhaps, in reaching back into his New England heritage, Nickerson would concur with Axtell that we judge history to appraise action, to do justice to the past (not pass sentence) and to advance our own moral education to learn from and, in effect, to be judged by the past.[86]

D.B.C.
Mashpee, Massachusetts

Notes

1. D. W. Meinig, *The Shaping of America: A Geographical Perspective on 500 Years of History* (New Haven: Yale University Press, 1986), 205-6.
2. John Noble Wilford, *The Mysterious History of Columbus: An Exploration of the Man, the Myth, the Legacy* (New York: Alfred A. Knopf, 1991), 274.
3. Ibid., x-xiii.
4. Ibid., 259-60.
5. Paul H. Chapman, *Discovering Columbus* (Columbus, Georgia: ISAC Press, 1991), 62. Chapman, believing Columbus to be of Jewish heritage, contended that the hereditary title of "Don," given only to non Jews, was especially important to Columbus as he desired to build a wall of protection around his family.
6. Wilford, *The Mysterious History of Columbus*, 230.
7. Ibid., 191.
8. Ibid., 96-97.
9. Ibid., 150.
10. David L. Bender and Bruno Leone, eds., *Christopher Columbus and His Legacy: Opposing Viewpoints* (San Diego: Greenhaven Press, Inc., 1992), 11.
11. Wilford, *The Mysterious History of Columbus*, 263.
12. Bender and Leone, *Christopher Columbus and His Legacy*, 14.
13. Ibid., 40.
14. Anthony Pagden, *European Encounters With the New World: From Renaissance to Romanticism* (New Haven: Yale University Press, 1993), 41-42.
15. Bender and Leone, *Christopher Columbus and His Legacy*, 91.
16. Kirkpatrick Sale, *The Conquest of Paradise: Christopher Columbus and the Columbian Legacy* (New York: Alfred A. Knopf, 1991), 31-33.
17. David E. Stannard's, *American Holocaust: Columbus and the Conquest of the New World* (New York: Oxford University Press, 1992) covers the pestilence and genocide, sexism, racism, and religious injustices, labeled "Holy War," from the perspective of the Native American.
18. Wilford, *The Mysterious History of Columbus*, 180-81.
19. James Axtell, *Beyond 1492: Encounters in Colonial North America* (New York: Oxford University Press, 1992), 87-90.
20. Ibid., 29.

21. Alfred W. Crosby Jr., *The Columbian Exchange: Biological and Cultural Consequences of 1492* (Westport: Greenwood Press, 1972), 31.
22. Bender and Leone, *Christopher Columbus and His Legacy*, 49.
23. John Yewell, Chris Dodge, Jan DeSirey, eds., *Confronting Columbus: An Anthology* (Jefferson, North Carolina: McFarland and Co., Inc., 1992), 139. This book is similar in purpose to the American Holocaust.
24. Axtell, *Beyond 1492*, 259.
25. Ibid., 99-100.
26. Bender and Leone, *Christopher Columbus and His Legacy*, 202-3.
27. Yewell, Dodge, and DeSirey, *Confronting Columbus*, 100.
28. Axtell, *Beyond 1492*, 26-27.
29. G. M. Gathorne-Hardy, *The Norse Discoverers of America* (Oxford: Clarendon Press, 1970), 196-220.
30. W. J. Eccles, *France in America* (New York: Harper Torchbooks, 1972), 3.
31. William Bradford, *Bradford's History "Of Plimoth Plantation"* (Boston: Wright and Potter Printing Co., State Printers, 1899), 100.
32. Ibid., 30.
33. Ibid.
34. Ibid., 32.
35. Ibid.
36. Ibid.
37. The situation would have been different if the Spanish had regained control of Holland. The Spanish were not known for their tolerance as can be witnessed in such measures as the Inquisition and the expulsion of the Jews and the Moors from Spain in 1492. The Spanish were certainly a threat to the Separatists but only if they controlled Holland. At the time that the Separatists made their decision to leave, the Spanish had no power in Holland and were only a minor consideration at most, though the Spanish king did not give up his claim to the Netherlands until 1648.
38. See W. Sears Nickerson's *Land Ho!—1620: A Seaman's Story of the Mayflower Her Construction, Her Navigation and Her First Landfall* (Boston: Houghton Mifflin Co., 1931) for his perspective on the subject.
39. Eugene Aubrey Stratton, *Plymouth County Its History and People 1620-1691* (Salt Lake City: Ancestry Publishing, 1986), 20.
40. Ibid., 142.
41. Ibid., 146.
42. For an example of kidnapping by Native Americans, see Mary Rowlandson, *The Narrative of the Captivity and Restoration of Mrs. Mary Rowlandson* (Lancaster, Massachusetts, 1903), 26.
43. Eccles, *France in America*, 21.
44. According to William Bennett Munro in *Crusaders of New France* ([New York: U.S. Publishers Association, Inc., 1918], 156), the French were primarily interested in making money. Only a small number of the French wanted to colonize New France in the manner the English colonized. Profit was always the driving force behind New France. In order to turn a profit, the fur trade had to succeed. The cooperation of several native peoples was

required to make the fur trade succeed since some of the groups acted as middlemen in the fur trade. Therefore, the French made an effort to adapt to the Native American way of life rather than trying to change them. (The exception here is missionary work in which the English also engaged.) Also, colonization required the acquisition of land, whereas the fur trade did not. Native Americans quickly learned that the French were more interested in trading whereas the English were more interested in taking their land. This was one of the reasons why they would later side with the French rather than the English during the French and Indian War.

45. Neal Salisbury, *Manitou and Providence Indians, Europeans, and the Making of New England, 1500-1643* (New York: Oxford University Press, 1982), 217.
46. Ibid., 222.
47. Ibid., 233.
48. The League of Augsburg consisted of England, Holland, Spain, Sweden, the Holy Roman Emperor, and various German states. This League battled Louis XIV of France for control of lands in Europe. It was basically an effort to prevent further French expansion in Europe and to keep a balance of power.
49. Francis Parkman, *France and England in North America* (New York: The Library of America, 1983), 2: 262.
50. Ibid., 264. This number is significantly different from the one in "How the Smiths Came to Cape Cod: Mary Smith of Oyster River," which was taken from Everett Stackpole, Lucien Thompson, and Winthrop Meserve, *The History of the Town of Durham, New Hampshire (Oyster River Plantation)* (Town of Durham, 1913). It is quite common for different sources to have different counts. It is equally impossible to resolve such differences.
51. The attack at Haverhill was another example of this brutal warfare. Stories of slaughter, as told by people like Hannah Duston and Mary Corliss Neff, could have been told by hundreds of others.
52. When the last Habsburg King of Spain had died with no heirs, a struggle began to decide which indirect heir would ascend the throne. The claimants were a Bourbon heir whose family also controlled France and an Austrian Habsburg whose family controlled the Holy Roman Empire. The balance of power in the colonies was also at stake since Spain had a vast overseas empire. If the French could gain control of these holdings by putting a Bourbon on the throne of Spain, French influence in the New World could have been enormous.
53. It is rather interesting that another young couple faced a situation similar to that of Elizabeth Vickery and her fiancee. Elisha Plaisted and Hannah Wheelwright were just married when Elisha was taken captive by Indians. Like Elizabeth Vickery, Elisha Plaisted's story had a happy ending as the newlyweds were reunited a few days later (Ibid., 370-72).
54. Ibid., 458.
55. Ibid.
56. Ousa Mekin, a Wamanoag, was also known as Rev. LeRoy C. Perry of Westerly, Rhode Island. On 17 February 1962, Nickerson wrote Russell H.

Gardner (Great Moose), Halifax, Massachusetts: "This Clarence Wixon belonged to the Dennisport family of Wixons as did my great-grandmother Jean (Wixon) Eldredge. He & other Wixons claimed to have Indian blood in their veins but had no substantial proof of it. It may be so: the old saying that it is a wise man who knoweth his father is true."

57. The National Algonquin Indian Council represented thirty-two tribes.

58. He died in January 1966.

59. Captain Atkins, representative of the sturdy stock from which Nickerson descended, came home empty-handed after the British had taken his ship and set him adrift in an open boat. He brought all his belongings tied up in a red bandanna handkerchief slung over his shoulder. "When great-grandma Mehitable met him at the door of the square-top, he laid the bandanna down at her feet and said: 'Well, Hit, here's all I've got left!' But it took more than a British seventy-four to sink Hit, as he called her. 'Oh, no! Josh!' she said. 'You've still got me!' And in his old Bible which lay open on his knees when he was found dead in his chair was written: 'She was a very comfortable woman to live with'" (W. Sears Nickerson, *The Bay—as I see it* [Published by his daughters, 1981], 22).

60. Nickerson, *The Bay—as I see it*, 12.

61. "I remember the day the four-masted schooner *Sarah W. Lawrence* was towed by, waterlogged and dismasted after being all but given up for lost in a winter blizzard. Her crew was frostbitten and she was a sorry-looking derelict, but she made port, and Oscar, who was her First Officer, said he saved his feet from freezing by pouring his ration rum into his boots instead of drinking it" (Nickerson, *The Bay—as I see it*, 13).

62. Nickerson, *The Bay—as I see it*, 12-13.

63. Ibid., 13.

64. Ibid., 32-33.

65. Ibid., 6.

66. John Billington became lost in the woods for some five days, living on berries until he came to a Native American plantation called Manamet, whereupon he was transferred to Nawsett. The Governor asked the Native Americans if they had seen the Billington boy; Massassoyt sent word where Billington was, and the Governor sent a shallop to retrieve him (Bradford, *Bradford's History "Of Plimoth Plantation,"* 124). Billington was executed ten years later for killing a man.

67. Nickerson, *The Bay—as I see it*, 16-19.

68. Ibid., 6.

69. Ibid., 7-8.

70. Ibid., 13.

71. Currently, Mary A. Marble, Jean C. Primavera, and Dorothy N. Ross (deceased).

72. Currently, Mary Atkins Nickerson (deceased) and Elizabeth W. Eldridge.

73. The information on Nickerson's occupations and family life comes from an article by Ed Fulke entitled "Success Story—1880-1952" (*Daytona News Journal*, 12 October 1952) and from Nickerson's daughter Jean C. Primavera.

74. Among the recipients were President Dwight David Eisenhower, Vice-President Richard Milhous Nixon, Senator Leverett Saltonstall, Senator John F. Kennedy, Senator Edward C. Stone, Queen Elizabeth II of England, and Captain Alan Villiers and the crew of *Mayflower II*.

The government wrote Nickerson during World War II and asked for the plates of *Land Ho!—1620* for the war effort which he gave them.

At Pilgrim Monument at Provincetown on display is an enlarged copy of his fold-out map (included in the back of *Land Ho!—1620*), and small maps are sold as souvenirs.

75. Morison taught American Colonial History at Harvard; he was three years chair of American History at Oxford and the official naval historian for World War II. He followed the voyages of Columbus in a sailing vessel before writing his famous biography *Admiral of the Ocean Sea*.

76. Joshua A. Nickerson, Sr. (1902-1990) was a Cape businessman, president of Nickerson Lumber Company, and a Cape benefactor as well as the author of *Days to Remember*.

77. The material described in this letter is in the Cape Cod National Seashore Archives, South Wellfleet, Massachusetts.

78. It is certain that Nickerson sent his material to the Museum of the American Indian Heye Foundation in New York, but that they returned it to him insured for $1,000. Today, they have none of his work.

79. The Society has three boxes. Boxes 1 and 2 contain family genealogy; box 3 is miscellaneous. One must be a member of the Society to examine their holdings.

80. Frank Gouldsmith Speck, an anthropologist with degrees from Columbia who taught at the University of Pennsylvania and Swarthemore College, did extensive field work among Indian tribes and wrote numerous books related to the field.

81. They were found in areas from two to eight feet below the surface, most commonly beside a fresh water spring on the southern side of a hill. He found bear, moose, and wolf skulls, occasionally a human skeleton, probably the bones of a captured enemy because Indian burial grounds were located elsewhere. Among Crowell's collection were arrowheads, pottery, a tobacco pipe, a bone fish harpoon, stone spears, a dark-colored, stone breast ornament, pieces of plumbago lead in the fashion of a stubbed pencil or marker, a bone comb or hair ornament made of a deer's antler, a pewter spoon, and enough pottery to enable him to trace the evolution of their pottery making.

82. The name of Smith's home was chosen in hopes of minimizing taxes on it.

83. Amelia Bingham, a Wampanoag from Mashpee, Massachusetts, who held no esteem for the white man's efforts to write down the Native American language, which is an oral language, explained to me that a word changed its meaning depending on a number of factors such as whether a man or a woman spoke it, what season of the year it was spoken in, what tone was used to say the word, etc.

84. Axtell, *Beyond 1492*, x.

85. Sale, *The Conquest of Paradise*, 368.

86. Axtell, *Beyond 1492*, 264.

I

Before the Mayflower: The Vikings and the French

The Wineland of Leif the Lucky

First Blood: The Death of the Carpenter of St. Malo

The Fight at Fortuné: Champlain at Stage Harbor

L ong before the arrival of W. Sears Nickerson's ancestors on the Mayflower, *the coast of North America was visited by Vikings and by French explorers. Nickerson describes the experiences of these earliest visitors in several of his writings, and his descriptions reflect the state of historical discussion of the early twentieth century.*

The Wineland of Leif the Lucky

*I*n *"The Wineland of Leif the Lucky," Nickerson relates a composite story of Viking sagas from the original sources. In this work,
Nickerson tries to prove that Leif's predecessor, Biarni, landed at Cape Cod.
The date of composition is unknown, but the idea was clearly fixed in his
mind in 1921. As far as sources or notes go, Nickerson starts his account by
writing, "It is based on the authorized Greenland and Icelandic versions of
the original Sagas as they are still preserved in the* Groenlendinga Pattr *and
the "Saga of Eric the Red" in the* Flatey Book *which itself was derived from
the* Landnamabok, *giving the story of the Iceland settlement." There are
three manuscripts that carry the accounts of the Vinland voyages:* Flatey
Book, Hauk's Book, *and a third vellum, A.M. 557. I have used Edward
F. Gray,* Leif Eriksson: Discoverer of America A.D. 1003 *and Arthur
Middleton Reeves, ed.,* The Finding of Wineland the Good: The History
of the Icelandic Discovery of America. *Ignoring the conflicts among the
three manuscripts, I have granted Nickerson his story and refer the interested reader to Gray's book.*

About the year 982 or 983, Eric the Red was banished from his home at
Ericsstadir in Iceland because of a quarrel, not of his own choosing but
which had resulted in the death of his neighbor Thorgest's two sons.
Instead of sailing back to Norway, he resolved to take a look at the land
to the west which his countryman Gunnbiorn, son of Ulf the Crow, had
sighted some years before, and for which he had left explicit sailing
directions.

Eric loaded his cattle, his farm implements, his household goods,
and his thralls onto his long-ship and with his wife Thorhild and their

children set sail from Iceland on the full of the moon as was the custom among the old Vikings when a voyage was to keep them at sea over night. The old Iceland records say that to reach Greenland one must sail due west for two days and two nights; then one should come in sight of Gunnbiorns-skerries.

Shaping his course by the sun by day and the moon by night, Eric kept his ship's nose to the west through two days and two nights and on the third morning raised the tide-washed ledges known as Gunnbiorns-skerries. Still heading to the west, he soon sighted the east coast of Greenland and, keeping the land aboard on the starboard side, rounded its southern tip at Cape Farewell and hauled to the northwest. Before long, he came to the fish-filled, sheltered fiords, the beautiful little islands, and the lush, green meadows of Greenland's west coast.

Scientists tell us that the Greenland area was much warmer at that particular period than at present, and the history of Eric's colony bears this out. As Eric saw it, here was a land free for the taking, wholly uninhabited, with plentiful food for his household and fodder for his cattle, and subject to no laws. He chose one of the many deep and protected inlets as his landing place and settled at Brattahlid in Ericsfirth.

Early in the summer of 985 or 986, the period of his exile from Iceland now being over, he sailed back to try to interest his old friends and neighbors in this green land to the west. Thirty-five ships followed Eric back to the west coast of Greenland; fourteen arrived safely. Among the company was Heriulf, the father of Biarni.

All this time, the softening influence of the Christian religion was gradually driving the pagan gods out of the Northland, but Eric the Red brought his Thor and Woden along with him to Brattahlid, never to forsake them. Only sixteen winters from the time Eric the Red went to colonize Greenland, his oldest son Leif sailed from Greenland to Drontheim, Norway where King Olaf Tryggvason converted him to Christianity and where he was accordingly baptized.

On his return to Ericsfirth in the spring, Leif heard a wonderful story from the lips of his friend Biarni, the son of Heriulf. Biarni, a Norse voyager of note, had, while sailing out of Norway the previous summer, touched at Iceland and then continued on to winter with his father in Greenland, where he had never been before. Before reaching the Greenland coast, he was caught in a howling nor'wester and obliged to scud before it to save his ship and crew. It drove him so far south that neither he nor any of his crew knew where they were except that according to their reckoning a north course should take them back to Greenland in the course of a few days.

At last, the wind changed and came in from the southward. Biarni headed to the north on a course which he calculated should bring them into Greenland waters in six or eight days if the fair wind held. Imagine his surprise when, before nightfall on that very same day, land was sighted on the port bow, a strange, new land, lying low in the west, which no man in his crew had ever seen or heard of before. Biarni hauled in close enough to make sure there were no mountains or glaciers in the backlands, as Greenland had been pictured to him. But the land was level, covered with woods and small hillocks, so he headed north again, and two days later sighted another forested coast, still on the port side and still nothing like what he expected the coast of Greenland to look like. His men wanted to go ashore and look over this new land, but Biarni decided to keep going as long as the south wind held, lest they should get caught in another norther and lose all they had gained.

Three days later, they saw a high, rocky, mountainous coast, with icy glaciers in the distance, but altogether too barren and forbidding to agree with the picture of Greenland he carried in his mind. But when four days later they again sighted land, this time right ahead on the starboard bow, Biarni is quoted as saying: "'This is likest Greenland, according to that which has been reported to me concerning it, and here we will steer to the land.'"[1] And that evening they rounded below a cape and found his father Heriulf's homestead.[2]

Leif Ericsson listened eagerly to Biarni's thrilling story and straightway made a vow to see this new land for himself. He memorized the number of days sailed with a fair wind and carefully estimated the mileage covered; he fixed in his mind's eye the prominent features peculiar to each landfall, and it was not long before he had a mental picture of the coastline as sharply etched in his memory as if a modern copy of the *Coast Pilot* lay open before him.

These old navigators had minds acutely trained to observe and register the details of outstanding landmarks, as well as the faculty of passing that knowledge along to other men. We of today depend so heavily on the printed word and accurate charts that their skill in picking up landmark after landmark would seem to us almost uncanny. With no charts to guide, no instrument with which to shoot the sun and get their position, and no compass to steer by, these old Vikings, by dead reckoning and sheer common sense, took their seventy-five foot long-ships where they wanted to go and brought them home again. No better seamen ever sailed the seven seas.

The next autumn, after the harvests were in, Leif loaded his long-ship with supplies for a winter's cruise and sailed boldly out of Ericsfirth. The Sagas tell us that Leif was a large and powerful man, of a most imposing bearing. It is not difficult to imagine him swaying against the great steering-sweep of his ship, as he strains his eyes ahead to catch the first glimpse of the landmarks which mark the way, resolved that he will land and winter on that new shore which Biarni had only seen from the deck of his vessel.

One by one the landmarks were picked up: "This was a level wooded land, and there were broad stretches of white sand, where they went, and the land was level by the sea."[3] Leif and his men landed on this island while yet the dew was heavy on the grass and " . . . it so happened that they touched the dew with their hands, and touched their hands to their mouths, and it seemed to them that they had never before tasted anything so sweet as this."[4] And never before, so far as the records show, had a white man ever stepped foot on the east coast of North America.

Back of the island lay a sheltered bay, its channel or river, as the Norsemen called it, leading into it from the eastward. The tide was on the ebb, and when Leif attempted to take his ship in, she grounded on a sand bar. While waiting for the next flood tide to float her, he put over a small boat and went on in to look the harbor over. He found a wide bay full of fish and fowl, lush tidal meadows fed by sweet-water springs, and forests heavily wooded with standing timber such as was extremely rare in his north country and which would make a rich cargo for the homeward-bound trip. But perhaps best of all, Old Tyrker, a member of Leif's crew who came from the wine-growing regions of Germany, discovered an abundance of wild grapes almost begging to be picked and made into wine. Because of this, Leif gave the new country the name of Vinland, or as we say it, Wineland.[5]

The next tide floated the ship, and they brought her in, pulled her ashore, unloaded her, and went to work putting up houses for winter quarters. They were astonished at the mildness of the climate, little if any snow falling all winter long and the grass in the meadow staying green. They loaded their ship with the best cuts of timber, filled the after boat with grapes which Old Tyrker had carefully dried, and with the coming of the first steady spring southerly swung her off before it for home.

There was great rejoicing when they sailed into Ericsfirth in Greenland, and the valuable cargo made Leif a rich man. Because of this voyage to Wineland, he became known to his generation and even down to this day as LEIF the LUCKY.[6]

Eric the Red died about this time, and the management of his farm, with its forty head of cattle, fell to Leif, he being the oldest son. Because of this, he was never able to go back to Wineland again, but his younger brother Thorvald borrowed his ship and his crew of thirty men and in 1007 set sail for the new country. He had no difficulty whatever in finding "Leifs-booths,"[7] and it is likely he planned to explore the surrounding country as to its possibility for a permanent settlement. But Thorvald was not as lucky as his brother Leif. Unfortunately, while exploring the coast, he ran his ship ashore on an outlying promontory in a heavy squall and damaged her keel, and it took so long to repair it that they gave the place the name of Kjalarnes or Keelness.

A short time afterwards, during a skirmish with the natives, an arrow flew in between his shield and the gunwale of the ship and struck him in the armpit. Realizing that it was a mortal wound, he asked his men to take his body to a certain headland for burial, where shortly before he had remarked that he would like to make his home there as it was such a pleasant place. ". . . thus it may be fulfilled, that the truth sprang to my lips, when I expressed the wish to abide there for a time. Ye shall bury me there, and place a cross at my head, and another at my feet, and call it Crossness,"[8] that is, Cross Cape.

Another one of Leif's brothers named Thorstein made an attempt in 1008 to reach Leifs-booths (some say with the intention of bringing home the body of Thorvald) but was forced, perhaps because of bad weather, to return empty handed without ever sighting Wineland.

In 1009, Thorfinn Karlsefni, a noted trader, came to Brattahlid to spend the winter with Leif the Lucky, who was his boyhood friend. While there, he fell in love with Gudrid, Leif's widowed sister-in-law, who was making her home in his household. Their wedding was celebrated at New Year's tide with great splendor and feasting because of Leif's generosity and the wealth of Karlsefni, both he and his bride being of noble blood.

After listening to the wonderful tales about the new lands to the southward, Karlsefni resolved to make a voyage there on his own account. Gudrid, true to her marriage vows, went along with him. There are said to have been sixty men and five women in the company, and they took along household goods and cattle. In Wineland, Gudrid gave birth to a son, whom they named Snorri. Karlsefni and Gudrid eventually made their home at Glaumboeiar-land in Iceland after their return from America. After his death, Gudrid ran the farm with the help of Snorri and after Snorri's marriage took the veil, entering the church which he had built in honor of Karlsefni. Many men of renown were descended from Karlsefni and Gudrid through their son Snorri.

Leif's sister Freydis, who seems to have been something of a Viking in her own right, in 1014, made the round trip successfully and also made a name for herself which is still remembered with shame in the annals of the Northmen. Freydis sailed in her own ship and was accompanied by another owned by two brothers, Helgi and Finnbogi, who had wintered in Greenland. They agreed to carry a crew of thirty men each, besides a few women, but right from the start Freydis showed her deceitfulness by concealing five extra men aboard her ship. They had no difficulty in finding Leifs-booths, but when they landed, Freydis informed them that Leif had agreed to let only her and her ship's company stay in his houses and that Helgi, Finnbogi, and their men and women would have to build new ones for themselves or go without.

These things bred hard feelings between them, and while the brothers went ahead and built their houses, the bad blood soon developed to the point where all visits between the two crews came to a stop. As winter merged into spring and the time drew near for the trip to Greenland, Freydis devised a devilish plan whereby she could secure for herself all the valuable goods and property of the two brothers. One night she dressed and went barefoot to the house of Helgi and Finnbogi, telling Finnbogi she had come because she would like to trade ships with them, theirs being the larger and she planning to sail for home before long with a large cargo. This he agreed to and then went back to bed, while Freydis returned to her own house.

When she climbed into bed, her husband Thorvard wanted to know where she had been and why her feet were so cold. She told him she had been to the house of the two brothers to ask them to trade ships, but that they had abused and mistreated her. ". . . what time thou," she said, "poor wretch, wilt neither avenge my shame nor thy own. . . ."[9] At last, unable to stand her taunts any longer, Thorvard called up his men and ordered them to arm and follow him. Catching the brothers and their men totally unarmed and unsuspecting, they slew every one, but when it came to the women, Thorvard's followers refused to murder them in cold blood. Whereupon, Freydis screamed, "Hand me an axe!"[10] and killed them all with her own hands.

She offered heavy bribes and threatened with death any of her own crew who should so much as hint when they got back to Ericsfirth at what had happened. But the story finally got to the ears of Leif, himself, who declared that he had no heart to punish his sister as she deserved. Nevertheless, the name of Freydis has always stood as a blot on the pages of the Old Norse Sagas.

Historians and laymen are still arguing as to the actual landing place of Leif the Lucky. Many harbors and inlets have laid claim to it, all the way from the Cape of Virginia to Greenland. I doubt if the location of Leifs-booths can ever be definitely settled unless some undeniable remains of that camp site are unearthed, such as have been found on the site of his father's farmstead at Brattahlid. Until that day, the possibility that he may have set up those houses right here on Cape Cod has as much in its favor as any other locality, and more than most.

Let us begin with the logical assumption that Leif, when he left Greenland, followed the instructions given him by Biarni and, in effect, back tracked on Biarni's course. He picked up landmark after landmark which had been described to him and finally, after he had run out the estimated distance, made his landing. Seventeen hundred miles down the coast by water from Greenland comes very close to Cape Cod.[11] If Leif got this far and missed the Cape, he is the only Western Ocean navigator who ever did so, but still I doubt if he got any farther south of Chatham. If he had attempted the dangerous stretch of shoals and rips lying off Chatham between Monomoy Point and Nantucket, which nearly wrecked Champlain's ship and turned the *Mayflower* back, he would have certainly mentioned an experience so totally foreign to his sea-going background, just as the Norse voyagers were so impressed by the long stretches of white sandy beaches, so typical of the Back Side of Cape Cod, that their Sagas still speak of them.

Just before he would reach The Shoals, however, and after he had coasted down by those intriguing white beaches which they tell of, he would come to the almost landlocked harbor of Pleasant Bay, right on the elbow of The Cape. No doubt it lay more open to the sea at that early date than now, but it agrees in almost every characteristic with the description of Leif's landing place. The distance from Greenland is approximately seventeen hundred miles. It lies in behind islands connected by sandy spits and beaches, just as they say. And it is an historical fact that its Inlet, which they call a river coming in from the east, did, as late as the seventeenth century, flow in from the ocean directly east of it. No doubt its channel in the year one thousand was as choked with sand bars on which Leif's ships would find no trouble to get aground, as its counterpart of today.

Its climate, even at the present time, would seem mild and gentle to men from Greenland. I, myself, have seen open winters on the Cape when almost no snow fell, ice houses went begging, and the "fresh meadow hay," as we Cape Codders call the fringe of short grass around the upland edge of our salt marshes, remained green throughout the winter. As to Old Tyrker's grapes, when I was a boy, before the cedar and huckleberry swamps around The Bay were torn up and converted into cranberry bogs, they were so overgrown and interlaced with a tough, unpruned network of wild grape vines that in the late fall we youngsters used to shin out on them over the slimy peat-water underneath and stuff ourself on overripe grapes until we were tipsy.

There is an excellent landing place for boats of any size up in the northwest corner of Pleasant Bay. Bold water can be carried right into a sandy beach where a tidal creek runs out under the highway bridge, draining a sizable stretch of meadow which is freshened in its upper reaches by a sweet-water spring and a little murmuring brook feeding into it from a crystal-clear pond back in the hills. A great grandfather of mine, who was also a sailor, bought this tract of upland and meadow from the Indians, built his house there and used to moor his trading schooner in front of it. Tradition, handed along by word of mouth just as were the original Norse Sagas, says that, when he cleared up his land, he unearthed what he called a Dutch oven, one of those clay-packed, domed-shaped, outdoor, cooking ovens still in use in certain parts of the world. It certainly was not of Indian origin, and no one as yet has come forward with a satisfactory explanation of why it chanced to be on grandfather's farm. Could it possibly be that the Norsemen who built Leifsbooths also set up a Dutch oven for their cooking needs?

The Norsemen never succeeded in establishing a permanent colony on the North American continent, as Eric the Red had done in Greenland. The shores of America were a long way from home. The climate also began to change for the worse, so that by the year 1341 it is recorded that Greenland-bound ships had to seek a more southerly course because of dangerous ice floes pushing down from the north. It was not long before the Greenland settlements themselves had to be abandoned to the advancing snow and ice, only to be remembered in the legends and Sagas of the Northmen. But as long-ships sailed to Greenland, the sea trail to the timber lands of North America must have been kept open, and in Columbus's day, not over a hundred years later, there must have been men living whose grandfathers had sailed it.

The breaking waves of many a long winter have filled the wakes of those half-pagan, half-Christian bands of bold Sea Rollers, who centuries before Columbus sighted the New World were driving down out of the Northern Seas to search out a land which one of their countrymen had but glimpsed from the deck of his long-ship, not knowing himself where he was. The shifting sands have covered their camp sites and their crosses. And yet, could we but turn time back on itself for nearly a thousand years, who knows but we might see Leif the Lucky nosing in out of a red sunrise on the Back Side of Cape Cod to cross the harbor bars of Pleasant Bay and shoot his ship ashore on old Strong Island to taste the morning's "dew so sweet." We might watch him sail up The Bay to great grandfather's old landing place, to set up a clay cooking oven and build Leifsbooths beside the green meadows, and while sampling Old Tyrker's wine, made from the native wild grapes, give to this strange new country the name of Wineland the Good.

Notes

1. Arthur Middleton Reeves, ed., *The Finding of Wineland the Good the History of the Icelandic Discovery of America* (New York: Burt Franklin, 1895), 64.
2. Since the discovery of Wineland by Biarni is not confirmed by any existing collateral evidence, Nickerson's position is strictly his opinion. Edward Gray and William Hovgaard agree that Biarni saw Newfoundland (Edward F. Gray, *Leif Eriksson: Discoverer of America A.D. 1003* [New York: Kraus Reprint Co., 1972]; William Hovgaard, *The Voyages of the Norsemen to America* [New York: American Scandinavian Foundation, 1914]). Nickerson argues, "According to Biarni's own statements, it was ten days after he first sighted the strange land before he tied up at his father's fiord in Greenland. All this time he had been running day and night before a southerly wind, sometimes of gale force. These ships of the Norsemen were well modeled, long and narrow, and with the wind over their shoulders would run like wild horses. I have had a wide experience in handling sailing craft of all kinds and sizes, and I believe a fair estimate of the hourly average of Biarni's ship when running free before a fresh breeze would be not less than seven miles per hour. This gives a daily average of nearly one hundred and seventy miles or a ten days run of approximately seventeen hundred miles. If we follow Biarni's course back along the coast for seventeen hundred miles, it will bring us just about to the tip of Cape Cod. Let us remember this and also remember that the first land sighted was a low-lying country, with rolling, wooded hills and wide, sandy beaches. Whatever the first land sighted, it is certain that Biarni and his men were the first white men ever to see the east coast of America and live to tell the tale." What bothers me significantly is that I can find no mention of sandy beaches in Biarni's account.
3. Reeves, *The Finding of Wineland the Good*, 65.
4. Ibid.
5. "A cargo sufficient for the ship was cut, and when the spring came, they made their ship ready, and sailed away; and from its products Leif gave the land a name, and called it Wineland" (Reeves, *The Finding of Wineland the Good*, 67).
6. Reeves avers that Leif was also known as lucky because of his rescue of fifteen persons from a wrecked skerry, along with as much of their cargo as he could carry. "Leif had now goodly store both of property and honour" (67-68). Gray mentions the rescue of the wrecked men as well as Leif's introduction of Christianity into the country as being the reasons for Leif's new name (45).
7. Reeves, *The Finding of Wineland the Good*, 68.
8. Ibid.
9. Ibid., 76.
10. Ibid.
11. Reeves, *The Finding of Wineland the Good*, 65.

First Blood: The Death of the Carpenter of St. Malo

" **F** *irst Blood: The Death of the Carpenter of St. Malo" is an account of the earliest authentic record of the killing of a white man by a Cape Cod Native American. Nickerson left no notes on "First Blood," except for the internal reference to* Voyages *of Sieur de Champlain. I have added all notes from the primary source and silently corrected all errors. I have combined two articles, what was possibly the original effort (which is undated) with the one printed 18 June 1959, in the* Cape Codder.

The earliest authentic record of the killing of a white man by a Cape Cod Indian is found in the *Voyages of Sieur de Champlain*. It took place on the beach outside Nawset Harbor in 1605.

In the year 1604, King Henry of France commissioned Pierre de Guast Lieutenant-General in Acadia, over a vast territory stretching vaguely from the Gulf of St. Lawrence to the Hudson River.[1] Among his distinguished company was Sieur de Champlain, Captain in Ordinary to the King and Royal Geographer, to whom we are indebted for our story.

De Guast, better known as de Monts, founded a settlement that same summer on an island at the mouth of the St. Croix River which separates Maine and New Brunswick. It was the first colony ever established by white men within the present limits of the New England states. Without losing time, Sieur de Monts proceeded to employ the workmen in building houses. Skilled artisans had been brought out from France, and barracks for the soldiers were soon knocked together. A kitchen, a bake-house, and a smithy took shape. Picturesque, peaked-roofed dwellings, after the fashion of the houses in Normandy, were raised for the priest, the carpenter, and other men of consequence. Surrounding

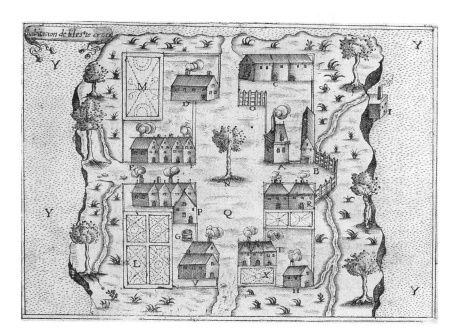

Champlain's drawing of the settlement on the island of Sainte Croix. By Permission of the Houghton Library.

them all, a strong stockade was strung along shore just above high water mark.[2] Among the artisans who converted the wooded Isle of St. Croix into a tight little fortress was a carpenter from St. Malo.[3] This carpenter hailed from the same port as the old sea-dog, Francois Gravé, the shipowner, more familiarly known as du Pont Gravé.

Champlain tells us that that winter in the new settlement "out of seventy-nine, who composed our party, thirty-five died, and more than twenty were on the point of death."[4] Because of this, they decided to go in search of a place with a better temperature. They set sail June 18, 1605, in a fifteen ton barque with a crew of twenty men, among them the Carpenter of St. Malo and Champlain as map-maker and keeper of the log.[5] They poked into every cove and inlet from St. Croix to Plymouth Harbor and at last on the morning of the 19th of July rounded the Head of Cape Cod which they called "Cap Blanc" because of the beauty of its white "sands and downs."[6] Taking a fair wind they ran down the Back Side as far as Nawset and anchored for the night off the Harbor Bars.

Next morning a storm was blowing up. A boat's crew had reported
that the Bars were bad but that there was a good harbor inside. De
Monts and Champlain were tough seamen, not to get caught on a lee
shore in an easterly gale, so they weighed anchor, picked their way in
through the dangerous Bars before the rising swell, and found a snug
berth under the lee of the Point of the North Beach. The turn of the
weather justified their judgment. Here they lay weatherbound by a cold,
howling north-easter which lasted four days. They were forced to break
out their great-coats to keep themselves warm in mid July; it was a perfectly understandable mid-summer "north-easter" to any native born
Cape Codder.[7]

Champlain improved his time by making a map of Nawset Harbor so
accurate that if today we allow for the changes in the Outer Beach and to
the shift in the magnetic north pole, it fits remarkably well the latest Coast
& Geodetic chart. It shows that where his ship lay was very close to Deep
Water Point, the Inlet of 1605 lying about midway between the headlands
of Eastham and East Orleans. On its south edge was a tough little island
which he says was covered with low shrubs and many vines and which
Captain John Smith called "Ile of Nausit." Our pioneer forefathers gave it
the less romantic sounding name of "a place on Pocha Beach called Slut's
Bush." When Slut's Bush washed away, almost within the memory of men
now living, the Inlet shifted rapidly south to its present location.[8]

From their anchorage it seemed to the Frenchmen that the Harbor
was entirely surrounded by the houses of the Indians for its whole circuit
of three or four leagues, each wigwam having around it as much land as
the occupant needed for his support. The Indian men and women paddled off in their dug-out canoes to visit the ship in the most friendly
manner, bringing with them generous gifts of their native tobacco and
bartering their bows, arrows, and quivers for the beads, buttons, and
other trade trinkets of the Frenchmen.[9]

On Thursday, the twenty-first, Sieur de Monts decided to go ashore
and pay them a return visit, so he made a landing with nine or ten armed
men on the North Point and marched about a league along the coast,
which must have brought them close to the site of the present Nawset
Coast Guard Station. Rounding the swamp at the head of the beach and
swinging inland, they crossed fields planted with Indian corn which was
in flower and five and a half feet high. There were Brazilian beans, many
squashes, tobacco, and some roots which tasted like artichokes. The
woods were filled with oaks, nut-trees, and beautiful cypresses of reddish
color, which gave off a very pleasant fragrance.[10]

Before the gale blew itself out, the ship's scuttle-butts were running
short of water. On the morning of Saturday, the 23rd of July, a squad of

four or five men, among them the carpenter of St. Malo, was set ashore carrying large kettles (prized by the aborigines above all articles possessed by the French) to get fresh water which was to be found in one of the sand banks which was a short distance from the barque.[11] The carpenter reached the spring first, filled his kettle, and had started to carry it back to the boats when suddenly he was surrounded by a band of Indians who twisted it out of his hands. As he ran for his life, the Indians shot several arrows at him from behind and brought him down. Then, they rushed upon him and despatched him with their knives.

His men attempted to drive off the Indians but were themselves chased down the beach to their boat, yelling for help. Their shipmates on the barque saw the skirmish and made a quick landing, firing as they came. In the confusion Champlain's musket exploded in his hands and nearly killed him.[12] The Indians, hearing the guns and seeing the landing party, turned and made for the Eastham mainland. The carpenter's companions were sure the band who had killed him were not the friendly Nawsets, with whom by now they had become fairly well acquainted. The Nawsets themselves seemed to be as much astonished as the Frenchmen at the surprise attack. The Sachem sent his Head Men down to the ship to explain that it was not they who had done this evil deed, but others farther off in the interior.[13] De Monts and Champlain were persuaded he was not to blame and released the man they were holding hostage.

That is the story as told by the men who took part in it, but that is not all. On his chart of Nawset Harbor, Champlain graphically sketched the death scene of the Carpenter of St. Malo. There we see him down in the sands, an Indian on top of him with knife poised for the death stroke, the Frenchmen rushing up the beach firing their guns as they came.

"We brought in the murdered man, and he was buried some hours later."[14] His burial place must have been very near where Henry Beston's Outermost House since stood. For utter loneliness, the group at the grave side must have been a scene hard to match—the sullen surf booming a dirge among the dunes, the new-turned sand checked by the hurrying storm wrack overhead, the little knot of hard-bitten Frenchmen, plumed hats in hand, guns primed for action, standing uncovered before their Maker, to say the last words for a dead comrade—the only white men on the whole eastern seaboard of North America between La Cadie and Spanish Florida.

Monday morning, the 25th, broke clear with a fair wind for St. Croix. Anchor was weighed, sails trimmed to the wind, and the brave little barque headed for the open Atlantic. Through a mistake of the pilots they came near being lost on the Bar,[15] but by God's good grace, they wallowed clear and shaped a course for home. The crude little cross marking the grave of their shipmate was soon lost to sight behind the beach knolls on the Point, and the carpenter of St. Malo was left to rest in peace under the white sands of Nawset Beach.

Notes

1. W. L. Grant, ed., *Voyages of Samuel de Champlain 1604-1618* (New York: Charles Scribner's Sons, 1907), 6.
2. Ibid., 42-44.
3. Ibid., 72. No mention is made of a carpenter in *Voyages of Samuel de Champlain 1604-1618* except that housing for carpenters is identified; the man slain in Champlain's account is referred to only as a sailor. I have not found Nickerson's source for the victim's profession; a profession possibly emerged from a simple desire to particularize the victim.
4. Grant, *Voyages of Samuel de Champlain*, 53.
5. Ibid., 56.
6. Ibid., 69.
7. Ibid., 71-72.
8. Currently the site of a Stop and Shop grocery store.
9. Grant, *Voyages of Samuel de Champlain*, 70-71.
10. Ibid., 71. The cypress is the red cedar, *Juniperus Virginiana.*
11. Grant, *Voyages of Samuel de Champlain*, 72.
12. Ibid., 72.
13. Ibid., 73. Nickerson speculates in the original version of this incident that the tribe farther off in the interior may have been Iyanno's tribesmen from Cummaquid.
14. Grant, *Voyages of Samuel de Champlain*, 72. Except for the possibility of Thorwald, son of Eric the Red, this sailor was the first white man to be buried on New England soil.
15. Grant, *Voyages of Samuel de Champlain*, 76.

The Fight at Fortuné: Champlain at Stage Harbor

Nickerson *left no notes for "The Fight at Fortuné," but three sources are apparent: Marc Lescarbot,* The History of New France; *W. L. Grant, ed.,* Voyages of Samuel de Champlain 1604-1618; *and William C. Smith,* A History of Chatham Massachusetts. *I have freely and silently edited this piece. The date of composition is unknown, probably after 1930.*

Tucked away under the crazy-bone of the ragged elbow of Cape Cod lies a little, landlocked cove known as Stage Harbor. As we pause near the stage or wharf which gives the Harbor its English name and read the tablet marking the spot where Champlain's Frenchmen died in 1606, it is hard to realize that the beach-plum-covered bluffs across the Harbor on Morris Island once echoed back the "Woach!" of the Indian war cry, the crack of spitting French arquebuses, and the death screams of dying men.

In 1606 a thriving Indian village called Seaquanset dotted the slopes where the marker stands. It was a comfortable settlement after the Indian fashion, where the foot of a white man had never trod, so far as the records show. Wide corn fields yellowed around it in the October sun, and oysters in abundance grew at its very doors. Frolicsome boys and girls romped among the piles of squashes and strings of tobacco ripening around the lodges. Smoke curled cheerily from the round-topped wigwams, and men and women moved busily about. The harvest moon had come, and the women were already lining their corn barns with bark and mats for the harvest home.

Two years before, in the spring of 1604, the French had made a settlement on the little Island of Dochet, or St. Croix as they called it, at the

mouth of the St. Croix River in Maine. Sieur de Monts, its founder, finding it unsuitable for a permanent colony, led an exploring expedition
south along the coast the following year looking for a better site as far as
Nawset, which they named Port de Mallebarre. On his return, it was
decided to give up the settlement on Dochet and relocate at Port Royal
on the Nova Scotia side. It was from here that the Baron de Poutrincourt
set sail on September 5, 1606, on another southward voyage. Theirs was
the only white settlement on the whole North American coast north of
the Spaniards in Florida.

De Poutrincourt's ship was armed with one small cannon, drew about
four feet of water, and carried a crew of some twenty sailors and soldiers
besides the officers. Champlain was official recorder and map-maker, and
Champdore was Master of the barque—the same berths they had filled on
the expedition to Nawset the year before under de Monts. The Baron de
Poutrincourt's son Biencourt went along, and young Robert, son of the
old ship owner Pont Gravé. Somewhere they had picked up an Englishman
by the name of Daniel Hay. The apothecary was Louis Hebert, and there
was a surgeon and a trumpeter.[1] Secondon, an Etechemin Indian chief,
who could talk with the Indians in the sign language if not in their own
dialect, was taken along as an interpreter—quite a sizable company to
squeeze into a fifteen ton vessel for a six week's cruise.

Nearly a month was used up in looking over the coasts of Maine and
Massachusetts which was all new country to de Poutrincourt. October
found them well down into Cape Cod Bay, and on the first day of the
month, they sounded in around Billingsgate and sampled the famous
oysters of Wellfleet on the half shell. Beating out around the tip of the
Cape that same afternoon, they rounded the Race and made a run down
the Back Side during the night. At daybreak next morning, the second of
October, they were off the Eastham shore.

Here the wind struck ahead, so they stood in to their old anchorage of
the year before under the lee of old Slut's Bush Island, which then lay
just to the south of the entrance of Nawset Harbor. Here they went
ashore for a visit with their Nawset Indian friends, as well as to pay a tribute of respect at the grave of their former shipmate, the Carpenter of St.
Malo who had been killed there the previous summer in a scrimmage
with another band of Indians.[2] The wind coming fair after about an
hour, they headed south again into what was new waters for them and
before sunset came to anchor close in to the beach off Chatham. They
attempted to make a landing in the ship's boat but found the breakers
too dangerous. The Monomoyick Indians, however, who were expert
canoe-men and knew every guzzle and shoal on Chatham Bars, launched
their dug-outs through the surf and came off to the ship to visit them.

The following morning, the third of October, broke fine and clear with a fair wind from the north. The Indians had told de Poutrincourt of a safe harbor farther around to the southward, so anchor was weighed, and the ship's head swung off in search of it. They had no way of knowing that almost under their bows lay one of the most dangerous stretches of navigable waters any where on the face of the earth. Almost before their anchor was fairly stoppered and their halyards coiled down, their little ship was in among the treacherous Shoals of Pollock Rip, the Great Rip of Mallebarre as the Frenchmen called it on their maps.

No better men ever handled a ship than these same Breton sailors, but there was not the ghost of a chance of beating back off the Shoals. Both wind and tide were driving them down into the Rips, and they had to find their way through or pile their ship up in the attempt. It is possible that Daniel Hay, the Englishman, may have been through the Shoals with Gosnold in the *Concord* and knew there was deeper water beyond. At any rate, with their pilot in the rigging where he could pick the blue water between the Rips and with their best helmsman at the tiller, they headed their ship in where it looked as if there were water enough to float her and prayed to St. Christopher to take her through.

Sometimes their sounding line showed as little as four and one half feet, with their ship drawing four. Sometimes the troughs of the running seas sat her down so hard on the hard-packed sands that the rudder began to split out of its ironwork. But "by the grace of God,"[3] almost the identical words used by the Pilgrims on the *Mayflower* in the same spot fourteen years later, they managed to con her through and around a sandy point into deeper water. There, a little to the westward of Monomoy Point, which they aptly named Batturier but which we natives still love to call Sandy Point, they let go their anchor in two fathoms and a half of water and went to work rigging a juryrudder.

Champlain calls the channel where they came through Pollock Rip Shoals a "very dangerous place,"[4] an expression he seldom uses in writing of his voyages, each day of which was crammed with more dangerous places than come to most men in a full lifetime. That he was a man of discrimination is attested by the fact that even today, with the best of government charts to steer by, with beacons, buoys, light-ships, and lighthouses to mark the dredged channel, this is still a very dangerous place.

While they were getting the rudder fit for use again, a boat under the command of Daniel Hay was sent in to the westward of the Point toward the main land. When they got in off the mouth of what is now Stage Harbor in Chatham, a Monomoyick Indian came dancing down the beach, chanting a "Yo, Yo, Yo,"[5] of welcome, as the Frenchmen put it.

He showed them the best anchoring ground outside Harding's Beach and then accompanied them back to the ship.

Before nightfall the barque was worked up to the roadstead, and the next morning, the fourth of October, came to anchor inside Stage Harbor, a little offshore from where the wharf now stands. The Frenchmen gave it the name of Port Fortuné, the port of mischance, or Unlucky Harbour, on account of the misfortune which happened to them there.[6]

The Indians let them land and set up a forge in which to weld the iron-work of the broken rudder. This is the first recorded instance of the ship-wright's trade being plied on Cape Cod, and this spot, still occupied by the ship-yard of the Stage, is still a favorite location. An oven for the baking of bread was built, and a sailcloth tent put up in which some of the men could sleep on shore to watch the tools and materials which could not be carried on board each night. Neither they nor their belongings were molested in any way.

The Indians bartered their tobacco, wampum, shell bracelets, and even their bows and arrows for the white men's iron hatchets and knives. They supplied the ship with fish, Indian corn, beans, and raisins and showed every hospitality in their power to the strangers. We do not know how the Native Americans felt when a company from the ship, armed to the teeth, marched through the village and circled into the back country, nor do we know their response when friends from the neighboring tribes gathered at Seaquanset [also Saquanset] to see the wonders of the white men of de Poutrincourt as he sent his soldiers among them brandishing their swords. It is probably safe to assume that the presence of Secondon, the Etechemin Indian chief, irritated them. The Etechemins had been the sworn enemies of every tribe south of Cape Ann from time immemorial, and the Monomoyicks possibly believed that Secondon's glittering knife itched to lift their scalps to carry back as trophies to his distant home on the Eastern Shore.

The work on the rudder pushed along. The lockers were filled with fresh bread. It is probable that de Poutrincourt would have gotten away without an open break had not some Indian tried to hide a French hatchet. Instead of reporting the loss to the Head Men of the tribe who undoubtedly would have brought the offender to justice according to Indian custom, the soldiers opened fire into a group of natives among whom the thief had taken refuge.

Almost in the twinkling of an eye, the Indian houses came down; the women and the children disappeared as if by magic, and with them went their bundles of household goods and provisions to some place of safety father inland. In no time at all the populous village of Seaquanset

The fight with the Indians on the 15th of October, 1606, at Chatham. By permission of the Houghton Library.

melted like snow before an April sun from the cleared slopes of Stage Harbor.[7]

This was the fourteenth of October, ten days after the arrival of the Frenchmen in the Harbor. The repairs to the rudder were completed without delay, and de Poutrincourt ordered everything on shore to be brought off to the ship that night. The cook and two companions who were making some bread and cakes were warned to hurry up with their baking in order that they, too, might get aboard before nightfall.

These three men, however, were evidently celebrating the winding up of their baking with a little party of their own. When the shallop was sent in for them at evening, one of them, who "was wont to play the braggart,"[8] as Lescarbot tells us, swore he would not go back with them because they would not let him get drunk on board ship. Two other men from the shallop also decided to join the shore party. So the rest of the boat's crew, disgusted with trying to get the tipsy rollickers on board, finally put off to the ship and left them to get as drunk as they pleased. De Poutrincourt had retired for the night, and no one awakened him to let him know that some of his men were still left on shore.[9] There may have been a little drinking going on aboard ship as well; otherwise, it is hard to understand how the officer of the deck ever allowed those five drunken sailors to stay ashore in what had become an unfriendly setting.

Before daybreak next morning, a Monomoyick war party was stealthily creeping through the underbrush behind the hill back of the tent where they slept. They came "to the number of four hundred, softly over a little hill"[10] in the half light, as an eye-witness describes it, and the Frenchmen, roused from their drunken sleep by the war cries of their opponents, ran out of the tent and down the slope for their lives. They were met by "such a volley of arrows that to rise up was death."[11] Two reached the water's edge and fell dead into it. Another dropped on the sands of the shore where he died soon after. A fourth, mortally wounded, was rescued by the men from the ship and lived to make the passage back to Port Royal, where he died soon after. The fifth, with an arrow in his breast, survived his wound and finally recovered.[12] Lescarbot says that the braggart of the night before who vowed he would not return to the ship made good his boast. They found him dead "face downwards, with a little dog upon his back, both transfixed and transpierced by the same arrow."[13]

The watchman on the ship hearing the unfamiliar shouts of the Indians and the death screams of his shipmates, shouted "To arms! They are killing our men!" Baron de Poutrincourt, together with Champlain, the apothecary Louis Hebert, the two youngsters Biencourt and Gravé, and seven or eight other men grabbed their arms and were into a landing boat before the echoes on Morris Island had scarcely died down from the hubbub. Their boat grounded the distance of a musket shot from dry land,[14] but they jumped knee deep into the water and splashed ashore. The Indians retreated out of gunshot while the Frenchmen gave chase, but finding it impossible to bring them within range, de Poutrincourt finally gave up and returned to gather up his dead and wounded.

The three dead Frenchmen were buried near the roadway which turns down into the head of the wharf today, near a cross that was erected the day before. The Indians were meanwhile taunting them while the last rites were being administered, which so enraged the white men that they again rushed after them but with as little success as before. At last, they took their two desperately wounded men back to the ship.

As soon as the coast was clear, the Indians came down to the shore, beat down the cross, dug up the dead bodies which had been thrown about amid the heath where the Indians had kindled a fire to burn them. The little brass cannon on the ship was trained on them, but they dropped to the ground whenever it was fired and let the shot go over their heads. Again, the exasperated Frenchmen rushed ashore and went after them, and again the Indians disappeared into the forest. The best the landing party could do was to put out the fire, reinter the bodies of their dead companions, and set the cross up again.[15] But they went back aboard this time with a solemn vow that "when it should please God" they would take full and complete revenge on the Indians.

Thus ended the day of the fifteenth of October, a bloody and disastrous one for de Poutrincourt's expedition. Hard luck had dogged them ever since they headed their ship's bow in over the Great Rip of Mallebarre as they called Pollock Rip Shoals and around Sandy Point. Disgusted with their stay at Fortuné and hoping to avoid the Shoals on their return trip, they set sail to the westward next morning, hoping never to see this unlucky harbor again. But head winds drove them back again that same night, and they lay wind-bound in their old anchorage through the seventeenth, the eighteenth, and the nineteenth, with no Indians sighted.

On the morning of the twentieth when the weather once more looked favorable, they tried again for the westward passage, but again the wind struck ahead, and for the second time they were forced back to Fortuné. Scarcely had they gotten their anchor down when young Gravé's musket exploded, blowing one of his hands completely off,[16] in spite of which he lived to become as noted a shipmaster and merchant as his father had been before him. To the exasperated Frenchmen, it seemed that the devil was aboard. Surgical supplies were running low, and the stench from the festering wounds of their stricken shipmates made living on board almost unbearable.[17] But to step foot on shore was to invite sudden death on the point of an arrow.

They decided, therefore, to carry out their vow of vengeance on the Monomoyicks, perhaps breaking the jinx that pursued them. They knew that to accomplish this it would first be necessary to again regain the confidence of the Indians. A squad of the strongest men on the ship was chosen to go ashore, apparently unarmed but with their weapons and those of the boat's crew carefully stowed out of sight in the long-boat. Each man was to carry a string of beads in plain sight on one arm as if for a peace offering; while on the other, he carried a rope of lighted match to make the Indians believe he came to light the peace-pipe of tobacco. They were to assure the Indians of their good faith and lure them if possible into their boat where they could be easily overpowered. Then, they would take them back to Port Royal as prisoners, to slave their lives away grinding corn at the stone hand-mills.

It was planned that if the Indians could not be enticed into the boat then each was to choose his man, approach him in the friendliest manner as if to hand the beads around his neck, and while so doing, to grab him, throw him, and truss him up with the rope of match. If by chance any could not be handled in this manner, then knives were to be passed out, and the Indian stabbed. Should any manage to escape from the strong men, the men in the boat were to surround them and finish them off with their swords. The ship's cannon was trained on the landing to keep the other Indians back if necessary.

It was so well carried out that the Indians were enticed down to the boat but evidently were not entirely fooled by this treacherous show of good will. The six or seven who did get near enough so that the Frenchmen were able to get ropes around them put up such a fight that they were butchered in cold blood. Not one was taken alive, and at last Secondon,[18] the Eastern Indian chieftain, was turned loose on them with his scalping knife to complete the bloody work.

After this, a day or two of quiet went by. Then, the Indians showed up again and, in their turn, attempted to lure the white men into an ambuscade. Nevertheless, Sieur de Poutrincourt landed with ten fully armed and mail-clad men. The Indians fell back to another ambuscade, only to be driven out with musket fire; after which, neither side resumed the fight again.[19] But the bitterness of it rankled in the hearts of the Monomoyicks for two generations to come. How many men the Indians lost besides the six or seven butchered in cold blood will never be known. They had been under point-blank musket fire several times and raked by cannon fire from the ship at least once, but they always carried away their dead and wounded from every skirmish. The death chant must have been heard for many a day in the lodges of the widowed and the fatherless.

At last the winds came fair. The Frenchmen cleared the Harbor, safely rounded Batturier, and gave the Shoals of Pollock Rip a wide berth. That same night they came to anchor off Nawset, and on the twenty-eighth of October, a cold, blowy day, with snow squalls off the land, they sailed away from Cape Cod forever.

The name which the Frenchmen gave to the Cape Cod harbors where they tarried epitomize their labors and their losses. To Nawset, where they left the first white man killed on the soil of New England and came so near to losing their ship in 1605, they gave the name of Mallebarre, bad bar. Stage Harbor, where they arrived in safety after pounding in over the Shoals and rounding Batturier, as they so aptly called Monomoy Point, they named Port Fortuné, and the Dutchmen, who knew the hard luck the French had encountered there, later designated it on their maps as Ungeluckige Haven.

As a result of the two seasons spent in exploring its shores, they took back with them a few specimens of native handicraft, two or three shipmates lying at death's door from their wounds, and a Monomoyick scalp or two dangling from the belt of Secondon, one of which was washed overboard before they reached Grand Menan, which caused the chief to weep openly and loudly.[20] They left behind four dead shipmates, one at Nawset and three at Stage Harbor. They also left behind such a memory of treachery and bloodshed that no white man ever again stepped foot on Cape Cod shores and got away with a whole skin until Pilgrim Governor Bradford made peace with the Indians in 1622. It was sixty years after that before the Monomoyicks ever gave in their allegiance to the Colonists.

They never came back to claim for their King the seaboard they had dyed with their blood, and Cape Cod became a part of New England instead of a province of Nouvelle France. Their dust has long since mingled with the alien soil of Port Fortuné, as forgotten as the Monomoyicks by whose arrows they fell.

Notes

1. William C. Smith, *A History of Chatham Massachusetts*, 4th ed. (Chatham: The Chatham Historical Society, Inc., 1992), 6.
2. See "First Blood: The Death of the Carpenter of St. Malo."
3. W. L. Grant, ed., *Voyages of Samuel de Champlain 1604-1618* (New York: Charles Scribner's Sons, 1907), 94.
4. Ibid.
5. Marc Lescarbot, *The History of New France*, ed. W. L. Grant (Toronto: The Champlain Society, 1911), vol. 2, book 4, 330; Smith, *A History of Chatham Massachusetts*, 8.
6. Grant, *Voyages of Samuel de Champlain*, 100; Lescarbot, *The History of New France*, 337.
7. Grant, *Voyages of Samuel de Champlain*, 97; Lescarbot, *The History of New France*, 332.
8. Lescarbot, *The History of New France*, 334-35.
9. Grant, *Voyages of Samuel de Champlain*, 99.
10. Ibid.
11. Ibid.
12. Lescarbot, *The History of New France*, 334. The survivor was Du Val, a locksmith, whose conspiracy against Champlain and subsequent hanging are told in Lescarbot's *The History of New France*, vol. 2, book 5, chapter 2 and in Samuel de Champlain, *Voyages in 1608-12* (1613), chapter 3.
13. Lescarbot, *The History of New France*, 335.
14. Grant, *Voyages of Samuel de Champlain*, 100.
15. Ibid. Lescarbot records that they dug up one of the dead, took off his shirt and put it on, and "made mock at us by taking sand in their two hands and casting it between their buttocks, yelping the while like wolves" (337).
16. Grant, *Voyages of Samuel de Champlain*, 101. According to Lescarbot, Gravé had three fingers blown off (336).
17. Grant, *Voyages of Samuel de Champlain*, 103-4.

18. Champlain calls him Secondon, but Lescarbot calls him Chkoudun (337-38).
19. Grant, *Voyages of Samuel de Champlain*, 102-3.
20. Lescarbot says, "The savage Chkoudun . . . carried off one of their heads, but by ill-luck it fell into the water, whereat he was so chagrined that he wept openly and loud" (338). However, he must have had some extra scalps because Champlain says, "we landed our savage with some supplies which we gave him. He was well pleased and satisfied at having made this voyage with us, and took away with him some heads of the savages that had been killed at Port Fortune" (105-6).

II

The Coming of the Mayflower

ince nine of Nickerson's ancestors were aboard the original Mayflower *when it made its historic voyage, it is not surprising that much of Nickerson's research was in that area. From this interest in his own genealogy, coupled with his sea-going knowledge, he wrote a book published in 1931 by Houghton Mifflin Company entitled* Land Ho!—1620: A Seaman's Story of the Mayflower Her Construction, Her Navigation and Her First Landfall *from which "That Bright Dawn When* Mayflower *I First Sighted Cape" was taken. He sought to establish the identity of the captain of the* Mayflower *and to solve the mystery as to what happened to Governor William Bradford's first wife. He also took issue with the accepted location of the "First Encounter" and wrote about the earliest recorded shipwreck on the Back Side of Cape Cod which was witnessed by Governor Bradford.*

The Captain of the *Mayflower*

Nickerson left no notes for this piece except for internal references such as "the Port Books show" and a second letter to Paul Harvey, American Broadcasting Co., written 22 February 1954, about the Thanksgiving Day broadcast where Paul Harvey named Tom Jones, the Pirate, as the captain of the Mayflower. In the letter, Nickerson lists eleven arguments that Christopher Jones was the captain, drawing on the High Court of Admiralty Records, the London Port Books, the Somerset House Prerogative Court Records, and the Rotherhithe Parish Register. An excellent argument for his position is in the "Somerset House Prerogative Court Records" (The Mayflower Descendant 1 [1899]: 230-31) which state that on 21 February 1620 (old style) that Christopher Jones witnessed the will of William Mullins, father of Priscilla, who told John to speak for himself, on board the Mayflower in Plymouth Harbor, Massachusetts. A copy of the will was made on 2 April 1621, probably the one to be carried back to England on the Mayflower. "The Captain of the Mayflower" was published in the Cape Codder 2 October 1958.

The Pilgrims who came over on the *Mayflower* refer to their captain simply as "Master Jones, Master," never once mentioning his given name. But the records of the British Admiralty, the King's Bench, the London Port Books, and the other authoritative sources are more explicit.[1] They contain entry after entry giving his full name and that of his ship for more than a dozen years before he sailed for America and until his death two years later. Here is a sample in good old Elizabethan English, quoted verbatim from the London Port Books: "In le Mayflower of Lond[on], Xpofer Jones Mr:—"[2] which translated into modern sea-going terms reads, the *"Mayflower of London,* Christopher Jones, Master."

Christopher Jones and his wife Joan married in the little seaport town of Harwich on the east coast of England.[3] The old church in which he and his wife were married and the house he lived in still stand much as they did when he left there over three hundred and fifty years ago.

By the year 1608, when he was still in his early twenties, he became part owner and skipper of the one hundred and eighty ton bark *Mayflower*—a good-sized merchant ship for his day. It is highly probable that for their honeymoon he took his bride around to London in their new ship because from that date we find the *Mayflower* hailing from the Port of London and the newlyweds making their home just across the Thames at Rotherhithe.[4]

For the next eight years he bucked the North Sea and Baltic runs, one of the coldest, toughest, and roughest salt water trade routes in the then known world. Once, homeward bound from Norway,[5] his deckload was washed overboard, and he nearly lost his ship in a terrible North Sea gale, only to be met with a lawsuit,[6] when he finally limped into port, because of his inability to deliver the lost goods. This must have been exasperating to Captain Jones, but the litigation which followed placed on record much of his life story and, in particular, brought out the high regard in which he was held by his shipmates. One old salt, Able Seaman Tom Thompson, who had sailed with him in the ship *Jason*[7] before he took over the *Mayflower*, testified that but for the superb seamanship of the captain the ship would probably have gone down with all hands.

In the year 1616 he switched into an altogether different trade.[8] Instead of bringing in the usual cargo of boards and pickled herring from the chilly northern countries, the Port Books tell us that he docked at London in midsummer with his ship loaded to the scuppers with the good "French wynes and redd wynes" as they put it, just in from a cruise to the South of Europe and the exotic Canary Islands. The wine trade employed only shipmasters of known integrity and sobriety and required that their ships be tight and sweet. Evidently Captain Jones and his *Mayflower* came up to those requirements. During the next four years, he landed shipload after shipload of wine for the London merchants, and as late as the spring of 1620, when the Pilgrims decided to emigrate to the New World and he decided to take them across, the Port Books show that he had just unloaded a full cargo of nearly one hundred and eighty "tonnes."[9]

We next pick him up in midsummer at Southhampton Water packing in the Pilgrims and their belongings, his ship overhauled and outfitted for overseas. His tough schooling in battling North Sea and Bay of Biscay gales had fitted him exceptionally well to take on the stormy Western Ocean. His passengers left an eyewitness account of one mid-ocean sifter in which on her beam ends "cracked" a main beam,[10] they say, and washed overboard a Pilgrim lad named John Howland.[11] With young Howland safe on board again, thanks to a trailing topsail halyard, Captain Jones jacked up the sprung beam, shored it securely in place,[12] and banged the *Mayflower* westward come hell or high water, until at last what he deemed to be Cape Cod loomed over the bow.

Historians in general have written off this landfall as hit upon purely by accident. This is emphatically not so; Captain Christopher Jones, an exceedingly skillful navigator, with his crude instrumental observations combined with the shrewdest kind of dead reckoning, was following in on the forty-second parallel of north latitude which he knew cuts across Cape Cod. He then intended to swing south and land his passengers somewhere in the vague Hudson River country as they had planned, but strong head winds and the treacherous shoals on the elbow of the Cape headed him off, and he was forced to seek temporary shelter in Provincetown before finally anchoring in Plymouth Harbor the day after Christmas.

Here he lay for three ghastly months while fifty per cent of his crew and passengers died[13] in the deadly epidemic which Governor Bradford called the general sickness. There is every reason to believe Captain Jones, himself, contracted the terrible malady but pulled through alive, never again to be a well man. It is a matter of record that when he cleared for Old England in the spring of 1621[14] he left buried with the Pilgrim dead almost half of their company, "many of their officers and lustyest men, as ye boatson, gunner, 3. quarter-maisters, the cooke, & others."[15] He sailed the *Mayflower* home to his wife and children, little Joan and Christopher, with only half a crew, but the tragic winter in New England had been too much for even his iron constitution. In a few short months, according to the Parish Register, he was laid to rest in the quiet of the old Rotherhithe Churchyard,—an unsung martyr to the landing of the Pilgrims.[16]

His widow Joan, who had kept the home fires burning through all these turbulent years, was appointed administrator of his estate by the Admiralty. These years had run fast since that bright day in 1608 when they came honeymooning up the Thames to register their new ship as the *"Mayflower of London*, Christopher Jones, Master." Now, with her sailor home from the sea and his last voyage ended, the probate records tell us that she was obliged to sell his share of that ship to wind up his worldly affairs.[17] A hint of heartbreak which went with it seems still to cling to the musty documents with which she closed the public record of an adventurous life lived dangerously.

Notes

1. G. Andrews Moriarty Jr., "Notes," in *The New England Historical and Genealogical Register* (Boston: The Society, 1929) quotes from the the Book of Imports into the Port of London for the year 1620 three entries from January through May: "In le *Mayflower of London*—Christopher Jones, Mr" (83: 251).
2. J. R. Hutchinson, "The 'Mayflower,' Her Identity and Tonnage" in *The New England Historical and Genealogical Register* (Boston: The Society, 1916) quotes from the Book of Imports into the Port of London an entry for 28 January 1619 (70: 341).
3. W. Sears Nickerson, who visited this little seaport town, was born in the Harwich on Cape Cod in New England which his Pilgrim forefathers, who settled it, named after the home town of the *Mayflower*'s captain.
4. R. G. Marsden, "The *Mayflower*," *The Mayflower Descendant* 18 (1916): 10; Marsden states that in 1618 Jones is described as of Redrith (Rotherhithe)."
5. Hutchinson, "The 'Mayflower,' Her Identity and Tonnage," 339.
6. Marsden, "The *Mayflower*," 8.
7. Marsden states that Jones was owner and master of the *Jason* (7).
8. Marsden, "The *Mayflower*," 9; Hutchinson, "The 'Mayflower,' Her Identity and Tonnage," 341.
9. Hutchinson, "The 'Mayflower,' Her Identity and Tonnage," 341; *The New England Historical and Genealogical Register*, 83: 251.
10. Marsden, "The *Mayflower*," 4.
11. William Bradford, *Bradford's History "Of Plimoth Plantation"* (Boston: Wright and Potter Printing Co., State Printers, 1899), 92-93.
12. Marsden, "The *Mayflower*," 4.
13. Bradford, *Bradford's History*, 111.
14. Bradford, *Bradford's History*, 120; Marsden, "The *Mayflower*," 5. She sailed on about 5 April and arrived 5 or 6 May.
15. Bradford, *Bradford's History*, 112.
16. Marsden states that he died before 26 August 1622 as on that day administration on his effects was granted to Joan, his widow (10). Also, see Hutchinson, "The 'Mayflower,' Her Identity and Tonnage," 340.
17. Marsden, "The *Mayflower*."

That Bright Dawn When *Mayflower I* First Sighted Cape

W. Sears Nickerson, a Mayflower descendent, discussed in his book, Land Ho!—1620: A Seaman's Story of the Mayflower, Her Construction, Her Navigation and Her First Landfall, *the controversial questions as to just what part of Cape Cod the* Mayflower *first sighted and where she spent her time between that first sighting and her final anchoring in Provincetown Harbor. He warns readers that one must allow for the change in the calendar when studying data on that first landing; to the Pilgrims they first saw land on 9 November 1620; by today's calendar, it was November 19. Nickerson left no notes for "That Bright Dawn," but his sources are clearly Dwight B. Heath, ed.,* Mourt's Relation A Journal of the Pilgrims at Plymouth, *William Bradford, Bradford's History "Of Plimoth Plantation," and Nickerson's own* Land Ho!—1620. *I have combined and freely and silently edited three articles: "First 'Town Meeting' Held On Mayflower Off Cape Tip," "Land Ho!—1620. Pilgrims' Progress Along the Backside of the Cape," and "That Bright Dawn When* Mayflower I *First Sighted Cape."*

Most of us have heard of the voyage of the *Mayflower* and the landing of the Pilgrims. How many of us have given a thought as to what it must have been like on board that good ship when she first sighted the coast of America?

It was about 6:30 on that morning of Thursday, November 19, 1620,[1] when the first streak of daylight hove up clear over the rim of a slick sea on the back side of Cape Cod. A waning quarter of the old moon hung high in mid-sky overhead. Twenty-five minutes later, at 5 minutes of 7, the splendor of the rising sun flooded the east with softest

75

rose and spilled westward until it broke against the lone ship lazily lifting and listing to the sleepy ground swell.

One moment she stood out weird and spectral against the backdrop of night; the next, lifting her high poop up out of a trough of shadows into the wake of the morning, every rippling fold of her idle canvas became a shimmering cloth of gold radiance; windowed galleries changed to sunbursts, and a weathered scroll, crusted with salt and bedimmed by the night's dew, turned to luster under the magic touch and blazed back the legend, *Mayflower of London.*

Captain Jones, straightening up from dreaming over the taffrail about his little Chris and Joan back there in Rotherhithe, stretched as a strong man does to shake off the lethargy of the night watches.

This was the 65th consecutive day since clearing from the Barbican in Plymouth in Old England that he had pounded his ship to the southwest across the Western Ocean. Unavoidable delays had hindered the start, and contrary winds dogged the westward passage. Unknown to him as to every navigator of his day, the set of the Gulf Stream had at times pushed him astern faster than his ship forged ahead through the waters. Scurvy was showing its hideous symptoms among the crew and passengers alike, and already one of the his own men had been buried at sea, followed in a few days by young Billie Butten, the first of the Pilgrims to go.[2]

One mother had already given birth to a baby boy on this long, overdue voyage, and another's time was nearly up.[3] Water was so low in the butts that none could be spared to the women for washing their clothes.[4] There was no firewood left even for cooking, and every westerly now came with the bite of winter in its maw. And still no land was in sight. A lesser man than Captain Christopher Jones or a less determined company than his Pilgrim passengers would long since have turned tail and made a fair wind of it for the English Channel.

At midnight the deep sea lead had found no bottom at 100 fathoms, nor had it at 4:00 when the watch was changed again. Then came the dawn of a new day, fair and clear. In the growing daylight, it almost seemed that the Indigo blue of the offshore depths was giving way to the emerald green of the coastal shelf, and perhaps a whiff of land was on the morning breeze. Sailors tend to forget the miseries of dark days at sea in the lure of the promise just over the horizon ahead. As the sails of the *Mayflower* filled with the breeze which comes up with the sun, Captain Jones snapped back to his job.

The marks and deeps on the leadline zipping through the knurled but experienced hand of the old leadsman, now stationed forward, disappeared into the mysterious blue. "By the mark!—By the deep!" His melodious singsong ritual chanted out the depths. Fifty fathoms—60 fathoms—70 fathoms"—and then a tense pause while he tried it again to make sure. Suddenly, his startled voice sang out in shrill staccato, its import clear and unmistakable.

"And BOTTOM sir!! at 80 FATHOMS!!"

As if to strike the high hour of victory, the ship's bell chimed out the hour of 7—"Ding-ding!—Ding—ding!—Ding-ding!" Its echoes were still tingling back from top—and spritsail when another shout, the most welcome that ever falls on sea-weary ears, rang out from the maintop lookout:

> "LA-A-ND HO-O!!
> LA-A-ND HO-O!!
> LAND! LAND!
> LA-A-ND HO!!"[5]

That hail, which they had longed for through so many weary days and nights, rang through the cabins and down to the 'tween decks of the *Mayflower!* It quickened the heart beat of every living soul in that devoted company from the aging elder of the flock to little sea-born Oceanus at his mother's breast. Half-dressed men, women, and children clambered to rail and rigging to peer ahead to the wooded shore of what is now Eastham whose rolling hills they were destined to people. Did these Pilgrims fathers and mothers of ours shout and dance, sing and pray, or were they silenced by the overwhelming solemnity of that ecstatic moment? William Bradford, who was one of them on that glad morning, writing of it in after years tells us, "they were not a litle joyfull."[6]

The first land sighted was the Eastham shore when the *Mayflower* was about nine miles offshore headed almost straight for the spot were the Nauset Coast Guard Station stands today.[7] The Pilgrims themselves tell us that "upon the ninth of November . . . by break of the day we espied land which we deemed to be Cape Cod, and so afterward it proved."[8] Captain Jones, no doubt, never brought his ship into much less than a hundred fathoms depth before daybreak that morning, even though it was clear weather and he had a small moon to light the way because old-time ship masters were as shy of coming in onto coastal shoal waters as the Devil is said to be of holy water. But after sunrise, with the sun striking full on the sand dunes ahead, eighty fathoms of water under his keel, and an off-shore breeze just ruffling the placid sea, he could take it by-the-wind and jog in to make sure of his landfall.

It was a beautiful, late-Indian summer day as the Pilgrims described it,[9] with a gentle breeze off the land in the morning, swinging out more from the north and northeast as the day wore on and coming in from the southward before night—what Cape Codders know as a "sea-turn day." A day or two of southerly wind almost certainly follows a sea-turn day, and no other sort of weather can logically account for the courses steered and the landmarks encountered by the *Mayflower* on that day and next.

The passengers have told us that they "deemed" it to be Cape Cod when they first sighted it. As they had no way of knowing the ship's position, it must be assumed that the captain had dropped them a hint; therefore, he must have felt pretty certain what landfall he had made before he headed his ship inshore.

Many historians claim that the *Mayflower* stumbled onto Cape Cod purely by accident, and even Captain Villiers, the commander of the *Mayflower II*, seems doubtful that Captain Jones knew his exact position at any time on the voyage across. It is true he had no way of knowing how far west his ship had gotten, the chronometer, which enabled later navigators to determine their distance west of Greenwich, not having come into usage. He did, however, have his cross staff, his old hog yoke, as he called it, and perhaps even an astrolabe with which to "shoot the sun" and get his distance north of the equator. In other words, he always knew approximately what parallel of north latitude his ship was on. Cape Cod lies on the 42nd parallel of north latitude, and then, as now, was the target for most ships sailing out of the north of Europe for America. Dutch skippers headed for the Hudson; English captains bound for Jamestown, explorers, slave stealers, and fishermen simply set their course so as to pick up the 42nd parallel a good safe distance off the American coast and then followed it until they raised the Cape and knew where they were. This prevented them from overrunning their reckoning and piling up on a strange coast some dark night.

Captain Christopher Jones certainly knew all this before he ever cleared from the English Channel. In addition, his town Master's Mates had been over this Western Ocean road before. So there can be little doubt he was following the usual course of experienced shipmasters. He was not the rum-soaked, half-pirate most writers, broadcasters, and the movies have pictured him.[10] Records made of that time and still in existence prove that he was, instead, a respected, young merchant skipper from Harwich, part owner of his *Mayflower* and a courageous and very capable navigator. It is, therefore, no small compliment to his skill as a navigator that after sixty-five days at sea out of sight of land, buffeted by equinoctial gales, pushed around by unknown currents, and navigating by dead reckoning and instruments alone, the *Mayflower* was on the 42nd parallel of north latitude and heading straight for Cape Cod when he made the land, that one known landmark from which all ships bound for Virginia from the north of Europe shaped their course.

Bradford goes on to tell us that ". . . Cape Cod; the which being made & certainly knowne to be it, they were not a litle joyfull. After some deliberation had amongst them selves & with ye mr. of ye ship, they tacked aboute and resolved to stande for ye southward (ye wind & weather being faire) to finde some place aboute Hudsons river for their habitation."[11] The eastern shore of Eastham which they had seen at daybreak "wooded to the brink of the sea"[12] might easily be mistaken for other similar low-lying areas on the American coast, but to have "certainly knowne" they had made Cape Cod, they must have gotten in close enough to clearly see the Highland of Truro.

Master's Mates Clarke and Coppin had sailed these waters before, and the Highland, rising a sheer one hundred feet above high water mark, once seen from offshore by an experienced seaman, is never confused with any other landmark on our eastern seaboard. Here was the proof that Captain Jones's old hog-yoke had proved pretty accurate. The position where they "tacked aboute" is very important in logging the day's work either forward or back. It was far enough to the north so that there was no mistaking the Highland of Truro. It was far enough south so that a half day's run brought the *Mayflower* to the shoals which turned her back, which at her known average speed of two and one-half miles an hour for six hours would be about twenty-one miles. And it had to be far enough off-shores that the "south south west"[13] course she steered after she tacked would clear the dangerous Chatham Bars. The one position which answers all these requirements places her about five miles off the South Wellfleet shore, some ten miles southeast of Highland Light and twenty-one miles north northeast of the shoals of Pollock Rip.[14]

The fact that she had to tack ship here to take a southerly course shows that up till now she had been standing in toward the land on a northwest course with the wind on the port or left side. Otherwise, she would not have had to tack to head to the south southwest. Assuming that at sunrise she was off in eighty fathoms of water, it would have taken her two hours to cover the five miles necessary to bring her in close enough to see clearly the Highland, and it would now be near 9:00 A.M.

If we backtrack five miles along the course which brought her to her 9:00 A.M. position, it must bring us to her daybreak position. Thus, we are able to pin-point the spot from which the Pilgrims first saw the land as just about nine miles east of the Nauset Coast Guard Station on the Eastham shore.

Had the wind favored them while they were hove to off South Wellfleet they would have then and there headed for Provincetown, which lay only a short distance to the north as shown on Captain John Smith's map which was part of the *Mayflower*'s equipment. They were on short rations of water, completely out of firewood; scurvy was breaking out, and in spite of the balmy weather that they were then enjoying, they knew winter might clamp down on them at any moment, as indeed it did a few days later. Simple prudence demanded that they make harbor soon, no matter where. But by the time they had finished their "deliberations,"[15] the sea-turn breeze was coming from the north, dead against them for a run to Provincetown, so there was no alternative but to swing the *Mayflower*'s head to the southward and make a try for the Hudson River country.

An eminent historian has argued that "South South West" was probably an error of the press for south southeast as such a course would have run the *Mayflower* ashore in short order. Evidently, he was unfamiliar with the erratic gyrations of the compass needle off back of the Cape. Champlain reported that in 1605 the magnetic variation from true north at Nauset was 18 degrees, 40 minutes west; in 1780 it had shrunk to 6 degrees, 50 minutes, but by 1929 it was back to 15 degrees, 30 minutes, and when one adjusts the *Mayflower*'s compass to the 13 degrees, 30 minutes west variation of the year 1620, one finds that the south southwest course which the Pilgrims gave was the true course and has never been improved upon to this day.

It is obvious to any seaman that as the coast lies today a competent shipmaster headed south southwest from a position five miles off the South Wellfleet shore would meet with no serious obstacle to navigation until he came to the shoals of Pollock Rip, south of Chatham.[16]

To make doubly sure, he took the off-shore, land breeze on the port tack and stood in until his men, who had seen it before, could clearly identify the hundred foot headland of the Highland of Truro. In the meantime, the wind shifted more to the north so that he had to "tack aboute" they tell us, in order to make a "South South west" course with a fair wind, hoping to reach some place "aboute Hudsons river" for a landing. The *Mayflower* ghosted along southward down the Nawset shore, slipped by the old inlet to Monomoyick Bay, now Pleasant Bay, and left the Great Hill of Chatham astern over her starboard quarter. The ocean ahead looked serene and inviting. Then suddenly, almost in the twinkling of an eye, she found herself snarled up among the "deangerous shoulds and roring breakers"[17] as they put it, of the Broken Part of Pollock Rip, one of the most deceitful stretches of navigable water on the American seaboard. There were no warning buoys or beacons to make the edge in 1620, and there could be no turning back for a square-rigged ship against that northerly wind which was crowding her in among the shoals. To anchor, drawing the twelve feet of water, meant that she would probably pound her bottom out on some unseen bar where she lay.

Just at this critical moment, when it looked as if the voyage was about ended, a seeming miracle took place, literally right out of the blue. The wind, which had hung from a northeasterly direction all day long, suddenly changed and struck "contrary"[18] as they express it, a good, strong, life-saving breeze from the south. Captain Jones praised the Lord, swung his ship's head around, squared his yards before it, and clewed her out through the treacherous rips into the blue water beyond. Before sundown he had her back off Chatham and hove to for the night with plenty of water under her kneel.

As a matter of fact, this sudden switch of winds was to be expected on the sort of day the Pilgrims describe in their comments on the wind and weather. They make it clear that this was what sea-going Cape Codders would have called a "sea turn day," one of those beautiful, clear, sunshiny days peculiar to the Cape, when the day-long, northeasterly breeze from the sea turns abruptly and comes in from the south just before night. It seemed like "Gods providence"[19] the Pilgrims say, and every old shellback in the forecastle would have sworn on Elder Brewster's Great Bible that he had indeed witnessed a miracle. Still, the hard fact remains that had it not happened just in the nick of time, the *Mayflower* might well have laid up in some forgotten slue in the Broken Part of Pollock Rip, as many a good ship has done since her day.

Captain Jones must have driven the old girl to the north for all she was worth while the daylight lasted, once he got her back into deep water again. With everything drawing alow and aloft before the freshening south wind and with a 2 knot tide kicking her right in the stern, the *Mayflower* would make five or six miles of northing before darkness shut down at 5:00 P.M. This would bring her by nightfall to a position about seven miles southeast by east from Chatham, not far outside the present anchorage of Pollock Lightship 110. With the weather clear and the wind and the tide both setting him away from the Shoals, no level-headed skipper like Captain Jones would take a chance on running further in the utter darkness of an unknown and uncharted coast, nor of losing a good mud-hook in twenty fathoms of water by anchoring for the night.

The logical thing to do would be to heave his ship to back his main topsail against the wind, to keep the lead line over the side to tell him if she ranged ahead or astern or did a little side-slipping, to twig his other sails to balance his backed topsail, and to let her hold her ground as near as possible until daylight hove up again in the east. Thus ends Thursday, November 19, 1620, the Pilgrim's first day on the American coast. It had been quite a day.

We now come to the historical controversy over the whereabouts of the *Mayflower* on Friday, November 20. The Pilgrims themselves give us little to go by, but they did amply record the fact that they did not get into Provincetown Harbor until the morning of Saturday, November 21.

With this in mind, we will pick her up at daybreak Friday morning just where we left her off Chatham at dark the night before. It so happened that there was about ten hours of daylight sailing time that day. It also happens that owing to a peculiar split of the tides off Nauset a ship leaving the shoals and heading north at just the right time of the tide can hold a head tide for the next ten hours. That is just what happened to the *Mayflower*. She had to buck a head tide from sunrise to sunset on November 20, for the whole fifty-odd miles up the coast from Chatham to the Head of the Cape. That she had gotten near enough to Provincetown by nightfall so that she could slip into the harbor on Saturday morning, November 21, is proof that she held a good, stiff, southerly wind over her shoulder all day Friday, or she never could have made it.

Of course, Captain Jones knew nothing of these witch tides, but he did know that this south wind ended for the present all hopes of reaching the Hudson River Country. On the other hand, it was a fine, leading breeze for Provincetown, which lay only a short distance to the north. The prudent thing to do was to swing her off the road he had so blithely run down the day before. In fact, there was no alternative, and it is plain, too, that the Pilgrims, themselves, agreed with him.

For turning back here he has been accused of everything from petty graft to downright treachery. His accusers do not understand how utterly impossible it was for him to beat his square-rigged ship south over the Shoals against a head wind, nor do they know the great risk he would have taken of losing her altogether on a lee shore had he hove to wait for a change of wind anywhere in the dangerous waters off back the Cape at this season of the year. No land lubber can even begin to imagine the almost unbearable living conditions which must have existed on board this old windjammer for passengers and crew alike, after almost ten long and dreary weeks at sea. The Pilgrims themselves, the men and women who were there and knew the answers, never criticized Captain Jones for this decision. No litigation ever arose because of it, and they held him in high regard to the end, even naming a river for him.

By 10:00 A.M.. he would have the *Mayflower* back off Nauset but a little closer inshore than the place from which her people first sighted the land the day before. The gullied clay banks of the Highland of Truro would be looming close aboard by 2:00 P.M., and by 4:55 that night, with High Head almost abeam on the port side, the Pilgrims would watch the sun go down behind the hill in Provincetown where three centuries later a grateful posterity would rear a monument to their memory. Whatever our pilgrim fathers and mothers may have seen in that sunset, Captain Jones, doubtless, watched it go down with a much easier mind than on the night before when he had just clewed his ship to safety out of the breakers of the broken part of Pollock Rip.

As darkness shut down, a gentle breeze from off the land would bring them the sweet scent of bayberry and savin-bush, and the tide which had headed them all day would turn fair and sweep them out by The Race into the deep waters of Cape Cod Bay, where the records of earlier navigators showed there twenty fathoms almost right up into the beach knolls. So long as the weather remained clear and the wind held from off the land, Captain Jones had only to keep his ship off the beach, not lose touch with the land, and let her jog on and off until daylight would show him the path into Provincetown Harbor.[20] Thus ends the Pilgrims' second day on the back side of Cape Cod, with the *Mayflower* holding her position off The Race for the night and waiting for the dawn.

Saturday morning, November 21, the sun rose clear again about 6:55. Undoubtedly, the wind still held from the south, but it makes little difference from which direction the wind comes in taking a sailing ship into Provincetown Harbor. She boxes the compass anyway, as sailors express it; that is, she heads to every point of the compass while rounding in to the anchorage, and a fair wind in one place is a head wind in another. Captain Jones caught a fair tide going in that morning, so with his fore and main courses clewed up he could feel his way along before the tide under easy sail with the hand lead going with whatever wind he could catch.

While he sounded in around the Point, below in the great cabin of the *Mayflower* was held the first New England town meeting. It was by now understood by all that their settlement would have to be made outside the jurisdiction of their English patent or charter, which was for Virginia and definitely not for New England. This left them with no constituted authority by which to preserve order and regulate the affairs of the proposed colony once they got ashore.

There was quite a large number in the Pilgrim company who were not members of the original Separatist congregation. They immediately asked the question as to who would govern the colony and by what right, now that they would be obligated to start their settlement wholly outside the jurisdiction of their English patent. The Pilgrims tell us that some of the strangers, as they called those who were not Pilgrims, made "discontented & mutinous speeches"[21] and threatened that " . . . when they came a shore they would use their owne libertie; for none had power to comand them, the patente they had being for Virginia, and not for Newengland."[22] They tell us in their own words, "This day before we came to harbour, observing some not well affected to unity and concord . . . it was thought good . . . that we should combine together into one body, and to submit to such government and governors as we should by common consent agree to make and choose, and set our hands to this that follows word for word."[23] It presented a very delicate situation for the leaders to handle. They were actually fewer in numbers than the strangers, and there was no precedent to go by. But most of the Pilgrims had lived long years of exile in the Netherlands where they had become accustomed to regulating the affairs of their Separatist congregation by majority vote. When faced with this dilemma, they immediately adapted this familiar procedure to their civil affairs so that the question might be settled before any person should be allowed to set foot on dry land.

And so it happened that on the following morning, while Captain Jones was cautiously sounding his way in around Race Point toward Provincetown, an open meeting was called in the great-cabin of the *Mayflower* before they came to harbour as they are so careful to state. Then and there a patent or charter of their own making was presented and after due deliberation adopted.

"In the presence of God," the Pilgrims wrote, "and one of another," the oldest elder and the youngest indentured servant and hired hand were required to walk to the table and there signify their willingness to abide by it by signing the document. There, under the uncertain light of the *Mayflower*'s cabin lamp, every man jack of them who was of legal age and a free man, whether "well affected" or otherwise, from John Carver, soon to be made their first governor, down to young John Alden, the hired hand who had been shipped in Southampton as a cooper, forty-one of them in all, walked up to the table and set their hands to this home-made constitution before the *Mayflower* came to anchor. After it was signed and sealed, John Carver was confirmed as governor of the colony with power to enforce the terms of their mutual agreement.

Known today as the "*Mayflower* Compact," it is one of the treasured documents of the English-speaking world. And the little gathering in the great-cabin of the *Mayflower* off Cape Cod on Saturday morning. November 21, 1620, when it was accepted and adopted, was the first New England town meeting. The "*Mayflower* Compact" or "combination," as the Pilgrims called it, became the basis on which their civil code was founded, "as firm as any patent, and in some respects more sure."

The "*Mayflower* Compact" that they signed follows:

"In ye name of God, Amen. We whose names are underwriten, the loyall subjects of our dread Soveraigne Lord, King James, by ye grace of God, of Great Britaine, Franc, & Ireland king, defender of ye faith, &c., haveing undertaken, for ye glorie of God, and advancemente of ye Christian faith, and honour of our king & countrie, a voyage to plant ye first colonie in ye Northerne parts of Virginia, doe by these presents solemnly & mutualy in ye presence of God, and one of another, covenant & combine our selves togeather into a civill body politick, for our better ordering & preservation & furtherance of ye ends aforesaid; and by vertue hereof to enacte, constitute, and frame such just & equall lawes, ordinances, acts, constitutions, & offices, from time to time, as shall be thought most meete & convenient for ye generall good of ye Colonie, unto which we promise all due submission and obedience. In witnes wherof we have hereunder subscribed our names at Cap-Codd, ye 11. of November, in ye year of ye raigne of our soveraigne lord, King James, of England, France, & Ireland ye eighteenth, and of Scotland ye fiftie fourth. Ano: Dom. 1620.”[24]

Before she sailed back to old England in the spring, half of those signers were in their graves, but the Compact survived and was the foundation on which the struggling colony based its laws for years to come. Not only that but also it set the pattern for other voluntary agreements among later colonists which finally culminated in our Declaration of Independence and put our country out in the forefront of the free nations of the world.

The Compact was signed and sealed; a governor was confirmed in office, and by 10:00 in the forenoon of Saturday, November 21, 1620, the *Mayflower of London*, sixty-seven days out of Plymouth in Old England backed her topsails just inside Long Point in Provincetown Harbor in New England. This ancient anchorage has seen many a famous ship ride its sheltered waters during its long history but never one so dear to America's heart as the old *Mayflower* as she let go her anchor in the waters of this New World, the mud of the Old still sticking to her flukes.

Here we will leave her, gently swinging in her moorings on the blue waters of the Bay, her Pilgrim passengers giving thanks to their “ . . . God of heaven, who had brought them over ye vast & furious ocean, and delivered them from all ye periles & miseries therof,”[25] the while they grimly trim their matchlocks for the work ahead.

Notes

1. Dwight B. Heath, ed., *Mourt's Relation A Journal of the Pilgrims at Plymouth* (Chester: Globe Pequot Press, 1963), 15.
2. William Bradford, *Bradford's History "Of Plimoth Plantation"* (Boston: Wright and Potter Printing Co., State Printers, 1899), 93.
3. Bradford, *Bradford's History*, 532; Heath, *Mourt's Relation*, 31. Oceanus Hopkins and Peregrine White were born on this voyage.
4. Heath, *Mourt's Relation*, 19.

5. W. Sears Nickerson, *Land Ho!—1620: A Seaman's Story of the Mayflower Her Construction, Her Navigation and Her First Landfall* (Boston: Houghton Mifflin Co., 1931), 11. This is historical fiction.
6. Bradford, *Bradford's History*, 93.
7. In giving his credentials for arriving at this conclusion, Nickerson writes, "By the grace of God I was born right on the ragged elbow of Cape Cod toward which the *Mayflower* was pointing her bowsprit when she made the land. I fished its shoals and battled its witch tides as a boy and as a young man sailed its waters in an old square-rigged ship not much larger than the *Mayflower*, just as Captain Jones had to do. There are perhaps few men alive today who can tackle this problem from any like prospective of background and training, certainly few who still hold papers from square-rigged ships of the United States Merchant Marine. I combed original records to find out just what conditions she actually encountered, what sort of ship she really was, and what state of affairs really existed on board among the passengers and crew when she came onto our coast. I gathered from *Bradford's History* and from *Mourt's Relation*, both written by men who were there. I witnessed testimony concerning the state of the weather, the directions from which they had the wind, the landmarks encountered, essential features of the ship, herself, and the condition of crew and passengers after two months at sea. I went to the Naval Observatory in Washington for the correct hours of the sunrise and sunset, the phase of the moon, and the time of high water on the back side of Cape Cod on that particular date over three hundred years ago. The British Admiralty and London Port Books came up with the history of the *Mayflower* and her commander for a dozen years before their transatlantic voyage, and these are but a few of the authentic authorities from which I have drawn. Add to these expert opinions given me by Shoals fishermen, light ship skippers, and coast guard captains on local eccentricities of wind and tide, coupled with my own intimate knowledge of this coast and how to navigate square-rigged ships, and it becomes clear that little was left to guess work in pin pointing the position of the *Mayflower*."
8. Heath, *Mourt's Relation*, 15.
9. Bradford, *Bradford's History*, 93.
10. See page 71.
11. Bradford, *Bradford's History*, 93.
12. Heath, *Mourt's Relation*, 15.
13. Ibid.
14. Nickerson spells this Pollack Rip and Pollock Rip. I have used the modern spelling.
15. Bradford, *Bradford's History*, 93.
16. To see if this were true in 1620, Nickerson studied the maps and journals of the early explorers from the year 1500 on down to current Coast Pilot, Coast and Geodetic Survey Charts. The results showed that except for a slight retrogression and a general straightening out of the coast line because of the washing away of old islands and out jutting points and filling in of

ancient harbor mouths, it is a fact that no radical changes which would affect off-shore navigation have taken place within historical times. As a matter of fact, the man who stood on the deck of the *Mayflower* some three hundred years ago and fixed the landmarks of the Backside in his mind would have little difficulty in recognizing them today, and Captain Christopher Jones would find the "deangerous shoulds and roring breakers" of the Shoals of Pollock Rip just about where he left them on the night of 19 November 1620.

17. Bradford, *Bradford's History*, 93.
18. Heath, *Mourt's Relation*, 16.
19. Bradford, *Bradford's History*, 93.
20. Heath, *Mourt's Relation*, 16n.2.
21. Bradford, *Bradford's History*, 109.
22. Ibid.
23. Heath, *Mourt's Relation*, 17.
24. Bradford, *Bradford's History*, 110.
25. Ibid., 94.

William Bradford's First Wife: A Suicide

Nickerson, who was descended from Governor Bradford's second wife and her first husband, draws on public records to support family tradition concerning the fate of Bradford's first wife.

Much Pilgrim lore never recorded in the archives of any society of *Mayflower* descendants was common table talk on Cape Cod. Probably seventy-five percent of the pioneer settlers on the Lower Cape were of *Mayflower* extraction, and they not only brought along to their new homes their religion and customs but also much of their unwritten family histories. One of the skeletons in the closet of *Mayflower* heritage was the love story of Governor William Bradford.

Family tradition held the opinion that Governor William Bradford's first wife loved him passionately but that her love was never fully reciprocated. It said that while he was a kind and faithful husband he had married her on the rebound, as it were, when refused the hand of his first and only love. It told that her death by drowning from the deck of the *Mayflower*, in Provincetown Harbor, was no accident but her own deliberate act and that later her husband's first love became his second wife.

One such Cape Cod family was W. Sears Nickerson's.[1] The old folks who handed down this old family tale had probably never heard of the ancient Dutch records, nor of Mather's *Magnalia*, nor *Bradford's History*, but they knew, or thought they did, that his first wife committed suicide and why.

William Bradford, the son of respectable and God-fearing country folk, was baptized on the nineteenth of March, 1589, in the little church known as St. Helens in Austerfield, Yorkshire, England.[2] His parents died when he was very young, leaving him to be brought up by an aged grandfather.

Austerfield, although in another county, lies only a very few miles distance across the fields from Scrooby in Nottinghamshire. As the lonely orphan lad grew into boyhood, he came more and more under the influence of William Brewster, who was later to be immortalized by the poet, Longfellow, as "The Excellent Elder of Plymouth." Brewster became almost a second father to Bradford, and the living example of that good man and the great lessons of simple brotherhood which he learned as he gathered with the Pilgrim band to worship in the old Scrooby Manor House moulded his whole life. While yet in his teens, he followed the Separatists into exile in the Low Countries and became an active worker in the struggling community in Leyden.

In the Reverend John Robinson's congregation in Leyden was the exiled family of Alexander Carpenter, consisting of his wife and their daughters, Mary, Agnes, Juliana, Priscilla, and Alice. Alice was about the same age as William Bradford,[3] and they were naturally thrown much into each other's company in the younger set of Leyden's Separatist society. She is described by those who knew her as of "good descent and holy predecessors"[4] and as comely as she was Godly.

Stalwart young Bradford and beautiful Alice Carpenter fell deeply in love there in the old Dutch city, as young men and maidens are said to have done even in staid old Pilgrim days. But father Carpenter frowned sternly on the relationship. Englishmen of that day, whether Pilgrim, Puritan, or Papist, were careful of the prestige and prerogatives of their families. Bradford was a poor boy of obscure lineage, scarce out of his teens and with no estate. Who could foresee in this lowly, fustian worker, diligently throwing the noisy shuttle of his loom back and forth on coarse corduroy and velveteen, a future Governor of a Colony whose name and fame would become a proud heritage of the English-speaking race? Love or no love, Alice must not marry below her station.

In the Leyden congregation, another young man's heart was also set on the comely Alice. Edward Southworth counted his descent through high lords and ladies back to Magna Carta barons. Wealth and influence were part of his inheritance. The ancient Southworth holdings in the Parish of Winwrick in Lancashire entailed from Norman knights whose names were on the Roll of Battle Abbey with that of William the Conqueror. Father Carpenter looked with favor on the suit of Edward Southworth. Alice, it is said, like a true Pilgrim daughter bowed her neck to the wishes of her father, but when William Bradford went out of her life, her heart went with him.

In the ancient *Echt Books* of Leyden, in quaint old Dutch, may still be seen the marriage record of Edward Southworth and Alice Carpenter. It tells us that "Edward Southworth, . . . single man, from England, accompanied by Thomas Southworth, his brother, Samuel Fuller, his brother-in-law, and Roger Wilson, his acquaintance," was married to "Alice Carpenter, single woman, also from England, accompanied by Anna Ross and Elizabeth Jennings, her acquaintances. . . . before Andries Jaspers van Vesanevelt and Jacob Paedts, Sheriffs, this 28th of May, 1613."[5]

It must have been a shrewd blow, as the future Governor of Plymouth Colony would have put it, when he saw Alice Carpenter returning from the wedding as the wife of Edward Southworth. Tradition says that then and there he made a vow that he would show the house of Carpenter that he could marry and marry well, despite his lowly station.

Be that as it may, the *Doop, Trouw* and *Begrafenis Registers* at Amsterdam testify that less than six months after the Southworth-Carpenter nuptials, the banns were up publishing the betrothal of William Bradford and Dorothy May of the New Dyke in Amsterdam. "William Bradford, from Austerfield, fustian weaver, 23 years old, living at Leyden, where the banns have been published, declaring that he has no parents," and "Dorothy May, 16 years old, from Wisbeach in England, at present living on the New Dyke, . . . declared that they were betrothed to one another with true covenants,. . . . and their banns are admitted."[6] There stand their intentions of marriage to this day, underwritten with their names; his, the compact, easily-read signature so familiar to every student of Pilgrim history; hers, the rare, almost childish handwriting of a sixteen-year-old girl.

The Leyden *Echt Book* also shows that William Bradford, unaccompanied, registered there his intentions of marriage to Dorothy May, she not appearing in person but being duly certified.[7] And on the sixteenth, twenty-third, and thirtieth of November, their banns were published in Leyden,[8] so that all the Separatist flock might read (perhaps especially the Carpenter family) that William Bradford was about to become the husband of Dorothy May.

They were married in Amsterdam. The original Dutch record in the old *Pui Book* of that city, when translated, runs thus: "The tenth of December, 1613, this stands confirmed in the (ecclesiastical) marriage records. . . . William Bradford, Englishman, fustian weaver, dwelling in Leyden, and Dorothy May, maiden from England, dwelling on the New Dyke.

Joris Joris   J. G. Hoing."[9]

Somehow, if one studied the entry in the *Echt Book* which records the marriage of Edward Southworth to Alice Carpenter only six months earlier, one cannot but have caught something of the sympathetic warmth and affection radiating out from the friends and family circle standing by. One feels the contagion of suppressed merriment pulsing among the bevy of young people making up that gay party. Then one turns back to the Amsterdam *Pui Book* which records the meager fact that William Bradford and Dorothy May were married. There is no hint that any one was present but what the law required to legalize the ceremony; there's nothing to show that neighbor or acquaintance came to gladden the nuptials.

A son, John, was born to the Bradfords in the years before 1620.[10] When the decision was made to seek a new home in the New World, Dorothy placed her baby boy in safe hands and sailed with her husband on the *Mayflower*.

It was a heart-breaking trip, that passage across the Western Ocean, over four months of it from Delfthaven to Cape Cod. The twisting wake of the *Mayflower* stretched ever longer and longer between her and her baby's arms reaching out to her from far away Holland. Dreary, monotonous days of gazing westward for the land that did not rise palled on her spirit. Crowded quarters, made more miserable by seasickness and aggravated by frightful gales, wore down her physical strength which, there is reason to believe, may not have been too robust. Strong bodies were needed on that ship as well as strong souls.

Winter and the *Mayflower* arrived at Cape Cod together.[11] They were completely out of fuel; the butts were almost empty of water, and scurvy was stalking in their midst. The words of Dorothy's husband best sum up the situation. He says, "they had now no freinds to wellcome them, . . . no houses . . . to repaire too, . . . which way soever they turnd their eys (save upward to ye heavens) they could have litle solace. . . . If they looked behind them, ther was ye mighty ocean . . . to seperate them from all ye civill parts of ye world."[12] Then, quoting the words of the Psalmist, he continues, "When they wandered in ye deserte willdernes out of ye way, and found no citie to dwell in, both hungrie, & thirstie, their sowle was overwhelmed in them."[13] Is it any wonder that the spirit of one poor woman should break under the strain, when the souls of such strong men as William Bradford were nigh overwhelmed?

Wednesday, the sixteenth of December, 1620, was a bitter, cold day. The wintry wind swooped spitefully down from off the Truro hills, with snow flurries in its breath. Dorothy Bradford must have shivered as she stood in the lee of the *Mayflower*'s rail and watched her husband and some ten of the ablest Pilgrims set off in their shallop from the anchorage

in Provincetown Harbor on their final search for a suitable site for the
settlement. She could see the glistening of the glaze on his great-coat as
the salt spray turned to ice where it struck. Perhaps the numbing chill of
it seemed to strike against her own naked heart. As his boat weathered
Long Point and set its sail to the east wind, his dear form fused into the
blur of the other men in the shallop and was gone from her sight.

It may be that her mind went back to that other Wednesday in
December, now seven years past, when she had stood by his side on the
New Dyke in Amsterdam, a sixteen-year-old bride, dreaming dreams of
love and happiness. Had those years in between taught her the bitter
lesson that, although his wedded wife and the mother of his son, she
could never hope to enter within that barrier which his first love had
built around his heart? Here, with every tie cut which ever moored her
to normal living, in this desolate wilderness from which even God,
Himself, whose spirit of grace she now so sorely needed, seemed absent,
the utter hopelessness of it all may have become greater than she could
bear.

One can imagine her turning wearily back to their meager living quarters in the great-cabin and mechanically setting to rights the disarray
which her husband had left behind. The great beams of the ship must
have seemed to crowd her down into the over-jammed space, and the
very presence of her fellow passengers, after long months of close confinement together, jangled on her taut nerves.[14] Only the steady slap . . .
slap . . . slap of the icy waters against the outside planking of the ship
seemed to hold anything of rhythm in all this chaotic world.

It was a long night of darkness, that night of the sixteenth of
December. Anxious wives, roused by a heavier gust of wind whipping
through the frayed rigging, raised themselves on elbow to listen and to
murmur silent prayers for their men out somewhere in the bitter night.
The whimpering moans of little Jasper More, sinking into his last sleep,
tore at the mother's heart of her, lying lonely in her bunk. Other tired
children mumbled restlessly in their sleep, haunted by childish fears at the
taking away of their little playmate. And through it all came that rhyth-
mic slap . . . slap . . . slapping of the eternal waters against the ship's side.

Perhaps that sound haunted her, as the tap-tapping of watch-beetles in
old woodwork, said to be numbering the years of a man's life, haunt the
listener. It may have lifted her distracted mind above and away from the
sordid sufferings, the hardships, and the turmoil all about her and offered
peace. How blessed it would be to slip away from it all into that soothing
harmony and be at peace forever.

Did they find her bunk empty when daylight filtered in through the
tiny cabin windows of the *Mayflower* the next morning? Or was she

missing when they returned from laying away the little body of Jasper More—poor little Jasper, who looked so pitifully small as they lowered him over the great side of the ship and rowed away with him to the burial place among the sandy beach knolls? Tradition does not recall, would not even remember the date but for the record. It only knows that here, in the dark waters of the bay, she ended her life.

It must have been another black day in the life of young William Bradford when they met him at the gangway of the *Mayflower* on his return a few days later and told him that his wife was drowned. He may have hoped that in this New World, and under new skies, the heartaches of the Old would fade into the past and that they two might begin a new life and a new love together. But her empty bunk, her cherished keepsakes in the tiny cabin—each spoke its mute story of broken hopes and a "soul overwhelmed." I am sure he was glad when the *Mayflower* sailed away from that tragic spot, where visions of her white face must have haunted him from the uneasy waters alongside.

The cryptic record of her death, written by his own hand, reads as follows: "William Bradford his wife dyed soone after their arivall."[15] That is all. There is not a hint that she died in any other way or manner than that in which others were dying all around her—not even that it occurred in Provincetown Harbor before the landing at Plymouth. Does it not seem strange that so shocking an event as the drowning of the wife of the most prominent man in the Colony, whether accidental or not, should never have been commented on in any way in the voluminous writings of her husband and his contemporaries? Is it not almost unbelievable that the death of the first Pilgrim woman—the first white woman ever to die anywhere on the shores of New England—should never have been referred to in any public manner by those she left behind? Her death in Provincetown Harbor, no matter what the cause, was evidently a closed incident, never to be openly discussed or alluded to by those Old Comers who came back alive with her husband out of the jaws of death of that first terrible winter.

It was not until some eighty years later that it was first made known to the public that Dorothy Bradford died by drowning. Mather's *Magnalia* then tells us that she accidentally fell overboard; and the Reverend Thomas Prince, writing at about the same period, states that she was drowned by falling over the ship's side. It seems to have been common knowledge among those who got their information by word of mouth from the last *Mayflower* survivors that she was drowned straight from the deck of the *Mayflower*. If there is truth in the half-told tale of Pilgrim tragedy and love, that she did in fact deliberately take her life, which was a fearful thing for one of her sect and upbringing to do, that would have been enough to seal the lips of her companions who seem truly to have gone out of their way to avoid comment as to how she died.

For a ship of the *Mayflower's* build, it borders very nearly on the absurd to try to imagine any circumstance under which this young woman of twenty-three could fall overboard accidentally, with the *Mayflower* lying safely at anchor in the smooth water under the lee of Long Point. Ships of that period had a bulwark or railing breast-high around their decks in most places and at all points high enough so that no one could possibly get over the side without considerable premeditated effort, unless washed overboard in heavy weather.

There is no record extant even hinting that her body was ever recovered. Cape Cod tides have a way of sanding up drowned bodies, just as the winds of winter drift snow over and around a fallen log. In sheltered bottoms, a body thus buried may rest secure through all eternity, and for aught we know, Dorothy Bradford still rests under the sands of the harbor bottom where the *Mayflower* swung at anchor on that Thursday in December, some three hundred years ago.

Off hand, taking tradition out of the picture altogether, it would be farfetched to suspect any connection between the drowning of Dorothy Bradford so soon after her arrival at Cape Cod and the death of Edward Southworth, Alice Carpenter's husband, in faraway England three months before, just after the *Mayflower* set sail for America.[16] But there was a connection, and a very vital one, as subsequent events emphatically prove.

When the *Mayflower* sailed back to Old England in the spring of 1621,[17] carrying the roster of the dead which that terrible first winter in New England had rolled up, Alice (Carpenter) Southworth, now the Widow Southworth and mistress of her own destiny, learned that William Bradford was as alone in the world as she. The next ship out of England for the Pilgrim Colony, after the return to London of the *Mayflower*, was the *Fortune*, which arrived at Plymouth in New England, in the fall of 1621.[18] There is little possibility that word of the death of Edward Southworth could have reached William Bradford before that time, unless by some chance fishing-smack or trading vessel which the Pilgrims have never mentioned. But it is certain that from that time on, for the next two years, love found some way to transmit intimate and personal messages across the Atlantic between the Widow Southworth and the Governor of Plymouth Colony.

On the very next ship to sail with passengers out of England for America, after the return of the *Fortune*,[19] we find Alice (Carpenter) Southworth flying as straight to the arms of William Bradford as an arrow to its mark. She, a widow, with no other possible motive to draw her to New England, did not place her own two boys in the care of her sister and strike out across the ocean alone on any haphazard adventure. Neither the Pilgrims themselves nor their financial backers in England would have tolerated such a move for a moment, at that critical period in the Old Colony's history. She was now a free, mature woman of means. No fond parent could say her nay. There cannot be the slightest doubt that she knew she was to become the wife of Bradford before she ever left Old England's shores. She came at the call of her man, to share his fish and fair spring water in the humble cabin she knew he had built for her in this New World.

It must have been a gala day in the Old Colony town when the good ship *Anne* rounded the Point of the Gurnet and sailed bravely into Plymouth Harbor, in that midsummer of 1623. Husbands clasped to their breasts wives and children they had never dared to hope to see again; sons and daughters grown into young men and women since the parting in Leyden joined the family circle once more. Patience Brewster tripped lightly ashore and rushed into the waiting arms of the Excellent Elder of Plymouth and his no less excellent wife, Mary. Myles Standish, his good sword for once in its scabbard, welcomed the comely Barbara, who had come to fill the place of his dead Rose. Tears of love and joy and thanksgiving must have filled every eye. Bradford, dressed in his Governor's cloak, as befitted the occasion and his own official position, stood in dignified confusion as a glorious vision of young womanhood came up the path to bend her knee at his feet.

There were some among the passengers from the *Anne*, who, " . . . when they saw their low and poore condition a shore, . . . some wished them selves in England againe; others fell a weeping, . . . many were ragged in aparell, & some litle beter then halfe naked; . . . The best dish they could presente their freinds with was a lobster, or a peece of fish, without bread or any thing els but a cupp of fair spring water."[20] The Widow Southworth was probably not among those who wished themselves back in Old England again. On the contrary, one might hear her spirit speaking through the words of Bradford when he says, "Only some of their old freinds rejoysed to see them, and yt it was no worse with them, for they could not expecte it should be better, and now hoped they should injoye better days togeather."[21] Indeed they did enjoy better days together. On the fourteenth day of August, 1623, scarce a month after she had set foot on dry land and just as soon as was permissible after the three weeks publication of the betrothal banns, Alice (Carpenter) Southworth became the bride of Governor William Bradford.[22]

Their simple dwelling, which stood just back from the site of the present Post Office building in Plymouth Town, was a home of open hospitality. Religious outcasts from the Puritan settlement at Boston, Roman

Catholic priests shipwrecked on New England's inhospitable shores, haughty Indian sagamores seeking for treaties of peace—one and all found a gracious welcome within its doors. Here three children were born to them: William, Mary, and Joseph and three others were brought overseas to live with them: her own two Southworth boys and Bradford's John, the son of Dorothy.

John died childless. Looking out eastward from the site of the Bradford homestead, where John grew to young manhood, beyond the Gurnet and across the waters of Cape Cod Bay, sometimes, on a clear day, the Pilgrim Monument at Provincetown can be seen looming above the horizon. It marks the place which was journey's end for John's mother. But no tablet guards the spot which was her final resting place, and not one drop of her blood flows today in the veins of all the vast multitude which peoples the shores she but glimpsed.

Governor Bradford lived to guide the destiny of the growing Colony for over thirty-five years. He died on Saturday, the 19th of May, 1657 (new style), in the sixty-eighth year of his age.[23] Mistress Alice Bradford kept alive the traditions of the home they had brought together through so much toil and suffering for another thirteen years. Nowhere, does the great love she bore William Bradford shine out more clearly than in the closing days of her life. Knowing that her end was drawing near—a sick and suffering old woman—she made the following remarkable request in her will:

"I Allis Bradford senir of the Towne of Plymouth in the Jurisdiction of New Plymouth widdow: being weake in body but of Disposing mind and prfect memory blessed be God; not knowing how soone the Lord may please to take mee out of this world unto himselfe: Doe make and ordaine this to be my last Will and Testament; in manor and forme as followeth; Impr I bequeath my soule to god that gave it and my body to the Dust in hope of a Joyfull resurrection unto Glory; Desiring that my body may be Intered as neare unto my Deceased husband; mr Willam Bradford: as Conveniently may be; . . . [24]

It is not her trusting faith that their souls would be united in the Great Beyond that is remarkable; that would be expected of a devoted Pilgrim of her day. But her overwhelming desire to sleep the last sleep so close to the earthly body of her beloved husband that their dust should mingle through all eternity, never more to be separated while earth shall last, transcends the bounds of convention and bespeaks an unashamed love as deep as time itself. There they sleep on the hill overlooking the town they wrought out of a wilderness.

The Plymouth Colony Vital Records still cherishes her memory in these words: "on the 26 Day of March 1670 Mistris Allic[e] Bradford senir: Changed this life for a better haveing attained to fourscore yeares of age or therabouts shee was a godly Matron; and much loved while shee lived and lamente[d] tho; aged when shee Died and was honorabley enterred on the 29 Day of the month aforsaid; att New Plymouth."[25] Here, as everywhere else that we come in contact with her memory, we catch a fleeting but none the less clear glimpse of a strong and noble character shining brightly out through the austerities and hardships of the days of our Pilgrim fathers and mothers.

Such is the uncanny way in which the ancient records run hand in hand with the old family legend. The basic truth of the old tradition, which has been handed along by word of mouth from generation to generation and which the recorded facts bolster up at every point, seems to be self-evident.

Notes

1. Governor Bradford's second wife was Alice (Carpenter) Southworth, widow of Edward Southworth. Her son, Constant Southworth, married Elizabeth Collier whose daughter, Mercy, married Samuel Freeman. Their daughter, Apphia, married Isaac Pepper whose daughter, Apphia, married Timothy Cole. Their daughter, Dorothy, married Thomas Freeman whose son, Thomas, married Esther Ryder. Their daughter Dorothy, married Elnathan Eldredge whose son, Elnathan, married Jean Wixon. Their daughter, Jane, married Warren Nickerson. Their son, Warren J., married Mary Atkins who were W. Sears Nickerson's parents.
2. The date from St. Helen's Parish Register is old style and would be 29 March 1590 by today's calendar. He was undoubtedly born just a few days previous to his baptism (George Ernest Bowman, "The Record of Governor Bradford's Baptism, on the Parish Register at Austerfield," *The Mayflower Descendant* 7 [1905]: 65-66).
3. "The Plymouth Colony Vital Records" say that when she died on 26 March 1670 she was "fourscore yeares of age or therabouts" which would place her birth close to 1590 (George Ernest Bowman, "Plymouth Colony Vital Records," *The Mayflower Descendant* 18 [1916]: 68).
4. From a poem to her memory by her sister's son, Nathaniel Morton.
5. George Ernest Bowman, "The Marriage of Edward Southworth and Alice Carpenter," *The Mayflower Descendant* 10 (1908): 1-2.
6. George Ernest Bowman, "The *Mayflower* Marriage Records at Leyden and Amsterdam," *The Mayflower Descendant* 9 (1907): 115-16; George Ernest Bowman, "The *Mayflower* Marriage Records at Leyden and Amsterdam," *The Mayflower Descendant* 22 (1920): 63-64.
7. "The *Mayflower* Marriage Records at Leyden and Amsterdam." *The Mayflower Descendant* 9 (1907): 116; "The *Mayflower* Marriage Records at Leyden and Amsterdam," *The Mayflower Descendant* 22 (1920): 64.

8. "The *Mayflower* Marriage Records at Leyden and Amsterdam," *The Mayflower Descendant* 9 (1907): 116.
9. Ibid., 117.
10. John Bradford was born about 1617 and died childless about 1677 (Albert H. Plumb, *William Bradford of Plymouth* [Boston: Gorham Press, 1920], 59).
11. The *Mayflower* arrived in Provincetown Harbor, 21 November 1620 (new style) (William Bradford, *Bradford's History "Of Plimoth Plantation"* [Boston: Wright and Potter Printing Co., State Printers, 1899], 110).
12. Bradford, *Bradford's History,* 94-96.
13. Ibid., 97.
14. It is a well-known fact among sailors that acute melancholia frequently results from scurvy.
15. Bradford, *Bradford's History,* 535.
16. He was apparently alive and in normal health when Robert Cushman wrote him on 17 August 1620, from Dartmouth, England. There is a copy of this letter in *Bradford's History* (86-90). His wife's nephew stated that they had been married seven years when Southworth died. As they were married 28 May 1613, he must have passed away very soon after the sailing of the *Mayflower* from England.
17. She sailed from Plymouth, Massachusetts, about the fifth of April 1621, and arrived in England the fifth or sixth of May (Marsden, R. G. "The *Mayflower*," *The Mayflower Descendant* 18 (1916): 13).
18. The *Fortune* arrived at Cape Cod 9 November 1621 (Bradford, *Bradford's History,* 127).
19. The *Anne* arrived at Plymouth, Massachusetts, during the latter part of July 1623. She and her consort brought about sixty passengers (Bradford, *Bradford's History,* 170-71).
20. Bradford, *Bradford's History,* 174-75.
21. Ibid., 175.
22. She did not arrive until the latter part of July, and the banns had to be published three consecutive weeks before she could be married to the Governor (George Ernest Bowman, "Plymouth First Church Records," *The Mayflower Descendant* 4 [1902]: 93).
23. Governor Bradford was sixty-seven years and nearly two months old when he died ("The Record of Governor Bradford's Baptism, on the Parish Register at Austerfield." *The Mayflower Descendant* 7 [1905]: 66).
24. "From 'Plymouth Colony Wills and Inventories,' vol. 3, part 1, pages 2-5." *The Mayflower Descendant* 3 (1901): 144.
25. "Plymouth Colony Vital Records." *The Mayflower Descendant* 18 (1916): 68.

The First Encounter

Nickerson's only information on his source for disagreement with the placement of the First Encounter follows: "This committee may have had information on which to base its choice of the particular spot which I have never run across in my many years of research into the lives and times of the Lower Cape Cod Indians. However, I have made a careful study of the events leading up to and including the fight as told in Bradford's History *and other sources by the men who were there and did the fighting. I regret to say I can find no evidence whatever to justify the opinion of the committee." Nickerson's date of composition is unknown.*

The Tercentenary Committee of 1920 placed a marker near Great Meadow in Eastham to commemorate the first encounter between the Pilgrims and the Indians.[1] This encounter took place during the third exploring expedition to set out from the *Mayflower* still anchored off Long Point in Provincetown Harbor. The men boarded the shallop at shipside on Wednesday, the 6th of December 1620, sailed directly to Grampus Bay near Wellfleet Harbor, and camped for the night. Next morning they split into two units; one under command of Captain Myles Standish was to march up the Cape by foot; the other was to work the boat alongshore southerly until signalled by him.

Standish and his men soon picked up the old Nawset Trail, that ancient super-footpath so well known to our forefathers, which ran the whole length of the Cape from Provincetown to Bournedale. The Pilgrims refer to it as the Indian Path in their description of that day's march, and it led them almost directly south to Great Meadow, right into the area where the committee claimed their fight with the Indians took place.

This claim, however, does not fit at all into the story told by the marchers themselves. They tell us, in so many words, that by ten o'clock that morning they had come to the ancient Nawset Indian Burying Ground. This can only mean they had already left the marker area far behind and followed the Trail as it swung to the eastward of Great Meadow. Now, in the middle of the forenoon, it had brought them into the vicinity of Herring Pond, near which the Burying Ground was located. This positive statement makes it seem extremely doubtful that they ever came near the spot where the marker stands. Even if we allow that they may have, what reason would they have had for bivouacing there before ten o'clock in the morning, with a clear trail and the better part of the day ahead? Or how can we imagine any tough, fighting man, such as we know Captain Standish to have been, picking this spot on which to build a barricade, surrounded on all sides as it must have been by forests to hide the approach of the enemy and with no creek to bring his boat and its men even within hailing distance?

After the company left the Burying Ground, they say that in the afternoon they went a long way before they left the Path and struck westward toward Cape Cod Bay to join their boat which they had not seen since morning. This must have brought them to the northern reaches of Boat Meadow. As his footsore, weary band slogged along toward the North Shore, Standish's trained eye undoubtedly sized up the point which makes down to the Boat Meadow Creek entrance as a likely place to camp for the night. Here, surrounded on three sides by water, with an unobstructed view of both bay and meadow, they need fear no enemy's unseen approach except from the land side, while a sharp bend in the creek made a snug anchorage and a sandy landing place for the boat within a stone's throw.

The Indians struck next morning, Friday the 8th of December, just as the Pilgrims were breaking camp.[2] Some were still in the barricade while others, who were just getting aboard the boat, had laid their guns down on the bankside, something they never would have done had the landing place been mucky saltmarsh. While the guns banged from the barricade and the arrows flew through it and through some of their jackets which hung in the barricade, one young Pilgrim grabbed up a burning log from the campfire and carried it on his shoulder to the men in the boat so they could light the fuses of their matchlocks and join in the fray. They shouted words of encouragement, "Be of good courage!" from the shallop along with screams of defiance to the blood-curdling "Woach woach ha ha hach woach" of the Indians, as they later tried to describe it. After a short but sharp scrimmage, the Indians broke and ran. The Pilgrims collected eighteen arrows, some headed with brass, others with harts' horn, and others with eagles' claws, to send back as souvenirs to their home folks in England.

This was the first encounter as told by the men who were there. It takes little imagination to fit the details of the fight into the lay of the land down at the point where Boat Meadow Creek empties into the Bay. Neither is it difficult to go back and follow the march up the Cape from Grampus Bay, if we but know something of the old Nawset trail, the Nawset Indian Burying Ground, and the area a long way up the Trail where they left the Path and came to the Field of the First Encounter.

Notes

1. See William Bradford, *Bradford's History "Of Plimoth Plantation"* (Boston: Wright and Potter Printing Co., State Printers, 1899), 97-107.

   Nickerson's article corresponds very closely to *Mourt's Relation*; see Dwight B. Heath, ed., *Mourt's Relation A Journal of the Pilgrims at Plymouth* (Chester: Globe Pequot Press, 1963), 19-37.

   It is very difficult for me personally to verify Nickerson's contention that the committee was wrong in choosing the spot of the First Encounter. I consulted his nephew, E. Carleton Nickerson, an octogenarian with a lifetime familiarity sailing the Cape Cod coast and with a thorough knowledge of the Cape, who, after a careful study of all available sources, basically concurred with W. Sears Nickerson's judgment. E. Carleton Nickerson said that with two seamen, three sailors, and two master's mates there was no way the shallop would have been left on the beach which is open to the ocean. He checked both a National Ocean Service's nautical chart and the actual locations and decided that the shallop could have been safely left either at Herring River (about six-tenths of a mile from the marker) or at Boat Meadow Creek (about one and four-tenths miles from the marker).

2. It is not surprising that the Native Americans were hostile after the behavior of the Pilgrims on their two previous explorations. They took a kettle, all the ears of corn they found, and as much loose corn as they could carry. Later, they returned to "Cornhill" and found the rest of the corn which they had buried—in all about ten bushels—and took it. They were thankful to find "seed" corn but gave no thought to what would happen to those from whom they had taken it. They rationalized that if they had the opportunity that they would satisfy them for the corn and return the kettle, but the Native Americans had no way of knowing that, nor a choice in the trade. They also dug into some graves, suspecting from the beginning that they were graves.

The *Sparrow Hawk*

A family named Sparrow settled in the vicinity of Old Ship Harbor in 1675. Mr. James L. Sparrow, a descendant, in 1863 stated that according to family tradition a vessel dating from the early days of the colony lay buried in the sands of Potanunaquut Harbor and that its name was Sparrow-Hawk. Nickerson left no notes on this article which I have revised from a clipping from the Cape Codder. His primary source is obviously Bradford.

The earliest recorded shipwreck on the Back Side of Cape Cod was that of the *Sparrow Hawk* in the fall of 1626.[1] Governor William Bradford, who was an eyewitness left the details of it in his history of Plimouth Plantation.[2]

The *Sparrow Hawk* was a small English ship loaded with emigrants bound for Virginia. After six weeks at sea with "ye maister . . . sick . . . of ye scurvie," they had "no water, nor beere, nor any woode left," and were steering a "desperate course" due west, hoping to "fall with some land, what soever it was they cared not," before "they should be starved at sea, or consumed with diseases. . . . "

She struck in the night on the harbor bars "right before . . . ye midle of Manamoyake Bay. . . . sprung ye but end of a planke or too" in pounding across and fetched up half full of water on a sand flat inside. By daylight, when the tide had ebbed, they found they could all wade ashore to the point of the beach on the north side of the inlet and "saved their lives & goods, though much were hurte with salt water. . . . "They had no idea where they were nor what they should do next. It was not long, however, before they sighted Indians paddling down channel toward

102

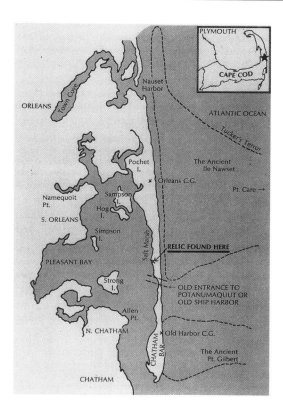

The site of the discovery of the *Sparrow Hawk*.
Courtesy of the Pilgrim Society, Plymouth, Massachusetts

them. Expecting to be attacked, the men primed their matchlocks and stood on their guard. What was their surprise when they were hailed in English by the canoe men who told them where they were, inquired if "they were the Gove'r of Plimoths men, or friends;" and offered to "bring them to ye English houses, or carry their letters."

The "Manamoyake Bay" of Bradford and the Indians is the Pleasant Bay of today, and at that time its inlet, as he says, opened out to sea almost directly east of it. This was less than six years after the landing of the Pilgrims; Plimoth Plantation was the only white settlement within hundreds of miles, and there was not a settler's cabin on all of Cape Cod. Nevertheless, Bradford had already rounded the Cape in a little trading sloop, with Squanto as pilot, and been in through this same inlet to buy corn and beans of the Bay Indians.

As soon as the friendly Indians brought two of the *Sparrow Hawk's* crew to Plymouth, Bradford mustered his boat's crew, loaded their shallop with oakum, spikes, and necessary tools with which to mend the sprung planks of the ship and set out to her relief. Coasting down the north shore of the Cape, they landed at the head of Namskaket Creek and portaged their supplies on their backs over the Indian trail to Arey's Pond in South Orleans. From here the Indians paddled them down to the wreck in their log canoes, and the Plymouth men must have looked like angels from heaven to the sick and sea-weary people huddled in the December cold under the lee of a beach knoll on the bleak and God-forsaken point.

The Pilgrims mended their ship for them, replenished their food supply, and rounded up some of the sea men who were run away among the Indians. They made the *Sparrow Hawk* shipshape and seaworthy again and then went home. But they had not been home many days before in came an Indian runner with the bad news that a great storm had driven her ashore again and so beaten and shaken her that she was now wholly unfit to go to sea. So the shipwrecked crew and passengers were brought to Plymouth where the settlers cared for them as well as they could until a couple of barks carried them away to Virginia the following summer.

The shifting sands soon buried the deserted hulk, and salt marsh grew over her grave. But Cape Cod traditions are as indestructible as its sands, and long after she was hidden from the sight of man, the point of the beach continued to be known as The Old Ship, and the inlet as Old Ship Harbor. The marsh grew to be valuable to the haymakers, and in the 1750 division of the meadow the Old Ship Lot became Lot Number Two on the Proprietors' Book. To verify tradition, enough of "ye antiente wracke," as our forefathers knew it, was uncovered in a 1782 hurricane but was soon sanded over for another eighty-one years.[3]

A gale of 1863 gouged out the old inlet, washed away the sand and sedge, and laid bare the *Sparrow Hawk*.[4] Her upper works had been chewed out by the sand-filled surf, and her stem-post and forefoot were entirely gone, but her rudder was found nearby. The rest of her hull had been well preserved in its almost hermetically sealed tomb. A group of public-spirited citizens, headed by Charles W. Livermore and Leander Crosby,[5] realizing the relic's historical value (and probably monetary profit), had the wreck removed to the mainland.[6]

After being reconditioned by the ship building firm of Peter E. Dolliver & Sylvester B. Sleeper (building yard in East Boston)[7] she was exhibited for a while on Boston Common, later at Providence, and finally presented to the Pilgrim Society of Plymouth which placed her in a museum where she still remains, safely dry docked.[8]

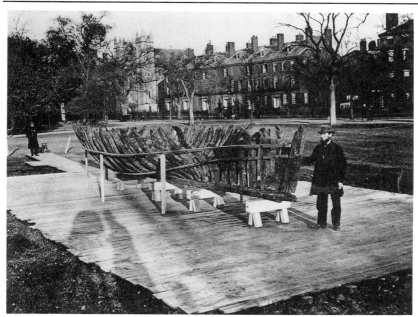

The *Sparrow Hawk*. Courtesy of the Pilgrim Society, Plymouth, Massachusetts.

The planks of this priceless relic of over three hundred and fifty years ago, while James the First was king, which once echoed back the voices of our Cape Cod Indians, still bear the marks of the handiwork of Governor Bradford and his Plymouth men. Like the Prairie schooner of our western plains, she represents an era in the development of our country. She and others of her kind brought the first pioneers across the Western Ocean to our shores. Nowhere in this wide world today is there another original survivor of that great fleet of Pilgrim days.

Notes

1. See H. H. Holly, *Sparrow-Hawk: A Seventeenth Century Vessel in Twentieth Century America* (Boston: The Nimrod Press, 1969), the booklet used by Pilgrim Hall to describe the remains housed there that is reputed by Cape Cod tradition to be the 1626 wreck described in William Bradford, *Bradford's History "Of Plimoth Plantation"* (Boston: Wright and Potter Printing Co., State Printers, 1899).
2. See *Bradford's History*, 261-66 for Bradford's account.
3. Nickerson notes that even in his boyhood the cod-fishing ground off shore from the old inlet was still known as the Old Ship Ground, though few of the fishermen knew why.

4. On May 6, it was discovered partly protruding from the marsh mud by Solomon Linnell 2nd and Alfred Rogers of Orleans. Linnell had not seen it two days previous. Three days later, it was visited by Leander Crosby of Orleans who was responsible for having it removed and preserved in partnership with Charles W. Livermore, a resident of Boston and a member of the City Council. It is also felt that Otis viewed the vessel before it was removed (Holly, *Sparrow-Hawk*, 8).

5. See Charles W. Livermore and Leander Crosby's anonymous pamphlet, *The Ancient Wreck, Loss of the Sparrow-Hawk in 1626, Remarkable Preservation and Recent Discovery of the Wreck,* anonymous pamphlet (Boston: Alfred Mudge and Son, 1865) which is taken in large part from Otis, Amos, "An Account of the Discovery of an Ancient Ship on the Eastern Shore of Cape Cod," in *The New England Historical and Genealogical Register* (Boston: The Society, 1864), 18: 37-44.

6. Nickerson's father, Warren Jenson Nickerson, saw the wreck where it lay and often pointed out the spot to him. It is just inside the outer beach, about a mile north of the Orleans Chatham boundary line, across the Bay from his boyhood home.

7. See Holly's *Sparrow-Hawk* for a letter from Dolliver and Sleeper and one from D. J. Lawlor, a famous designer of schooners who made a model of the *Sparrow-Hawk* (8-11).

8. She was exhibited at P. T. Barnum's Museum and other showplaces for curiosities (Holly, *Sparrow-Hawk*, 4).

III

The French, the English, and the Indians: War in the Colonies, 1690-1745

Mary Corliss Neff

How the Smiths Came to Cape Cod

Honor Bright: Elizabeth Vickery and the French Privateers

Exploit of a Cape Cod Indian at Louisbourg, 1745

Nickerson wrote about the exploits of several people during the French and Indian wars. These wars were in fact a series of conflicts that corresponded to larger conflicts on the European continent. The first of these wars was known as King William's War (1688-1697) in the colonies. It was during this war that the events inspiring stories about Mary Corliss Neff and Mary Smith took place. In this guerrilla warfare, surprise attacks were made against defenseless towns whose inhabitants had done nothing to provoke them. Innocent people on both sides were massacred or taken prisoner. The Oyster River attack in 1694 and the attack at Haverhill are just two examples. Another war, one that served as a backdrop for Nickerson's story of the adventure of Elizabeth Vickery, was Queen Anne's War (1702-1713). In the colonies King George's War broke out in 1744 when France declared war on England. The most famous incident in this struggle was the taking of the French fortress at Louisbourg. Nickerson describes the exploit of an Indian from Cape Cod during the taking of the Grand Battery at Louisbourg.

Mary Corliss Neff

Nickerson left no sources for his Mary Corliss Neff story, but there are numerous options from the storehouse of material on Mary's companion, Hannah Duston (also spelled Dustin, Dustan, and Dustun). The primary sources for this are Cotton Mather and Samuel Sewall who interviewed Hannah Duston. Of the three times Mather set pen to this account, I recommend Cotton Mather, Magnalia Christi Americana, volume 1, 4th book, 550-52 and Samuel Sewall, "Diary," 1: 452-53.

Among the scholars who have reviewed the primary, secondary, and literary sources on Hannah and her two companions, see Robert D. Arner, "The Story of Hannah Duston: Cotton Mather to Thoreau"; Glenn Todd, "Introduction," in Captivity Narrative of Hannah Duston related by Cotton Mather, John Greenleaf Whittier, Nathaniel Hawthorne and Henry David Thoreau, four versions of events in 1697, interspersed with thirty-five wood-block prints by Richard Bosman; and Kathryn Whitford, "Hannah Dustin: The Judgement of History." Also of interest is Mary Harrower Morse, "Murderess or Heroine?" and Laurel Thatcher Ulrich, Good Wives: Image and Reality in the Lives of Women in Northern New England 1650-1750.

Among early secondary sources which Nickerson might have used, see Robert B. Caverly, Heroism of Hannah Duston, together with The Indian Wars of New England; George Wingate Chase, The History of Haverhill, Massachusetts; and B. L. Mirick, History of Haverhill, Massachusetts.

The genre of the captivity narrative interested several prominent literary figures. The evolution of historical judgment on the trio of captives seems to be what most interests scholars in addressing the literary works. (Six of the ten scalped were children, evoking the issue of genocide. Only two were men. W. Sears Nickerson does not make a point of this.) Later writers made Mr. Duston the hero, not one suggesting what is apparent to me that his action of

*turning away from the direct conflict and following the children could be
interpreted as less than noble. Nathaniel Hawthorne in "The Escape of the
Dustons" called Cotton Mather "an old hard-hearted, pedantic bigot" and
said of Hannah, "Would that the bloody old hag had been drowned in crossing Contocook river, or that she had sunk over head and ears in the swamp,
and been there buried, till summoned forth to confront her victims at the
day of Judgment. . . . " John Greenleaf Whittier in "The Mother's Revenge"
granted her temporary insanity, "It was the thirst of revenge; and from that
moment her purpose was fixed. There was a thought of death at her heart—
an insatiate longing for blood. An instantaneous change had been wrought
in her very nature; the angel had become a demon,—and she followed her
captors, with a stern determination to embrace the earliest opportunity for a
bloody retribution." Henry David Thoreau in A Week on the* Concord and
Merrimack Rivers *gives a straightforward recording of the traditional facts.*

*The subject matter found its way into various art forms. The first statue
was erected at Haverhill in 1861 in marble (five feet square and twenty-
four feet high), said to be the first statue ever erected in this country to honor
a woman; there is another in marble at the confluence of the Merrimack
and Contocook rivers, Penacook, New Hampshire, done in 1874 by William
Andrews, and there is a bronze one on the Haverhill Commons of Hannah
by Calvin H. Weeks, 1879. A granite boulder (1908) marks the site where
Hannah was living at the time of her death. Matthew Thornton Chapter of
the D.A.R. in 1902 erected a marker to point out the land of John Lovewell,
where Hannah spent the night after her escape from the Indians at
Penacook Island. Similarly, a bronze tablet in front of Col. Tyngs' house,
Tyngsboro, marks the location of Hannah's first night after captivity. A mill
stone in Haverhill on the Merrimack River was erected by Ezra W. B.
Taylor to mark the landing Place of Hannah on her return from captivity.
The Haverhill Historical Society has the hatchet head she used to scalp the
Native Americans, her darning needle, a bowl, a coverlet made by her, and
her letter asking permission to join the church, a letter whose controversy split
the congregation. In addition to Richard Bosman's wood-block prints and
certainly among others are the engraving of the raid by John W. Barber,
1841 and G. W. Fasel's "Duston Covering the Retreat of His Seven
Children," 1851, currently in the Haverhill Public Library.*

*In light of the large body of material, I will reference primarily those
facts having to do with Mary Corliss Neff, referring the reader to the primary and early secondary sources for the general story. Controversy has followed several of the details which probably are best taken as oral tradition.
Questions of whether Mr. Duston fired his gun as he fled with the children,
for example, or whether Mrs. Duston really had on only one shoe through this
ordeal have never been resolved.*

Statue of Hannah Dustin. Photo by Robert J. Gibeau. Courtesy Trustees of the Haverhill Public Library.

❦

Most New Englanders are more or less familiar with the Hannah Duston story, but few have ever heard of her companion Mary Neff who was with her from first to last and took an equal part in that bloody exploit. She was the daughter of George and Joanne (Davis) Corliss.[1] She was born Mary Corliss on the 8th day of September, 1646, in the house her father had built for his bride the year before. It stood in the neighborhood of the present three hundred block of Highland Street in Haverhill, Massachusetts. He was one of Haverhill's first settlers, and their wedding was the second marriage in the frontier town. Mary grew up in a bloody period of the old French and Indian Wars, and her father, his son John, and all his grandsons were noted Indian fighters.

Mary Corliss became Mary Neff on the 23rd of January 1665, when she married William Neff, another tough Indian fighter. They had six children: William, Mary, Joseph, John, Clement, and Thomas. The oldest, Will, came close to being hanged as a pirate down on Cape Cod because he was one of the crew of the pirate ship *Good Speed* under the command of the notorious buccaneer Thomas Pound when she was captured in Tarpaulin Cove. Many of his shipmates went to the gallows, but after Will had convinced the court that he had been kidnapped at Falmouth, Maine, and forced into Pound's service, he was set free.[2]

Mary Neff's husband was killed and scalped by the Indians in the winter of 1690 when he was only forty-seven. Not long after that, her brother John and his son John were both killed and scalped, and soon this was the fate of two of her brothers-in-law, Samuel Ladd[3] and John Robie. Her aunt Jane Davis, three of her cousins, and thirteen of their children were killed and scalped all in one day in the Indian massacre at Oyster River in 1694. Her cousin Judith, one of the forty-nine wretched captives carried off to Canada at that time, was the wife of Samuel Emerson, Hannah Duston's brother. Four years later, after Judith had been given up for dead, a Yankee fur trader discovered her living as a slave with the dogs in a Canadian Indian village, bought her for two shirts, and returned her to her husband.

The widow Mary Neff was the nurse in the Duston Home when Hannah's baby girl was born on the 9th of March 1697. Six days later, on the morning of the 15th, when Thomas, Hannah's husband, fresh-primed his loaded musket, hitched up his team, and went out to work on his farm as usual, everything seemed all right. His wife would be up and around in a week or so; little Martha was a healthy, husky baby; nurse Neff was keeping the rest of the children well scrubbed and well fed, and spring was in the air and stirring in the earth under his feet. If thoughts like this ran through his mind, it was not for long. Suddenly the dread cry, "The Indians are coming! The Indians are coming!" rang through the village. It took but a few short moments for him to unhitch the horse from the wagon, jump on the horse's back, grab his gun, and gallop pell mell for home. By the time he got all of his children except the baby on the run across the fields toward the garrison house, the Indians were breaking out of the woods, but using his horse as a barricade, he stood them off until every one of the youngsters were safe inside. Now the Indians were dancing around his own house, making their war cries and waving flaming torches. It made him sick at heart to think of what might be going on inside, but he could not reach them, and the only thing left for him was to get into the garrison house and add his gun to the defense of his children there.

Mary Neff had snatched up the baby and started on the run toward the garrison house also, but the Indians headed her off and chased her back into the house. They dragged Hannah Duston from her bed, shoved both women into chairs, and lashed them to the chair backs. They then proceeded to plunder the house, making the loot into packets wrapped in quilts and bed linen which they strapped to the backs of the women, whom they now released and pushed out of doors just as they set fire to the house. With their arms still tied behind them, neither woman could pick up the baby. A large, painted Indian grabbed her up, and reaching the Duston's orchard, he seized her by the feet, swung her around his head, and smashed her brains out against the trunk of an apple tree. For many, many years, old timers pointed out that tree as "Baby Martha's Apple Tree."

Half a dozen other houses were pillaged and burnt, and twenty-nine persons killed or made captive. Before the raiders started north for home, they split up into two or more bands to make it more difficult for the aroused settlers to track them down. The party who took Mary and Hannah along was led by the same Indian who had killed Hannah's baby. In spite of the fact that both were loaded down with plunder and Hannah had given birth to her baby only six days before, he forced them to march twelve miles on foot that day. According to tradition, Hannah was still in her lying-in clothes and had on only one shoe. That night they reached the canoes of the raiders hidden on the banks of the Merrimack, guarded by a couple of Indian women and a white lad, Samuel Leonardson, who had been their captive for nearly a year.

The band worked slowly up the stream for many days, hiding, and sleeping by day and paddling by night. When they reached Penacook, a few miles above the present Concord, New Hampshire, where they felt safe from the avenging guns of the white men, they dug in for a rest and built a wigwam big enough to sleep them all: the twelve Indians and their three captives. The Indians delighted in telling the two women prisoners how when they reached their Canadian home village they would be stripped naked and made to run the gauntlet of tomahawks, knives, and clubs to entertain the women and youngsters. They knew from reports of ransomed captives that if they survived the gauntlet it would only be to become the wives of some Indian or made slaves to eat and sleep with the dogs. They had long since determined to escape should there be the least possible chance, even though they knew that if caught in the attempt it would probably mean slow death by torture. To the minds of Mary Neff and Hannah Duston that sort of death would be preferable to the living death awaiting them in Canada.

They plotted with the white lad to make believe he liked the Indian way of life so well he wanted to grow up to be a great warrior. One of the Indians showed him just how to strike a death blow with a tomahawk, saying "Strike um here," pointing to his temple. Then, he demonstrated the proper technique of ripping off a scalp with a twist of the scalping knife. Their plans were well matured when along toward the latter end of April the lad, who had learned the Indian tongue, overheard the leaders planning to break camp soon, now that the ice and snow were nearly gone out of the canoe streams and the woodland trails to the north.

The three captives must have spent many sleepless night waiting to catch the Indians off guard and in deep slumber all at one time. Their chance came some time after midnight on the morning of the 30th of April. Moving stealthily as a cat and as silently, they secured the tomahawks of the sleeping Indians. Then, in one concerted action, all striking at a signal, they killed ten out of the twelve almost instantly. One woman only, badly wounded, and a young boy managed to get away alive. Hannah had the satisfaction of tomahawking the man who had bashed out the brains of her baby, the one who had taught the young lad how to "Strike um here."

They scuttled every canoe but one, loading that with arms and provisions that they could gather up and were ready to push off down the Merrimack when, tradition says, they realized that if they got home alive, no one would believe such a fantastic tale. So back to the wigwam they went, took the ten scalps, wrapped them in some of Hannah's looted bed linen, and carried them along as proof. These thrifty New England women may just possibly have also remembered that there was a possibility of bounty being paid for scalps.[4]

What a day it must have been in old Haverhill town when Mary Neff, Hannah Duston, and the Leonardson lad came paddling in to the canoe landing! It was like a return from the dead, and the story they told was no less incredible. But there was the Indians' canoe loaded with the Indians' tomahawks, their scalping knives, their guns, and some of the captured plunder from the Duston home, and last, but by no means least, the ten carefully wrapped scalps. Not long afterward, a ransomed Haverhill captive returned and corroborated their story. She had been in another camp of the raiders when the half-dead Indian had dragged herself in and told of the killings just as the two women had described it.

When the next General Court was in session in Boston, the two women and the boy appeared on the floor of the House, presented before the eyes of the legislators the ten Indian scalps they, themselves, had taken, and asked that they be paid a bounty by the Province of the Massachusetts Bay. It still stands on the record that their request was granted without debate.

Mary Neff's share in the scalp money was twelve pounds and ten shillings. In addition the Government later gave her son Thomas two hundred acres of land at Penacook, including the spot where the wigwam stood in which his mother had tomahawked and scalped her Indian captors. She never married again after her husband was killed by the Indians in 1690. She died peacefully in bed on the 17th of October 1722, when she was seventy-six years old.

Notes

1. I have verified all the genealogical material on Mary and her family from Dorothy Neff Curry, *The Descendants of William Neff who Married Mary Corliss January 23, 1665 Haverhill, Massachusetts*. W. Sears Nickerson's wife, Donna Corliss, is directly descended through their son John, Mary's brother. Her maternal grandparents James and Cicely Davis are ancestors of W. Sears Nickerson through their great-granddaughter Mary Smith who was rescued from an Indian massacre at Oyster River, New Hampshire, and brought to Cape Cod by Captain Tom Freeman, later to become his bride and a great-grandmother of W. Sears Nickerson.
2. See Elizabeth Reynard, *The Narrow Land: Folk Chronicles of Old Cape Cod* (Chatham: The Chatham Historical Society, Inc., 1985), 236-45 for "The Secret of Tarpaulin Cove." See Dorothy Neff Curry, *The Descendants of William Neff who Married Mary Corliss* for the court information on their son Will as it relates to this case.
3. George Wingate Chase, *The History of Haverhill, Massachusetts* (Shelburne, Vermont: New England History Press for Haverhill Historical Society, 1983), 199, 201.
4. "In 1694 a bounty of fifty pounds had been placed on Indian scalps, reduced to twenty-five pounds in 1695, and revoked completely on Dec. 16, 1696. . . . he [Thomas Duston] took the two women and the boy to

Boston, where they arrived with the trophies on April 21, 1697. Here he filed a petition to the Governor and Council, which was read on June 8, 1697 in the House (Mass. Archives vol. 70, 350) . . . claiming the reward, pleading that 'the merit of the Action remains the same' and claiming that 'your Petitioner haveing Lost his Estate in that Calamity wherein his wife was carryed into her captivity renders him the fitter object for what consideracon the publick Bounty shall judge proper for what hath been herein done'. . . . The same day the General Court voted payment of a bounty of twenty-five pounds 'unto Thomas Dunston of Haverhill, on behalf of Hannah his wife', and twelve pounds ten shillings each to Mary Neff and Samuel. This was approved on June 16, 1697, and the order in Council for the payment of the several allowances was passed Dec. 4, 1697. (Chapter 10, Province Laws, Mass. Archives)" (*The Duston-Dustin Family Thomas and Elizabeth [Wheeler] Duston and their Descendants* [Compiled by The Duston-Dustin Family Association Genealogists], 26-27). Governor Nicholson of Maryland sent complimentary presents to them as well.

How the Smiths Came to Cape Cod: Mary Smith of Oyster River

N ickerson gave no sources for this undated story about his great grandmother. I have edited and included additional information from the sources that I located in researching the subject. Most of the material on the massacre comes from Everett Stackpole, Lucien Thompson, and Winthrop Meserve, The History of the Town of Durham, New Hampshire (Oyster River Plantation), *which draws heavily on Rev. John Pike's Journal (A. H. Quint, ed.,* Journal of the Rev. John Pike of Dover, New Hampshire), *and Jeremy Belknap,* The History of New Hampshire.

In the days of the French and Indian Wars, the lovely, old, college town of Durham, New Hampshire, went by the name of the Oyster River Parish of Dover or just Oyster River for short. Six or eight garrison houses, loopholed and palisaded, to which the settlers could flee in times of danger guarded the scattered farmhouses. Nothing lay between the settlement and Quebec but the unbroken wilderness known only to the Indians, the fur traders, and the marauding war parties sent out against each other by Catholic Canada and Protestant New England. Both countries looked upon this conflict as a sort of holy war, and priests or ministers went along with the raiders to give their blessing in the name of religion to the horrible atrocities of their Indian allies. Both countries offered bounties for scalps. The five pounds paid by Massachusetts made the hair of a human scalp worth more than a prime beaver skin.

Mary Smith,[1] whose father and mother, James and Sarah (Davis) Smith, kept the inn just above the falls on the south side of the river, was born on the 24th day of May 1685. Her father James, who was listed in

1662 as a tailor in Oyster River, apparently had a mind of his own. In 1663 he was "set by the heels for keeping his hat on in court after admonition; fined next day for absence from meeting several months and going once to a Quaker meeting." Here, Mary grew up in a world of tomahawk and scalping knife. Among her earliest recollections was the day when the blood-stained men and terror-stricken women and children straggled into the inn after neighboring Cochecho, now the bustling city of Dover, had been sacked and burned by the French and Indians. Twenty-five of its people had been killed and scalped, and twenty-nine others were carried off captive to Canada. The Huggins garrison on the outskirts of her own village was cut off and burned the next day, all of its men tomahawked and scalped and their women and children made prisoners. But the Indians got no nearer for the time being.

The following summer, on July 4, 1690, a war party fell on nearby Newmarket, killing and scalping seven and taking captive several others. Then, they headed for Oyster River but were finally driven off by the settlers on July 6 after a bloody, running fight in which Mary's father was one of the sixteen killed near Wheelwright's Pond just behind the town. James Smith "'died of a surfeit which he got by running to assist Capt. Floyd at Wheelwright's pond.'"[2] After her husband's death, her mother took the five children and moved in with her brother, Ensign John Davis, at his garrison house close by.

Then came the terrible Massacre at Oyster River itself, breaking the peace treaty made at Pemaquid. Before day-break on the morning of the 18th of July 1694, some two hundred and thirty Indians led by twenty French-Canadians and two Catholic priests burst without warning on the sleeping village. Before the sun was two hours high, forty-five of its people, tomahawked and scalped, lay in grotesque heaps among the smoldering timbers of their homes. Forty-nine had been made captive, and three garrisons and thirteen farmhouses burned to the ground.[3]

The garrison house of Ensign Davis was surrounded so quickly that none of the neighboring settlers had a chance to flee to it with their weapons. When one of the French leaders and a priest promised safety for him and his household if he surrendered, he took them at their word and accepted, realizing all too well that alone he could not hold out long against this mob. The instant he unbolted his front door he was rushed upon by the Indians, tomahawked and scalped together with his wife and two of their children, while the two older girls were seized as captives. When Mary's mother saw what was happening, she grabbed her tiny Jim and Sammy in her arms and shouted for her three other children to run for their lives out the back door. Somehow, in the confusion, Mary, her sister Sarah, and brother John made it across the clearing and hid in the woods where they listened in horror to the death shrieks of their mother and little brothers being butchered.[4]

Mary's grandmother Jane Peasley Davis of Haverhill, Massachusetts and Aunt Judith Emerson, alone in the Emerson farmhouse, were awakened by the gunfire and war whoops. They started to run to the safety of Jones'garrison but were headed off by the Indians who tied Judith up as a prisoner.[5] Perhaps because she was so old and feeble, they released Judith's mother, who hid in a nearby cornfield only to be discovered by another band who killed her for the bounty on her old, gray-haired scalp.[6] Aunt Rebecca Adams and her husband, together with their nine children, some of whom were grown boys big enough to handle a gun, held off the Indians until their garrison house was set on fire and burned down over their heads. As they were driven out by the flames, the Indians killed in revenge every one of the whole family of eleven who were buried in one grave near Mathes Cemetery.[7] Twenty-eight of Mary's closest relatives met death that bloody morning, and as many more were carried away captive, most of them never to be heard from again.

The garrison house of Captain John Woodman[8] was one of the few not taken and burned. When the scalping and looting around it was ended, the forty-nine wretched prisoners were rounded up in front of it just out of gunshot. Here, they were strung together on rawhide leashes like cattle and loaded down with the plunder from their own homes. While the now half-drunken Indians danced around them, flaunting the still dripping scalps of their loved ones in their faces and before the eyes of the helpless Woodman garrison, the two Catholic priests celebrated Mass. According to tradition, the priests made chalk-marks on the pulpit of Parson Buss' church which were thought to be some verse from the Bible or Credo.[9] Then, the captives were driven off into the forest on the long, cruel trail to Quebec. Some would die on the way; some would be killed for the price of their scalps; and many would become slaves in the Indian villages with a remote chance of being ransomed.

Mary heard in after years that several little boys and girls were tomahawked and scalped soon after they disappeared into the wilderness because they could not keep up with the pace set by the raiders for the prisoners. When they made camp at Lake Winnepesauke, probably near Alton Bay, a grown lad was made to run the gauntlet of the two hundred and thirty Indians until he was cut down and killed. She learned also that her cousin Mary, one of the Davis girls, became a Sister of St. Benedict at the Ursuline Convent in Quebec, while the other was finally ransomed and brought home to become the wife of Peter Mason. Another cousin was educated in the Canadian parochial schools and became a Catholic priest there.[10] Her Aunt Judith, after living four years[11] as a slave with the

dogs in a Canadian Indian village and given up for dead, was at last recognized by a Yankee fur trader, a Mr. Morrill, who bought her for two
shirts, one of which he took from his back and returned her to the arms
of her husband Samuel Emerson, a brother of the famous Hannah
Duston. Samuel Emerson, believing his wife was dead, was in
Portsmouth to arrange for a second marriage. In sharing his plans with
an old acquaintance who knew that some captives had just arrived from
Canada and that Mrs. Emerson was among them, he must have been
ambivalent on hearing his acquaintance reply, "'I bet a double drink of
grog your wife is in town.'"[12] Samuel Emerson lost the bet!

On that fateful July morning in 1694, Captain Tom Freeman from
Cape Cod was heading his little lumber schooner in toward Oyster River
for a load of sawn boards. The first he knew of the massacre was when he
began to pick up canoe loads of frightened and bewildered people who had
escaped down-stream and to rescue from the river bank others who had
hidden in the woods. He loaded no lumber that trip; instead, after he and
his shipmates had helped in the gruesome task of burying the forty-five
dead, he brought out a shipload of refugees who had lost their loved ones,
their homes, and possessions and prayed only to get to a place free from
the constant fear of French and Indian tomahawk and scalping knife. Thus
it was that early New Hampshire settlers with such names as Emery, Rich,
Jones, Small, Davis, Smith, and others were transplanted to Cape Cod.

He also brought back with him the orphaned Mary Smith.[13] She was
taken into the home of his father, Deacon Thomas, whose farm covered
much of what is now the very center of the town of Brewster but then a
part of Harwich. The Deacon was a great grandson of Elder William and
Mary Brewster of the *Mayflower* through Governor Thomas and Patience
(Brewster) Prence and Major John and Mercy (Prence) Freeman, and Mary
was reared and educated in the best family tradition of these fine people.
When she grew to young womanhood, she became the bride of the youth-
ful sea-captain who had rescued her from the Oyster River Massacre.

Mary kept in her family Bible a record, beautifully written, almost
script-like, in a hand of which Elder Brewster himself might well have
been proud. Her first entry, carrying a note of joy after all the tragedy in
her young life, reads: "Mary Smith born May 24: 1685—married november 13: 1707."[14] But the shadow of sorrow seemed always to fall across
her path; in a short ten years her beloved husband was dead, and she, at
thirty-two, a widow with four little ones.

The final line of the record, though written in as clear and firm hand
as the first, reaches down to us with the unspoken anguish of this strong
woman: "My Husband Thomas Freeman : Deseased march 22:
1718/19."[15]

Notes

1. Mary Smith is the great grandmother of W. Sears Nickerson. As our early ancestors seldom went far outside the home to pick a mate, Nickerson was baffled by not finding in local records a Mary Smith who married Thomas Freeman in 1707. He mentioned his dilemma to his good friend, Stanley W. Smith, who suggested that Nickerson take a look at the Smith refugees from New Hampshire who fled to the Cape after the Oyster River Massacre. It is there he found her.
2. Everett Stackpole, Lucien Thompson, and Winthrop Meserve, *The History of the Town of Durham, New Hampshire (Oyster River Plantation)* (Town of Durham, 1913), 88. Nickerson records fifteen killed near Wheelwright's Pond; I have changed it to sixteen to agree with Stackpole's account. It is possible that Nickerson used a source that listed fifteen.
3. Stackpole, Thompson, and Meserve, *The History of the Town of Durham, New Hampshire*, 89.
4. Ibid., 90.
5. Emma Lewis Coleman, *New England Captives Carried to Canada: Between 1677 and 1760 During the French and Indian Wars* (Portland: The Southworth Press, 1925), volume 1, chapter 10.
6. Stackpole, Thompson, and Meserve, *The History of the Town of Durham, New Hampshire*, 99.
7. Ibid., 94. The numbers do not clearly agree. Stackpole writes, "This garrison was burned, and Charles Adams and wife, his son, Samuel, and wife, and eleven others were killed."
8. Woodman, a noted Indian fighter, was an ancestor of Nickerson's second wife, Donna Corliss.
9. Stackpole, Thompson, and Meserve, *The History of the Town of Durham, New Hampshire*, 101.
10. Ibid., 90.
11. Ibid., 99. "Among the captives remaining in the hands of the Indians, 17 January 1698/9, was Judah [Judith] Emerson" (Collection of Maine Historical Society, 2nd Series, vol. 5, 516).
12. Stackpole, Thompson, and Meserve, *The History of the Town of Durham, New Hampshire*, 99-100.
13. Mary Smith became the grandmother of Dorothy Freeman who married Elnathan Eldredge "The Miller" and was the grandmother of Nickerson's grandmother Jane (Eldredge) Nickerson. In addition, both Nickerson and his wife are descended from James and Cicely Davis, pioneer settlers of Haverhill, Massachusetts, whose son John was the maternal grandfather of Mary Smith of Oyster River, and whose daughter Joanna became the wife of George Corliss from whom Nickerson's wife Donna Corliss was a direct descendant, making Nickerson and Donna Corliss eighth cousins.
14. *Freeman Genealogy* (Boston: Franklin Press, Rand, Avery, and Co., 1875) confirms this marriage date on page 56; however, page 36 dates the marriage as 17 October 1707.

15. *Freeman Genealogy* records his death date as "March 22, 1716-17"; it states that administration was granted to Mary, widow, on May 15, 1717 and that the estate was settled July 30, 1718 (56). *The Doane Family* (Boston: Alfred Alder Doane, 1902) reads, "Hezekiah Doane. . . . Married second, about 1717, Mary (Smith) Freeman, widow of Thomas Freeman of Harwich. She died after 1742" (57). A Smith genealogy lists his death as 22 March 1717-8. I have adjusted her age at the time of Freeman's death to agree with two of the published sources. Perhaps, she recorded the date in the Bible at a later time and was mistaken. Possibly, Nickerson made a mistake in either reading the entry or in transcribing it. Of course, at least one of the published sources is in error.

Honor Bright: Elizabeth Vickery and the French Privateers

This account is a combination of oral tradition and genealogical research. Nickerson writes, "I have never attempted to prove or disprove its historical accuracy, but I know it persists in other branches of the family besides my own." I found his source from another branch of the family with his note, "The above was sent me by a descendant of Elizabeth Vickery, & although I believe Elizabeth was the daughter of Rev. Jonathan, instead of granddaughter, the essential facts of the tradition are as I knew them from my branch of the family." I have silently corrected spelling and punctuation in the version below, told by the other branch of the family.

"Elizabeth Vickery, daughter of Deacon Jonathan and granddaughter of Rev. Jonathan, when 18 years of age, took passage in a fishing vessel from Truro to Boston. This was during the French war. The vessel was taken, and four Frenchmen were put on the prize. During the excitement, Miss Vickery was left behind and found later by the men who took charge. They started with their prize for Louisbourg. A heavy gale overtook them, and they were shipwrecked on the Isle of Sable. It was now winter, and no communication could be had till the ice would allow passage from the mainland in the spring. From the wreck, the four men built a hut where they passed the long winter. When the Island was visited in the late spring, they were all made prisoners by the English. At the earnest solicitation of the Frenchmen, Miss Vickery was liberated, carried to Halifax, and from there sent home. To the honor of these French sailors, be it remembered that during all these trying experiences they never failed in their kindness or honorable protection to the helpless prisoner and that she received only marked respect from their hands. She was married to Jonathan Collins and became the mother of many generations."

Nickerson left two versions of this story, "Honor Bright" and a much shorter account which was published on 25 February 1960, in the Cape Codder. *I have rewritten the piece combining the two.*

123

The story of how Elizabeth Vickery was made captive by a French privateer has been told and retold by many a Cape Cod fireside while the spin-
drift out of a howling northeaster sifted against the window panes. She
was the daughter of the Reverend Jonathan Vickery, the first ordained
minister at Chatham, Massachusetts, and his wife, Elizabeth Hudson, and
was about twenty years old when the Boston-bound Cape Cod packet on
which she was a passenger was taken by the French. The banns for her
marriage to young Jonathan Collins had been posted on the door of the
Meeting House on the hill, and they were to be wed as soon as she
returned from buying her wedding outfit in the big town.

Jonathan was the son of Joseph and Ruth (Knowles) Collins known to
her neighbors as Duty Knowles, the daughter of Richard and Ruth
(Bower) Knowles, pioneer settlers of Nawset. He was born, according to
the time-worn Eastham Town Book, on the 20th of August 1682, and
already at twenty-four was high-liner in the whaleboat fleet just as
Elizabeth's father had been until he was lost on Chatham Bars two years
previously.[1]

It was September of the year 1704, and Queen Anne's War, raging in
Europe, meant in New England a fresh outbreak of bloody French and
Indian massacres on our northern borders and the piratical plundering of
our shipping on the high seas. Although this sea-going folk reckoned
lightly of the ordinary perils of the short trip across the Bay to Boston, in
the days of the old French wars no one knew when some swift-heeled
privateer might slip down from the Canada ports to cut out a Yankee
prize. It was still fresh in their minds how the gay party of "Gorham wed-
deners," as an old diary tells us, bound across the Sound from Hyannis to
Nantucket had been cleaned out of everything but the clothes they stood
in, so that the groom landed at the door of his prospective bride clad
only in his shift.

No such foreboding thoughts filled the mind of pretty Elizabeth
Vickery. For months her deft fingers had caressingly patted the golden
butter into enticing patterns for the Boston market. Day by day, row
upon row, the bayberry wax candles had been patiently dipped and hung.
At last, the returning stream of bright shillings which were to buy her
wedding trousseau had spilled over the sides of the old pewter dram cup
that was her bank. Now, with the little hoard safely sewed inside her
modest bodice and with a mind filled with visions of dainty dimities and
fine damasks, she was off for the mainland a-shopping. She laughed at
the manly fears of Jonathan Collins and told him she would be back by
sabbath day, never fear, with the best of Boston under her arm.

The skipper of the corn-cracker, as the Cape Codders called their little trading sloops, saw that Nature was setting up her storm signals as his ship swung off down the Harbor before the tide. The sun, which at rising had thrown a lurid wake athwart the oily sea, was soon swallowed by two green sun-dogs in the sky. The wind began to puff in cat's paws out of the east, but it would be a free sheet and a following sea to Boston, so he stood boldly out into the empty ocean. The tawny shore line of the Cape sunk to a glimmering mirage over the taffrail astern, and under the lee ahead the loom of the black rocks of Cohasset began to notch the horizon on the heave of the swells. Everything looked serene for a quick and uneventful passage across Cape Cod Bay.

Before noon the North Shore was up in sight. Somewhere off toward Nahant, hull down, a lone sail was made out, standing in for Boston. She might be a trader from Kittery or the Kennebec, but the wary skipper kept his weather eye open. Both ships were running free on different tacks before the freshening easterly and drew together pretty rapidly. Whoever the stranger proved to be, it soon became apparent that she would cross the bow of the corn-cracker before they reached the roads of Nantasket.

The suspicion which had lurked in the back of the mind of the Cape Cod captain ever since he raised the strange sail grew to a certainty as soon as he could make out the rake of her masts and the wealth of duck she carried. Soon her white gun ports could be seen and then the tri-colored flag at her mizzen. He immediately ordered his passengers below and cleared his decks for action. It was useless to turn back; the Frenchmen could sail two feet to his one. His only chance lay in getting a lucky slant of wind which might let him squeeze by into the shelter of the guns of the Harbor forts.

The privateer was a bold lad, however. With guns run out and men at battle stations, she took up a position to rake the cracker fore and aft should he attempt to pass in. With all that helpless bunch of men and women crowded below, the skipper knew that to risk a point blank broadside would mean a bloody mess. But he would rather haul his flag down to the devil, himself, than to a bead-telling French-Canuck. Quick as lightning, he shoved his tiller hard a-starboard, gibed his little sloop over with everything standing and before the enemy realized what he was up to was around on the other tack and headed in for the shoal water of the ledges off Cohasset.

Masts snapped and cracked, but they stood the strain. For a time, it looked almost as if he would win the day by his audacious trick, but the Frenchmen could out sail and out point him, and before he could work in onto safe water, he was again looking into the guns of the privateer.

This time the Frenchman took no chances on the slippery Bible-back. Luffing out on his weather quarter where he could rake him whichever way he attempted to dodge, he gave him a couple of shots through the rigging and another into the bulwarks, sending the splinters flying across decks. There was no alternative for the Cape Cod skipper but to surrender or be sunk. Reluctantly, he nosed his little corn-cracker around into the wind, and the jig was up.

A smart boarding crew was soon on deck with orders to set the crew and passengers adrift in their boats and take the sloop to Louisburg as a prize of war. The easterly, which had been pricking steadily on since daylight, was now kicking up a nasty, little sea. The Yankee was as anxious to get his crowded boats to land as the Frenchman was to clear out from a hostile shore. In a short half-hour the sloop was headed for Canseau, manned by a French prize crew, while her life-boats, loaded to the gunwales, were bobbing in before the wind toward the Nantasket shore. Here they all made a safe land—all, that is, except Elizabeth Vickery, the sweetheart of Jonathan Collins.

Elizabeth, thinking the French would follow their usual customs and simply loot the cargo and passengers, slipped unnoticed out of the crowded cabin and hid herself in the black darkness of the ship's bends, just as she had done time and again playing hide-and-hoot in the tidewashed wrecks along shore at home. Muffled sounds came to her through the thick partition planking as the boarding party rifled the helpless passengers of their valuables. If she could but keep hidden until the Frenchmen had looted the ship, then, her own little treasure might be saved. An officer came out into the hold and rummaged around among the casks and boxes until he felt sure no one was hiding there. Elizabeth flattened her lithe body into the blackness between the great oaken knees of the ship, holding her breath and clutching her priceless hoard of hard-earned coins tightly against her breast.

When she heard a boat pushing away from the side of the packet, she felt sure it was the privateersmen leaving with their plunder and believed that she had outwitted them. Mounting the cabin steps, she got the surprise of her life. There, at the helm, steering for the open sea, was a French sailor, while two or three others were busily trimming sails and coiling down ropes. Leaning against the weather rail with his back to her was a nattily dressed French officer intently watching the boats of her companions bobbing in toward the shore. The astonishment was mutual. At an astounded exclamation from the helmsman, the officer whirled on his heel, and the amazed look on his face as he met her bewildered gaze almost made her laugh in spite of her fears. It was no part of his orders to carry off helpless Yankee maidens in undermanned prize ships. By their excited gesticulations, although she could not understand a word of their language, she knew but for the threatening storm they would have then and there turned back and landed her among her shipmates where they sincerely wished she had kept herself in the first place.

While they debated, the storm broke. A white squall whipped a sheet of rain and a dollop of spray across deck. The officer, with a God's-will-be-done shrug of the shoulders, ordered sail to be shortened, shook his head in disgust, and walking over to where she stood, courteously threw his cape around her shoulders.

The easterly blow soon developed into a regular fall twister, one of those September gales before which little made of wood and canvass can stand. Within forty-eight hours, despite the superb seamanship of those privateersmen, the snappy Cape Cod packet was a half-dismasted, water-logged derelict, pounding herself to pieces on the pitiless, white hell of the Northeast Bar of Sable Island. The officer and one man, all who were left of the dandy crew who had taken over such a short time before, fastened Elizabeth between them by a life-line and lashed her to the main rigging along with themselves.

Raised high on rushing crags of toppling green, only to be smashed down into a clutching undertow of sand and water which scoured the clothes from their bodies and the very skin from their flesh, they were whiplashed and battered into a merciful stupor of insensibility. Finally, a giant roller picked them up and threw them high and dry on the beach out of the reach of the killing breakers. Slowly, it seeped into their numbed consciousness that they were at rest; whether in this world or the next, it mattered little. At last awakening to the full realization that, though bruised and battered, they still lived, papist Frenchmen and Pilgrim maiden knelt side by side amid the tangle of ropes and wreckage and thanked their God.

The news leaked back through the lines, as news always has in war times, that the Cape Cod packet had never arrived at Louisburg and was listed as lost at sea with all hands. Jonathan Collins quit his farm and his fishing, sailed his whaleboat to Boston, and signed up on the first man of war bound out to fight the French. One bright December morning as they were lazily fanning along just off the Northeast Bar of Sable Island, the deck was snapped out of its usual routine by the lookout's hail that he had sighted a signal flag on the island. Jonathan Collins, boatsteerer for the landing party,[2] was too busy conning them in through the breakers to see what the signal meant. Then, as he stepped ashore and looked up, there stood his Elizabeth, his betrothed, emaciated and haggard, her nakedness covered with pieces of sailcloth, supported between two half-naked, half-starved men. Regardless of navy discipline, he rushed forward and gathered that frail reality into his arms before it should become a vision again and float away.

On board ship, fed and rested, she told her story of capture, hurricane, and shipwreck. She described the hut these men had built out of pieces from the wreckage with a separate room for her and how they had at last got fire with the flints from their pistols to keep them from freezing. She told of their digging shellfish almost with their bare hands and setting dead falls for wild pigs to stave off actual starvation. She stated clearly and without reservation that not once since they met her as a stowaway had they ever treated her with anything but the greatest respect and kindness. Then, standing by their side, she begged that they be treated as the gallant gentleman they were, no matter what their status might be now as prisoners of war.

Tradition does not say what became of these two French privateersmen. As for Elizabeth Vickery, the sequel to her story is verified by this quaintly spelled entry which has been preserved for over two hundred and fifty years in the musty, old pages of the early Eastham records. Like the weathered face of some old sailor who has in his heart the secrets of the sea, the parched and crackly, old paper does not even hint at the tale it holds. "Jonathan Collens and Ealisabeth vickerie were married at Easthem by mr. Sam*ll* Treat the 27th day of Januarie 1704/5." Held to the light, the stamp of the English crown safe guarded between rampant lion and unicorn still attests the maker's skill. For over two centuries it has held in its bond the precious entry which links a tradition with real lives.

Elizabeth lived only a short ten years after her marriage, probably because of the terrible physical hardships she endured on Sable Island, but that was long enough so that her story was passed along to her children and her children's children and down through to her many living descendants.

Notes

1. According to Nickerson, her father was the first minister at Chatham, a lay preacher, and, like many a Cape Cod parson of those days, varied the monotony of his ministerial duties by the more lucrative avocation of whaling. He was drowned 30 April 1702, together with Lieut. Nicholas Eldredge, William Cahoon, and Edward Small, when their whale-boat capsized while crossing Chatham Bars. Both Small and Cahoon were Nickerson's grandfathers of that generation as was the Rev. Vickery, himself.
2. The reader cannot help but wonder after reading the introductory note if Nickerson's branch of the family believed that Elizabeth was rescued by her

husband-to-be or if Nickerson added it as a romantic touch. Nickerson did confess, "Were I writing a scenario for the movies instead of a simple old tale of everyday Cape Cod folk, I would have Elizabeth and the gallant French officer fall deeply in love down there on Sable Island. Then the other privateersman could turn a deep-dyed villain and . . . but then I would not be here as proof that she was true to Jonathan Collins."

Exploit of a Cape Cod Indian at Louisbourg, 1745

This is one of the few articles where I found any notes or sources. Notes clearly indicate that Nickerson used the following sources: Francis Parkman, France and England in North America; Mary Rogers Bangs, Old Cape Cod The Land: The Men The Sea; Charles F. Swift, History of Old Yarmouth; Charles F. Swift, Genealogical Notes of Barnstable Families, Being a Reprint of the Amos Otis Papers; and Herbert Milton Sylvester, Indian Wars of New England.

"The Indian Rangers" appeared in the Cape Codder, 26 November 1959.

There is an ancient drinking toast which runs something like this: "Claret for boys, port for men, but brandy for heros!" Thereby hangs a tale of the taking of Louisbourg.

Louisbourg, a city on Cape Breton Island at the entrance to the St. Lawrence, was the heavily fortified headquarters of the French on our eastern seaboard at the outbreak of the War of the Austrian Succession in Europe. As soon as the French and English took sides against each other, it became a hornet's nest of French privateers which drove our fishing fleet from the Grand Banks, sacked and burned its fish houses and drying flakes at Canseau, and harried our coast from Matinicus to Cape Cod. Our people cared little what royal puppet succeeded to the throne of Austria, but they stood ready to fight the devil, himself, if he meddled with their fishing empire.

In the early spring of 1745, Governor Shirley of the Province of the Massachusetts Bay, which then included most of Maine and New Hampshire, called for volunteers for the "reduction of Canada" and placed Sir William Pepperell of Kittery in supreme command. A hard-bitten bunch of Cape Codders known as Gorham's Rangers[1] immediately joined the 7th Massachusetts Regiment under Major John Thacher. Many of them were native Cape Cod Indians, and all of them were dead-shot marksmen as well as superb scouts.

These rangers, their fathers, and grandfathers had fought the French and Indian on our frontiers under a Gorham ever since Captain John Gorham led them into the Great Swamp Fight against King Philip in 1675. A fatal Indian bullet smashed his powder horn into his chest, but his son John Jr. was there to finish that fight and many more until he finally turned them over to his son, Shubael, long after the Deerfield Massacre of 1704. Now Colonel Shubael was their leader as they set out for Louisbourg, his son, another Captain John, among them.

Any man was proud to be known as one of Gorham's Rangers. Stephen Nickerson was one of them.[2] So, too, was Captain Elisha Doane, who now sleeps peacefully under a forgotten, moss-grown stone in Wellfleet's Old Duck Creek Cemetery which tells us he was "in the army for the reduction of Canada." Parson Moody, who, it is said, always carried a well whetted tomahawk tucked in his belt with which to hack down the Romish altars, was their chaplain. Most Cape Codders can claim descent from some member of this rugged bunch.

An Indian buddy, the noted Sachem Cap'n Jeethro,[3] used to tie his Canuck captives to the stake, pile up the brush, and dance around them, swinging a flaming torch and chanting how strong some roasted French meat would make his heart. The Gorhams, however, never let him touch fire to the brush.

The Indian Doggamus served thirty years in the Rangers. Once he and Captain Doane were made captive together by the St. Francis Indians but managed to escape with their scalps on. Then, there were Isaac Jeems, Micah Rafe, Sr., and Indian Ned, who boasted just before he enlisted that he had agreed with the devil to kill God. It is likely Parson Moody persuaded Ned it would be best first to kill a few Frenchmen before he attempted to kill God.

On May 2, the day after Pepperell established a beachhead a short distance west of Louisbourg at Fresh Water Cove, Bill Vaughan, a dare-devil Indian trader, Harvard graduated, volunteered to lead a raiding party around the city and burn the enemy storehouses east of it. This would be an extremely dangerous, all-night mission, as the storehouse lay directly under the guns of the Royal Battery and the French would unquestionably have a cordon of scouts thrown out around the city. Such an adventure as this was just what the Rangers were itching for, and many joined Vaughan's group.

By midnight they had stealthily circled the city; their Indians had sneaked up on the unsuspecting watchmen and tomahawked them, and the stores were going up in flames. At daylight, they were well back toward Fresh Water Cove. Here Vaughan halted them while he chose sixteen of the toughest out of the ranks and sent the rest on to camp, loaded with plunder.

With this little squad of picked men, he worked out through the forest to a high knoll where they could get a bird's eye look at the city. Almost at their feet lay the Royal Battery, commanding the Harbor and all approaches to the city. They could scarcely believe their bloodshot eyes! No flag flew over the battlements! No sentry paced the ramparts! For all they could see it might have been a citadel of the dead! Smoke from the burning stores was billowing down over the city, and they rightly guessed that so acrid a pall had settled down on the battery as to drive out the garrison.

Within moments Vaughan had stationed three men as a rear guard while the other thirteen were on the run down the slope toward the fortress. They never stopped until brought up short by the ten-foot deep moat which surrounded it. Pulling a looted bottle of French brandy from his pocket, Vaughan waved it aloft and shouted that the man who would swim the moat, scale the wall, and open the gates would get the brandy.[4]

It is a matter of record that a Cape Cod Indian was first to answer. Stripped to breechcloth, tomahawk, and scalping knife, he had swum the icy water, squirmed up the rough masonry wall and through a gun embrasure almost before Vaughan's voice had ceased to echo back from the turrets.

For one long, tense minute his buddies held their breaths and their muskets at the ready. Then came the sound of bolts and bars being pulled back; the drawbridge slid down into place; the great doors swung slowly open, and there stood the Cape Cod Indian waving them in. Lieutenant Thierry, the French Commander, spiked his guns, cut the signal halyard, and took the tricolor with him when he was forced out, but a young hellion promptly shinned the flagpole, tied his own red coat by its sleeves to the masthead as a British flag.[5] The Indian got his bottle of brandy, and the fabled Royal Battery was theirs.

What must have been the astonishment of Sir William Pepperell! They turned every gun within range on Vaughan and his thirteen men, but the Royal Battery was still theirs with the red coat flying over it as a flag. As soon as gunsmith Pomeroy drilled out the spiked touchholes of the cannon, they poured hot shot down into the city until "it made its women weep,"[6] as one eyewitness described it.

The fall of the Royal Battery was the high point of the siege, but the city held out for long, weary months. Between French bullets and deadly camp fever, the death toll was terribly high. Colonel Shubael Gorham went to a soldier's grave under the walls of Louisbourg, and Isaac Jeems, Micah Rafe, Sr., and Indian Ned never came back. When young Captain John brought his Rangers home to be mustered out, scarce one in four answered the last roll call.

Notes

1. For information on the Gorham family and the Gorham Rangers, see Charles F. Swift, *Genealogical Notes of Barnstable Families, Being a Reprint of the Amos Otis Papers* (Barnstable: F. B. and F. P. Goss, 1888), 119; Mary Rogers Bangs, *Old Cape Cod The Land: The Men The Sea* (Boston: Houghton Mifflin Co., 1920), 108-10; Frank William Sprague, *Barnstable Gorhams: The Old House in which they lived, and Their Services in the Colonial Wars* (Boston: the author, 1896), 1-4; and Frank William Sprague, *Col. John Gorham's "Wast Book"* (Boston: David Clapp and Son, 1898), 3-5.

2. A great grandfather of W. Sears Nickerson.

3. For all known material on the Native Americans in this piece, see Nickerson's manuscript, "Some Lower Cape Cod Indians," in the archives at the Cape Cod National Seashore.

4. See Francis Parkman, *France and England in North America* (The Library of America, 1983), 2: 641; Bangs, *Old Cape Cod The Land,* 110; and Charles F. Swift, *History of Old Yarmouth* (Yarmouth Port: the author, 1884), 143-44.

5. "The rest of the party followed, and one of them, William Tufts, of Medford, a boy of eighteen, climbed the flagstaff, holding in his teeth his red coat, which he made fast at the top, as a substitute for the British flag,—a proceeding that drew upon him a volley of unsuccessful cannon-shot from the town batteries" (Parkman, *France and England in North America,* 642). Parkman's source was John Langdon Sibley, "William Vaughan and William Tufts Jr at Louisburg, 1745," *New England History and General Register,* 25: 377. Nickerson has in his notes the name of the lad.

6. See Parkman for the exact quotation, "'damaged the houses and made the women cry'" (643).

IV

Life and Legend on Cape Cod

A Cape Cod Colonial: Uncle Elathun's House

The Wading Place Path

Pompmo and the Legend of Paw Waw's Pond

Old Maushope's Smoke: A Cape Cod Indian Fog Legend

The architecture of the early settlers in New England and the ancient foot paths of the Native Americans are monuments to those earlier periods. Nickerson described the architecture of a Cape Cod home in "A Cape Cod Colonial—Uncle Elathun's House," which was built just previous to the Revolution while Cape Cod was part of the Province of Massachusetts Bay. One of the old foot paths of the Native Americans, which soon widened into cartways, many of which developed into today's highways, is mapped out in "The Wading Place Path," an ancient, single-file trail from the Land of the Monomoyicks down the Cape into the Nawset Country, which was followed closely by Route 28 between Chatham and Orleans.

Included in this section are new versions of two legends. Nickerson attempts to fuse legend to historical fact in "Pompmo and the Legend of Paw Waw Pond," giving a different tale from those commonly known. In "Old Maushope's Smoke—A Cape Cod Indian Fog Legend," he gives a new version of the legend, telling why the fog pushes in from the Sound, covering Cape Cod under a sea of mist.

A Cape Cod Colonial: Uncle Elathun's House

This was written about 1925, before Elnathan Eldredge's house was moved to West Yarmouth. Although I have freely cut this piece and edited the mechanics, I have otherwise left it in Nickerson's words, believing that part of its charm rests in his first person point of view and in his addressing the reader in the second person, thereby creating a cozy ambience for his exploration of a significant form of colonial architecture, the Cape Cod home.

Uncle Elathun's house was built just previous to the Revolution while yet Cape Cod was a part, and a very important part, of the Province of Massachusetts Bay. After a hundred and fifty years, it stands foursquare as the day it was built, on the same corner stones which Uncle Elathun laid under it with his own hands while he was still a more or less loyal subject of King George, the Third.

Elathun was not his real given name. He was christened Elnathan, but like many another good Christian name, it got a peculiar twist in the Cape Cod mouthing of it. So, in the unpredictable crucible, Elnathan had simmered down to Elathun with all the accent on the El.

Uncle Elathun was born in another old Colonial built by his great grandfather Covel soon after 1665. I have heard that the ancestor of Lovell & Covel candy fame was also born in that same old house. It stood on the Neck between Ryder's Cove and Crow's Pond in Chathamport until long after 1800. When it was built, there was presumably only one other white man's house in all Chatham, that of William Nickerson the immigrant whose daughter Sarah was Nathaniel Covel's wife. Covell died a few years after it was completed, but the house he built survived him for a hundred years, and I have no doubt that its hand-hewn beams are still part of the fabric of some old house or barn in that locality to this day. The old Covel house where Elathun was born and the one he built for his bride in 1772 housed the successive generations of Eldredges for two hundred and fifty years in an unbroken line.

I suspect that when Elathun drew his plans for his own house he took as a model the one in which he was born and raised. I was born and raised in one of these old Colonials, myself, which was built in 1807 in the "time of the bargo," as the old folks used to say, and modeled after the same pattern.

Uncle Elathun's grandfather, Jehosaphat, was of the Yarmouth Branch of the Eldredges who harked back to the Eldreds of Saxonham in England. Jehosaphat came to Chatham soon after Nathaniel Covel died and married Covel's daughter, Elizabeth. They set up housekeeping in the house her father had built and where she was born, and here they raised a large family. Among them was one whom they named Ebenezer, a fine, strapping, blue-eyed boy with ruddy cheeks and yellow hair like his Saxon forbearers. Time passed, and although many a Cape Cod lass set her cap for Ebenezer, it looked as if he would end his days a bachelor.

One fine morning, however, a little baby girl was born to his neighbor, William "Red Stockings" and his wife, Sarah Nickerson. Her dark hair curled in ringlets over her little, round head, and her brown eyes were as deep as the pools in the native Italian lakes of her Lombard ancestors. They named her Deliverance for her grandmother Nickerson, and when the staid Ebenezer saw her, he made a vow then and there that he would wait for her to grow up and make her his wife. Jacob waiting his seven years for Rachel had nothing on Ebenezer. When Deliverance reached her fifteenth birthday, she became his wife, and in spite of the disparity of over twenty years in their ages, they lived happily ever after. Among the twelve children she bore him was Elathun.

Uncle Elathun early learned the trade of cordwainer from his mother's people who had been tanners and workers in leather since the founding of the settlement. He became so skillful at his trade that people came from miles around to have their shoes made and fitted by the young cordwainer. Among them was Dorothy Freeman who lived over near Round Cove in East Harwich. She was of the blood of Elder William and Mary Brewster who came on the *Mayflower*, and she counted descent through Governor Thomas Prence of Plymouth Colony. Before the waxed-ends had frayed on the shoes which Elathun fitted to her dainty feet, the poor cordwainer had become her Prince Charming, and the palace of their dreams was the old Cape Cod Colonial which still stands by the side of the road.

I have before me as I write the little account book which he made with his own hands about this time and whose leaves crackle like parchment under the touch. It is filled with quaint, old entries, such as making shoes for "Granny Sary Nickerson" and fashioning leather bands for the cattle of "Micah Rafe," the last full-blooded Indian on the Monomoyick lands. But probably the most important to him, and certainly to me, was the one in 1770 when he made the note "Dorothy Freeman, one pair shoes, L1:6."

Perhaps she wore those same shoes on her wedding day because she became his wife before the year was out. And that made her my great, great grandmother as well, for although I call him, as all the neighbors did, Uncle Elathun, he was in reality my father's great grandfather. From that time on, his little account book is bursting with entries about the land they bought of Crisp Rogers for L29 and the timbers and "shingalls" and nails which they accumulated to go into their new house at Wequasset, on the north side of Round Cove in East Harwich.

The "Raisin'" was in the spring. Uncle Elathun had patiently and lovingly hewed the timbers and sills from square, and the rafters were tenoned. The plates were mortised and the trunnels were worked down to size and laid ready to hang. Bricks, boards, and shingles had been landed in the Cove below the Hay Field by the corn-crackers which traded "longshore." The well was dug, and the cornerstone was laid. Everything was in readiness, even to the "Raisin'" rum. Elathun was a strictly temperate man, himself, but for this occasion he furnished an ample supply as his notebook shows. It is the only time that he ever bought a gallon of rum so far as I have learned from the many papers of his in my possession.

Eben the Fiddler was there with every cat-gut tuned to race the flying feet of sweet Lizzie Arey whose heart was as elusive to the Fiddler as her feet to his hornpipes. His brother Stephen, my Nickerson great great grandfather, whose fife was to pipe many of this same merry crowd to arms and war a few years later, blew an accompaniment to Eben's fiddle that would make a jitterbug jazz player dizzy with envy.

The Freemans, the Rogerses, the Sparrows, the Hopkinses, and the Snows from down Skaket and Tonset and Barley Neck way were there, as well as the Covels, the Eldreds, and the Nickersons from across the Bay at Monomoyick. The Whites from White's Brook who counted kin with little Peregrine White, born in a cabin of the *Mayflower*, and many another rugged pioneer family came to the Raisin'. Nearly all were *Mayflower* descendants, and all were relatives of either Elathun or Dorothy.

After a brief blessing by Parson Osborn in the new home aborning for those who would live in it and after a generous cup all around to properly wet the waiting sill, the young men went lustily to work. Father Ebenezer and Mother Deliverance sat high to oversee the Raisin' and to start their son's new house aright. By noon the studs stood straight under the chamber floor joists. Before sunset the rafters held the ridgepoles firm in their arms. And before curfew I suspect many a swain was doing the same with his blushing sweetheart as he beamed her home in the gloaming.

When I first remember Uncle Elathun's House, it was over a hundred years old. It was gray and weather beaten with age, yet it stood in simple dignity as if it had grown out of the soil and was proud of its heritage and its memories. The nether millstone doorstep was worn smooth by a century of Eldredge feet scuffing in and out the kitchen door, and the brass thumb latch on the front door was tapered almost to a knife edge by the wear of countless hands. Uncle Elathun and Dorothy, his wife, had long since joined their forebears in the old churchyard, and the feet of their children and grandchildren who once kept the grass bare around the doorstone had wandered far afloat and ashore. Some carried the flag of the new Republic to unknown shores and through uncharted seas in their clipper ships. Some followed the Mormon Elders across the Plains in the covered wagons. For some, the light had shone vainly out through the little window panes waiting the return of those who carried a vision of this little house to a watery grave on the Grand Banks.

I saw it mellowed by time, with the patina of age upon it. But, when Uncle Elathun carried Dorothy over the doorsill a hundred years before, she saw it with eyes filled with love-light for all the young cordwainer had built into it for her. The shingles were bright and cheerful in their yellow newness. There was no sag to the lintel of the kitchen door, and the redbrick fireplace looked as if it were just beckoning a welcome home while the orchard trees were bursting with their first bloom of apple blossoms.

Now come with me into Uncle Elathun's House in proper, old-fashioned, Cape Cod style. When I was a boy, no native Cape Codder ever thought of using the front door of his neighbor's house when making a casual, friendly call. He just simply dropped in through the back door without apology or restraint, joined the current of household affairs which set strong in the kitchen from sun-up till bed time, and drifted along with the tide. The busy day's work would not stop for the caller, and because of that, he felt all the more welcome. Except on special occasions he never got any farther than the kitchen, which was the living-room par excellence, and living, not loafing, was the order of the day in colonial times.

If you were a moderately tall man, you had to look out and not bump your head on the low-lying lintel of the back door as you entered. If you were raised in a true Cape Cod Colonial, you probably never entirely got over the habit of instinctively ducking your head when you passed through a doorway. And when you got inside, you found that the kitchen floor was only on a level with the millstone doorstep which had raised you over the well-worn sill. By standing on tiptoes, you could push the tip of your head hard against the ceiling. But what this kitchen may have lacked in headroom, it more than made up in the girth and breadth of its hospitality.

The kitchen occupied nearly half of the back half of the house, and the kitchen fireplace, flanked by its built-in, brick oven, took up over half of the south side of the kitchen, which is true for practically all original Cape Cod colonial houses. They were set with due regard for the cardinal points of the compass, and like the Great Pyramid at Gizeh, a straight line through the center of any one of them would cut the North Star. So true was this that they were habitually used as sundials by men working in the fields, on the cranberry bogs, or even off in the Bay in their boats.

Of course, the fireplace was the nucleus about which all the inner life of the family centered. Its great iron firedogs grimly kept the greenwood back log in place so that the dry wood could crackle its cheery warmth out over the ample hearth and into the chimney corners. The kettle sang and bubbled merrily on the crane while wet mittens and shoes steamed and dried at a more respectful distance. The bellows and the fire tongs looked down in disdain on the diminutive pipe tongs from where they leaned against the jamb. Old Tabby, stretched in perfect bliss on the hearth rug, dreamed that she already was in one of the many heavens which must intervene between the nine lives of a cat.

No dust-catching mantel surmounted Uncle Elathun's kitchen fireplace. A simple, hand-carved molding marked the line where the brush work ended and the paneling began, clothing it with neatness and dignity. A handy closet on the left, balanced the Dutch oven on the right, and the waist-high wainscoting which went around the room matched the panels over the fireplace. From the depths of the brick oven exuded the seductive aroma of baked beans and brown bread, molasses cookies and apple pie or perhaps a golden brown Indian pudding with its jade green whey an inch thick on the top.

The sail cloth carpet on the kitchen floor was the remnant of some weather-beaten topsail which perhaps once filled to the push of the Northeast Trades or swayed among the stars while rolling the easting in the Roaring Forties. Painted green and spattered with white, with its wide-lapped seams still proclaiming its origin, it was practically impervious to wear or water. No modern homemaker has ever been able to quite equal the skills with which the old-time Cape Cod housewife embossed those needle point spatters of white on the greens and grays of her kitchen floors and stairways. With nothing but her deft hands and a bough of pine needles from the nearest tree, she set a pattern which has been the envy of every imitator since her day. And when the old sail cloth carpet would lift and bellow under her feet with a Northeast gale seeking every crack and cranny under the kitchen floor, it gave her a feeling of closer companionship with her sailorman somewhere out on the stormy Atlantic.

Uncle Elathun's House had a small "butt'ry," as it was called in the Cape vernacular, on the east side of the house next to the kitchen door. Pan after pan of creamy milk filled the shelves, and the dash-churn stood ready to separate the thick cream to the chant of "Come, butter, come! Sears wants some! There he stands by the gate; all he wants is a butter cake! Come, butter, come!" And then, there was the wonder of the sheaf of wheat, standing out in bold relief on the top of the golden-yellow butter ball when it came out of the butter mould. Under the shelf was the cookie jar filled with thick molasses cookies, and down through the trap door into the little round cellar was an apple pie, where among the cobwebs lurked the jars of cranberry jelly, crocks of piccalilli, and perhaps a demi-john or two of native juices which cheered but never inebriated.

Two tiny bedrooms, one on the east and one on the west side of the kitchen, were the only "finished off" sleeping quarters in the house. They were just large enough to squeeze in a four-poster bed and leave room to walk in on one side afterwards. But the great rough "open chamber," as the whole upper floor was known, with its ample supply of cord cribs and spool bedsteads, easily took care of the overflow. It was also a happy hunting ground for us youngsters on stormy days. I can remember now the muted whir of the wings of the swallows nesting in the great chimney, which stood naked and unashamed in the center of the upper chamber, as we romped in "Blind Man's Bluff" around it. And the dark corners under the eaves were filled with the discarded spring wheels and broken bedsteads of yesteryear.

You reached the open chamber by a narrow stairway just to the right of the brick oven. The chamber door, at the front of the stairway, opened out into the kitchen and revealed the high risers and narrow treads leading to the boy's paradise above. Through the second riser from the bottom opened the round "cat-hole," polished smooth around the edges by countless generations of Eldredge cats immigrating and emigrating to and from the open chamber and the great outdoors. This simple device gave ready access at all times, in all weathers, for feline raids on marauding rats and mice lurking in the dark recesses above to loot the rows of dried apples and seed corn hanging so temptingly from the roof rafters.

Perhaps you, being a stranger, should have been taken around to the front door of Uncle Elathun's House and received as a honored guest. The front door was reserved for such rare visitors as the minister or the undertaker.

The six-panel front door swung on its hammered brass "T" hinges into a small front entry which in turn opened to right and left into the Front Room and the Best Room. The Front Room was no more to the front than the Best Room, but I suppose it got its traditional name because it was relatively front from the kitchen. The Front Room was also commonly called the Sitting Room, probably because there was precious little time for sitting down in the kitchen except to eat, and when the day's work was through or the Sunday hush had fallen over the busy household, the Front Room was a welcome sitting place.

Here the more formal caller was entertained, and here of an evening the family and neighbors gathered around the Mason and Hamlin organ for a Sing. Their mixed voices ran the gamut from "Old Hundred" ("Praise God from whom All blessings Flow"), which their Pilgrim forefathers and mothers sang on the way over in the *Mayflower*, to "Seeing Nellie Home" and "When You and I were Young, Maggie." Sometimes a fiddle or an accordion would accompany some sailor lad as he gave them a salty fo'cas'le ballad or a deepwater chantey picked up in the far reaches of the seven seas.

When a wedding or a funeral was to take place, the sacred precincts of the Best Room were thrown open to the curious eyes of the world. Instead of the cheerful, red chintzes and the colorful, braided mats of the Front Room, the somber-toned, carpeted floors and the black, hair-cloth, walnut furniture gave the Best Room a semi-funereal atmosphere at best. Delicately tinted shells from the South Seas, carefully protected in their domes of glass, and the painstakingly needled mottoes over the doors, reminding the Almighty in no uncertain terms of his duty to this home and its inmates, did their best to brighten the gloom. The reason so much of this Best Room furniture is on display in showrooms of the antique dealers today is because it was so uncomfortable and so unfitted for any practical use that it survived the ravages of the normal wear and tear of a large Cape Cod family.

When I played as a boy around Uncle Elathun's House, great cedar trees on monstrous hummocks stood where now are cranberry bogs between it and my father's place. The common route for us youngsters in making the passages across was to shinny up to the top of the first cedar on our side of the swamp, and then by swinging this tree back and forth until we could swing to the top of the next one, continue on until we gained the land on Uncle Elathun's side. Then, with a stop at the little flag swamp below the house to sample the succulent sweet flags which grew waist deep among the snake flags and cat-o-nine tails, we raced on to bury our faces in the old oaken bucket which hung at the end of the old, wooden well sweep. How well I remember peering down over the edge of the moss-grown bricks and seeing far below in the still waters a little boy's face looking straight up at me as if from the other side of the world.

On the side hill above the well grew the most wonderful apples: yellow-skinned summer sweets, red-streaked rattleseeds (whose seeds you could hear rattle when you gave them a lusty shaking), spicy pignoses, which despite their name and resemblance of their bud ends to a pig's snout made the most luscious apple dumplings, all casting their first fruits onto the magic carpet of white and blue violets or yellow buttercups around the well's rim. In the deep, tangled, wild wood beyond the well, you could peek through the brambles on a hot summer's day and watch the whip-poor-will nesting on a dead limb in the cool, dark shade. If there are Sylvan dells where the fairies and the pixies love to dwell, then surely that hollow where Uncle Elathun dug his well was part of Fairyland.

We might race to the old barn and romp in the hay mows above the oaken stanchions worn smooth by the necking of contented cattle. The lofts were sweet with the scent of salt and English hay, and a long festoon of cobwebs looped down from the rafters where year after year the barn swallows came back to rebuild their homes of clay. The massive, curved ox yokes and the rotting ox carts under the sheds, the harnesses, the plows, and the grain chests—all went to make up our playground.

So this is how Uncle Elathun's House looked to me as a boy. Its worn timbers were tenoned and tree nailed; trunneled, the old folks would say; its eighteen-inch floor boards were handplaned, and its walls were sealed with plaster made from the shells of some Indian's kitchen midden, laid on overhand shaved laths, pinned on with hand-whittled pegs.

Uncle Elathun's house still stands, but its old barn has long since gone to decay. The well sweep no longer balances the old oaken bucket, and its whip-poor-will nests no more in the tangled thicket. Times have changed since George, the Third was king, and the indescribable glow of hospitality which enfolded you when you crossed its worn threshold died out with the last embers on the kitchen hearth.

The Wading Place Path

The Wading-Place Path" was published in a local newspaper, the Cape Codder, on 5 October 1961, but it is clear from Nickerson's correspondence with Cleon Stanley Crowell (1891-1961) that he had worked on it for decades. Cleon Crowell and his father, Anthony Elmer Crowell (1862-1952), were master decoy makers of East Harwich, Massachusetts. Elmer Crowell painted The Wading Place Bridge in 1890, probably as a wedding present to his wife, Laura. The scene depicts the buggy of Dr. Charles Burtel Worthing crossing the bridge on the end of Pleasant Bay Cove on the Chatham town line. The man waving in the boat is thought to be a self portrait of Crowell. In a letter to Cleon, 11 May 1932, Nickerson asks permission to mention Cleon's father's painting in an article on Micah Rafe. On May 23, he says it is o.k. with his father; then, on 20 October 1933, Cleon Crowell sends Nickerson a photo of the painting.

When our pioneer forefathers pushed down the Cape to make their homes here, their only means of communication by land was over the old footpaths of the Indians. They soon widened these into cartways, many of which have developed into our busy highways of today.

Route 28 between Chatham and Orleans follows very closely what was once the Wading-Place Path of the Indians. Packed hard by countless generations of moccasined feet, this ancient single-file trail[1] was the Indian highway from the Land of the Monomoyicks down the Cape into the Nawset Country. It came out of the Indians' Cotchpinicut [or Cotchpinecote], Chatham's Old Harbor of today, and crossed the little creek near the present Acme Laundry[2] which they called Pamuet,[3] the

145

**Detail from *The Wading Place Bridge* (1890) painted by Elmer Crowell.
Courtesy of The Cape Cod Five Cents Savings Bank and Heritage
Plantation of Sandwich.**

Step Stones, from the fact that they had rolled big boulders into it so
they could step across dry shod from stone to stone. Route 28 crosses at
exactly the same spot.

From the Step Stones it followed along the Ryder's Cove shore to the
lodge of Mattaquason, the Old Sagamore of the Monomoyicks, which
stood near where the Christopher Ryder House stands today.[4] Nearby
was the grave of the Pilgrims' famous Indian friend Squanto who died
here after he had piloted Governor Bradford in over the Bars and up to
the headquarters village. Just across The Path the immigrants William
Nickerson and his goodwife Anne raised their cabin, the first settlers in
the town of Chatham, and on the knoll beyond, their graves still over-
look the homestead they hacked out of a wilderness.

The Path continued on over the hill and down to the shore where the
Monomoyick River of the Indians empties into Pleasant Bay. A short distance upstream on the Harwich bank of the river stood the "English-
built" house of Micah Rafe, the last full-blood in these parts, whom my
grandfather could remember well. Just below the present causeway, the
Indians on the trail could wade the river on the clean, yellow sands at its
mouth. This was Askaonkton, their Wading-Place, and it gave its name
not only to The Path which crossed it but also to the whole locality
roundabout.

Leaving The Wading-Place behind, The Path wound along the Bay
shore to Wequasset, where on the west side of Round Cove stood the
"Indian-built" wigwam of Isaac Jeems, known in this vicinity, and his

mother Wahenanun, the granddaughter of the Old Sagamore. After his death my great-grandfather bought the wigwam site from Micah Rafe, and I was born and grew up nearby, while yet the spot was still known as Isaac Jeems's Wigwam.

The Path swung inland from Round Cove into Indian Hollow to avoid the mucky, cedar swamps which lay ahead in those days. Route 28 does not follow it here but picks it up again just beyond Baker's Tar Kiln Meadow in South Orleans. In my boyhood a short stretch of the original Wading-Place Path still remained intact in the Hollow, just as the Indians who made it left it. Worn deep into the hillside, it had never been plowed under by the white man nor over laid by one of his roads. It was still in everyday use by my neighbors and still known by its original name. It was a little spooky, too, for a small boy, because it ran right between the Squaws' Grieving Stone and a group of field stones marking Indian graves, probably those of Isaac Jeems and his mother Wahenanon among them. Tradition had it that the curious cup-like holes sunk into the top of the boulder had been chipped out by Indian women sitting there to mourn their dead. I often took The Path on my way to school in East Harwich and always held my breath until I was safely past this scary spot. One day in the summer of 1960 my daughter Dorothy took me and her children into Indian Hollow to see if any trace of The Wading Place Path could still be found. What used to be pasture field was now overgrown with the underbrush and forest trees of nearly three quarters of a century. Still we had little difficulty in locating the old path which was plainly marked by a dip in the earth running north and south under the leaves. There, too, stood the lonely, old Grieving Stone with the curious holes in its top, just as it did when I scurried past it as a schoolboy. A rabbit had made his home under the downhill side and in The Path beside it red Indian-pipes were prowling.

Learned archaeologists will tell you that those curious holes were made by Indians in which to grind smooth their fish sinkers and other stone implements.[5] But if he could talk our language, I'll bet Mister Rabbit would tell you that on some moonlit, misty nights in summer when he comes out of his hole, he wonders why the wraiths of old Indian women sit chipping on his rock.

After leaving the Hollow, The Path swung around the cedar swamps, nearly cutting my father's dooryard in two, and from there made a bee-line for Baker's Tar Kiln. I followed this well-worn path on foot all during my student days at Orleans High School and believe it was a relic of the old Wading-Place Path although it had lost its name and its identity. My path took me on a single log across the beautiful little brook which babbles down into the Meadow and through the open field marked only

An Indian Rock. Cape Cod National Seashore.

by the small-pox gravestone of Thomas Freeman, one of my nearly forgotten great-grandfathers. On the high hill overlooking the Bay, Route
28 again picks up the trail which it left at Round Cove and follows it in a
general way down to Arey's Pond where once the remnant of the powerful Nawset Tribe clustered around the wigwam of their last sachem, John
Sipson.

The old trail must have sent a branch from Arey's Pond down into
Pochet[6] and certainly one to Namskaket[7] over which Governor Bradford
tells us he toted supplies for the shipwrecked *Sparrow Hawk*.
Undoubtedly, the main trail went on straight ahead across the General
Fields to Town Cove in Orleans where it merged into the great Nawset
Trail from up the Cape and continued on to all the Lower Cape Indian
villages in The Nawset Country.[8]

Notes

1. In a letter to Nickerson, Cleon Crowell had written that his father's grandmother, Diana Rogers of Orleans, wife of Bangs Nickerson, lived next
   house east of his father's old home and that "Those Indians came from
   Cliff Pond and trailed by her Barn on their way to wading place & stepping
   stones in Chathamport to do a days trading at Stage harbor. Those Indians

trailed single file and when the first one got to the wading place the last one would just be going by her barn and they would hoot all along the line this was their custom."

2. Acme Laundry has moved because of environmental requirements; nothing is there now.
3. "Pamuet" is Wampanoag for "going-over place" or "ford." The creek is now called Frost Bite.
4. The Christopher Ryder House has been converted into condominiums.
5. Cleon Crowell and Nickerson held a mutual interest in these stones. On 20 October 1933, Crowell sent Nickerson a photo of "our much talked about Indian rock, a short distance from Asa Roger's.

Say you know, I believe, the Indians used the different size holes in that rock to grind down and shape their plummets or sinkers as some call them. You can imagine the Indians picking up a stone somewhere near the shape that he wanted and then by carefully twisting and grinding in the different size holes he brings the implement down to the dimensions he wants it. You will probably remember those holes are about the right size of plummets.

Now the material which this rock is composed of is very abrasive and tough, it would cut other stone material fast. The old Indian knew this too.

There again he could shape up the ends to his pestles and similar ends to other implements. Think it over and I bet you say the mystery is solved."

Nickerson obviously preferred the romantic, traditional theory to Crowell's more logical one.

One such rock, formerly off Henenway Landing, Eastham, was moved from the swamp to the top of Skill Hill, Eastham where it is currently on display by the National Seashore.

6. "Pochet" is Wampanoag for "at the narrow place" or possibly "at the turning place."
7. "Namskaket" is Wampanoag for "a fishing place."
8. Joshua A. Nickerson, a nephew of W. Sears Nickerson, subsequently acquired land for his home which was adjacent to and included a part of Muddy Creek and the Wading Place. He later gave most of that portion of his property to the Chatham Conservation Foundation.

Pompmo and the Legend of Paw Waw's Pond

*N*ickerson attempts in *"Pompmo and the Legend of Paw Waw's Pond"* to fuse legend to historical fact. He fails to acknowledge the legend as it existed in the area, which he surely must have known. A historical marker at the pond (I have seen a picture of it published in 1976) which according to William Quinn, caretaker of historical markers in the town of Orleans, washed out in a storm read as follows: "Pau Wah Pond, named for Pau Wah, Chief of the Potonamequoits who drowned herein after Chief Quanset refused marriage to his daughter Wild Dove. Fable says— Cast a pinch of tobacco in the pond and Pau Wah gives you good fishing." The information for the marker which was placed at the pond in the 1950s came from Albert S. Snow (deceased) who had gotten it from his grandfather. The town refused to spend the $500 to replace the marker, which is one way a legend can die.

For a detailed account of the legend, see Elizabeth Reynard, The Narrow Land: Folk Chronicles of Old Cape Cod. *Reynard received her information from John Kenrick of South Orleans. The name is usually spelled "Kendrick." I recently saw the Kendrick home of four generations which held the Post Office at one time; across the road is the town pump of which a John Kendrick was officially elected keeper. In brief sketch, Reynard's "The Water-Being of Pau Wah Pond" has Quansett refusing Pau Wah's request for his daughter Wild Dove. Pau Wah raided Quansett's wigwam but failed to secure the princess. In shame over his defeat, Pau Wah moved onto a pond near Namequoit to avoid the hunters' trails. Failing to make an offering to the Water Spirit, Niba-nahbeezik, Pau Wah was sent immediately to the bottom of the ice-covered pond where he lives, unfortunately, without Wild Dove and without tobacco. In order to make a trade with Pau Wah for fish, one must throw in the pond a piece of tobacco and make the deal, "Pau Wah, Pau Wah, Pau Wah, give me fish and I give you tabac."*

Possibly Nickerson gave his account of the legend because he knew from historical fact that Pompmo lived to be well over seventy, that he was married, had children, and was not a chief. See Nickerson's Some Lower Cape Cod Indians, Group II, "The Nawsets," 195-203 for the genealogy and legal transactions of Pompmo. Nickerson's well-indexed manuscript contains many references to all of the Native Americans mentioned in this piece as well as references to Quansett.

There are various spellings of Paw Waw. In Names of the Land: Cape Cod, Nantucket, Martha's Vineyard, and the Elizabeth Islands *Eugene Green and William L. Sachse, identify the pond as "an inlet of Pleasant Bay, off Portanimicut Road in Orleans. Pompo the powwow (Paw Wah is an irregular spelling of the Algonquian word for conjurer) had much land in early Orleans. He apparently drowned in the pond; thereafter, fishermen would drop a quid of tobacco into the waters as an offering to him and say, `Paw Waw, I give you tobac'. You give me some fish." This indicates how varied the spelling can be even in the same work; therefore, I have granted Nickerson his spelling.*

A version entitled "Indian Legend of Paw Waw's Pond" was published by Nickerson in the Cape Codder *on 21 February 1957.*

There is a beautiful little tidewater pond down in the northeastern corner of South Orleans known today as Lockwood's Pond. It nestles in behind Namacoick[1] Point, and but for the narrow Run which connects it with the ebb and flow of the waters of Little Bay and the ocean beyond, it would be entirely landlocked. Its ancient Indian name was Ottinamut, but when I was a boy, it was always spoken of by the old settlers as Paw Waw's Pond. Likewise, the whole countryside roundabout, including the little village nearby, was known as Paw Waw except when Harwich Hairleggers go under the skin of our neighbors, the Paw Waw Yallerbellies, by referring to their home place by its other colloquial title, Skunks' Misery.[2] Tradition has it that the pond got its name because a noted Indian paw waw or medicine man, named Pompmo, once lived by its shores and was drowned in its waters. The early records prove that there was in truth an Indian by that name who was a large land owner there. Among other children he had a son named Simon. Pompmo was a clever real estate operator, and it was a puzzle for many years how he managed to assume property rights in the hereditary lands of the Nawset and Monomoyick sachemries. The Indian custom of that period was to make their land sales through their sachems and then only after the tribe had given its consent in assembled council. This paw waw, who was never a Lower Cape sachem, sold land around Little Bay, Pleasant Bay, and even as far west as Oyster Island, without getting anyone's consent as far as the records show. No objections were raised by either red man or white when he and his son Simon made a sale of the salt-marsh Aquaquesset, which lay just a short distance south alongshore from Paw Waw's Pond. Joseph Rogers, who came over on the *Mayflower* and whose farm lay nearby on Barley Neck, was the buyer, and it still went by the name of Deacon Rogers' Meadow in my boyhood. When, however, he attempted to sell the adjacent Fort Hill and Hosey's Swamp, he ran head on into the old Indian land law and the claim of the Nawset sachem John Sipson, from whose daughter the swamp took its name.

Fort Hill was once the headquarters of the remnant of the Nawset tribe, their ancient Attacospa, and John Sipson was their last recognized sachem. This was almost sacred ground to the Indians. They said that in the olden days they had a palisaded fort there surrounding a sweet-water boiling spring, and this was why it was called Fort Hill. A spring on a hill is quite a rarity on the Lower Cape, but the Indians explained that once upon a time a great whale swam in under the land and getting short of air right there attempted to blow. He found the weight of the hill too much for him and succeeded only in starting this spring flowing. So he swam on to the west until he got under the swamp, where he really spouted. And to this day the tiny pondhole in the middle of Hosey's Swamp still goes by the name of The Whale Hole.

The files of the Massachusetts Superior Court of Judicature finally gave the answer as to why old Pompmo had been allowed to get away with so much on the Lower Cape. Sachem John Sipson, in the year 1715, when he was a very old man, made a sworn statement in a land suit before the Court that he knew Simon Pompmo to be the son of Old Pompmo and that Pompmo, himself, was the son of Pekswat.[3]

Pekswat was one of the war captains of the great sachem Chicatawbut of the Massachusetts Bay Indians and a ringleader in the plot of 1623 to wipe out the Pilgrim Plantation. Captain Myles Standish with his brave little squad of Plymouth men took the field against the conspirators and closed in on them at Neponset. In the fight that ensued, Standish, in a hand-to-hand scrimmage with Pekswat, killed him with his own knife. In his "The Courtship of Miles Standish," the poet Longfellow captured in vivid verse an almost verbatim eye-witness description of the death of Pekswat.[4]

> *Then stood Pecksuot forth, self-vaunting,*
> *insulting Miles Standish:*
> *While with his fingers he patted the*
> *knife that hung at his bosom,*
> *Drawing it half from its sheath,*
> *and plunging it back, as he muttered,*
> *'By and by it shall see; it shall eat;*
> *ah, ha! but shall speak not!*
> *This is the mighty Captain the*
> *white men have sent to destroy us!*
> *He is a little man; let him go and*
> *work with the women!'*

Standish took this taunt and insult until he could stand it no longer.

> *All the hot blood of his race, of*
> *Sir Hugh and of Thurston de Standish,*
> *Boiled and beat in his heart, and*
> *swelled in the veins of his temples.*
> *Headlong he leaped on the boaster,*
> *and, snatching his knife from its scabbard,*
> *Plunged it into his heart, and,*
> *reeling backward, the savage*
> *Fell with his face to the sky. . . .*

After Pekswat's death and the defeat of the plot to exterminate the settlers, word soon leaked into Plymouth that the ringleaders, including Sachem Aspinet of Nawset and Sachem Iyanno of Mattakeese, had crawled off into the swamps and died of starvation. This was good Indian propaganda, but it seems highly improbable. It is more likely that they simply went underground until such time as they could again safely appear under new names, of which they always had a plenty. Probably Pekswat's family quickly slipped into a safe asylum among Chicatawbut's relatives on the Lower Cape, which in 1623, along with the rest of New England, was practically an unknown wilderness. It is said that Chicatawbut's mother was from Pamet, and it is a matter of record that he and his son Josias Wampatuck were blood kin to other Lower Cape tribesmen and closely allied with them. This then would account for the prestige of Pompmo, the son of Pekswat, among the Indians which he seems to have used to ignore their time-honored customs and to further his own shady land deals.[5]

Returning to Paw Waw's Pond, the story goes that one cold winter when his pond seemed to be icebound for the season, old Pompmo moved his lodge out on its frozen surface so that he and his wife might sit snugly by the fire, smoke their home-grown tobacco, and fish comfortably through a hole in the ice inside their wigwam, as was the old Indian custom. But Cape Cod salt water ice has a reputation for being treacherous, and one stormy night with a sweeping, high tide accompanied by a warm rain, a regular January thaw set in and caught him napping. When morning broke, every vestige of ice was gone from the pond, and old Pompmo, his wigwam, and his wife were nevermore to be seen in this life.

The Indians said, however, that he was never really contented in the Happy Hunting Grounds of his fathers, and so powerful was his mystic medicine that his spirit enabled him to travel back to haunt the waters of the pond he loved so well. Be that as it may, old timers will tell you that even to this day if you expect to have any luck fishing in the pond, you had better first drop a little quid of tobacco over the side of your boat as an offering and address him prayerfully, something like this: "Paw Waw, Paw Waw, I give you tobacco. You give me some fish?"

Notes

1. Currently spelled "Namequoit."
2. Nickerson writes, "I picked many a six-quart measure of cranberries on my father's Paw Waw bog, which was reclaimed from part of the Indians' Seanesot Cedar Swamp and lay just west of the pond. A well-preserved quiver of arrows was uncovered in one of the hummocks while the virgin trees were being ripped out to make way for the cranberry vines."
3. Nickerson writes, "This Pekswat, or Peksuot or Pecksuot as it is sometimes spelled, was an old acquaintance of mine, both from his place in verse and in the cold script of the early records; but I never should have speculated, if it had not been for the old sachem, that Pompmo, the paw waw, was his son. Perhaps even the white Cape Codders of his day did not suspect it either."
4. Gov. Edward Winslow, *Good News from New England, The Story of the Pilgrim Fathers, 1606-1623 A.D.; as told by Themselves, their Friends, and their Enemies*, edited by Edward Arber (Boston: Houghton, Mifflin and Co., 1897), 567-69.
5. Pompmo sold a parcel of land to Josias Cooke which William Nickerson (Nickerson's pioneer ancestor) had purchased from Sachem John Quason Towsowet on 10 April 1665, six months previous to Cooke's purchase. W. Sears Nickerson wrote, "I suspect Sachem John Quason Towsowet and his father The Old Sagamore got together with Old Pompmo forthwith and played Cooke off against Nickerson, because the feud over this strip of land

lasted between the Cookes and Nickerson[s] for three generations, until their great-grandchildren married and buried the hatchet, thereby making Cooke an ancestor of mine also." See Nickerson's Some Lower Cape Cod Indians, Group II, "The Nawsets," 197-98.

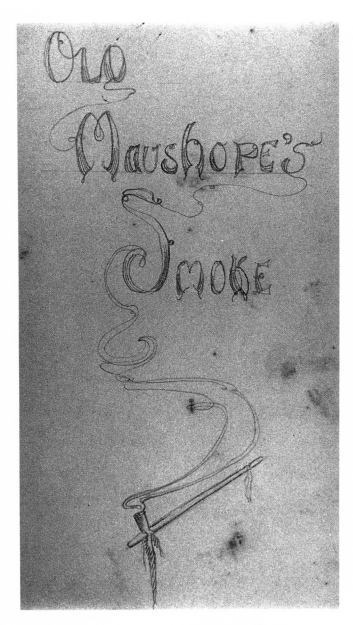

Drawing from the papers of W. Sears Nickerson.
Cape Cod National Seashore.

Old Maushope's Smoke: A Cape Cod Indian Fog Legend

Nickerson was familiar with several versions of the Maushope legend. In his papers I found one sheet with nine legends listed, with only three of them described. Under Maushope's Smoke, Nickerson notes,

> Also a tradition that Nantucket was unknown until a great bird carried off in his talon little children & the giant Maushope waded out and followed him to the island & found the children's bones under a tree. Whereupon he sat down to smoke & the smoke was carried across to the mainland[.] The true origin of fog is the sound.
>
> Another legend had it that Nantucket was formed from the ashes of his pipe.
>
> Still another that Nantucket was discovered by the parents of a child who followed the great bird in their canoe.

The only reference Nickerson gives for his source is "It was told by the Mattakeese Indians who lived at Iyanno's Town on the south shore of Barnstable Bay." I do not know, but I surmise that Nickerson's account is either derived from written accounts of oral traditions and/or from the white man's oral tradition. Nickerson wrote, "So far as I know none of them [versions of the fog legend] is given in anything like the Indian's own words. Scattered remnants of what the Indian believed, told in the white man's way, are all that remain." I can imagine his learning about the legend from his friend Stanley Smith or Cleon Crowell or perhaps even his father. Oral tradition on Maushope among whites continues in 1992. I spoke to Chris Burden (New Seabury Real Estate) about an area within New Seabury named Maushop Village. He said that it was named by his uncle,

Malcolm Chace, in the 1940s for a giant who protected small children from an eagle. He added that the giant on becoming angry over something threw some dirt which formed the islands. His source would be Wampanoag (Mashpee), not Mattakeese.

Nickerson wrote "Old Maushope's Smoke" twice. The factual content is basically the same, but the style is significantly different. Although I have drawn on both, I have primarily used the embellished account as being in harmony with the oral style of a story teller. The more objective, more fact-oriented version appeared in the Cape Codder *on 24 July 1958.*

William S. Simmons, Spirit of the New England Tribes: Indian History and Folklore, 1620-1984 *is the definitive word on the Maushope legend. See his chapter, "Giants: Maushop and Squant," 172-234 for numerous accounts of the legend and 258-70 of his conclusion. Simmons in a review of the Nickerson material for a potential publisher recognized Nickerson's "Old Maushope's Smoke" as a new version of the legend.*

I have maintained Nickerson's spelling of Maushope; the name according to Simmons (whose source is Roger Williams) is derived from the Proto-Algonquian word meaning "big man" or "giant." The word has several spellings: Maushop, Moshup, Moshop, Manshope, and Maushope.

See also Elizabeth Reynard, The Narrow Land: Folk Chronicles of Old Cape Cod.

❦

Would you like to know why the fog pushes in from the Sound on a summer's afternoon, stealing up the valleys like a great, gray, timber wolf and drawing its dripping veil across the burning face of the sun until Cape Cod lies submerged under a sea of mist? Then, listen to an Indian legend as old as the fog itself.

Nishkenon was a very, very old woman, so old that there was no one living who could remember when she was not old. Kiehtan, the Great Spirit, had smiled when she was born. He had bestowed upon her the gift of second sight—that wonderful power of divination by which those born under a caul are said to be able to peer through the thick darkness which veils the future.

Her father, Old Maushope, himself a noted medicine man and magician, rejoicing in the happy omens attending her birth, consecrated her girlhood to that semi-seclusion which the Indians imposed on certain children marked for special priestly education. He taught her all the ancient lore of his people so that when he should be called to join his fathers in the great Southwest Land of the Spirits his little nunksqua could carry the knowledge on to generations yet to come.

Drawing from the papers of W. Sears Nickerson.
Cape Cod National Seashore.

Tonight she sat beside the door of her lodge in the gathering twilight, dreamily watching the afternoon fog as it drifted in around the Indian village. Little boys put aside their tiny bows and arrows and, leaving their mimic warfare until another day, gathered around her as she sat. Little girls, bringing their corn-cob dollies and make-believe wigwams, squatted at her feet. Tired hunters, in from the trail, threw themselves down within hearing distance of her words. No Indian man or woman between Manomet in Plymouth and Meeshawn at Provincetown could tell the old tales quite so well as Nishkenon.

As the fog wraiths streamed in between the wigwams and eddied around her aged head, this is what she told them, sitting there beside her lodge door in the twilight.

Many, many summers ago, while she was yet a little girl, smaller than most in her group of listeners, there lived a great eagle over across the Sound on the Isle of Capoge or Martha's Vineyard. He was so huge that when he soared across the Cape his shadow fell on the fields as if a black cloud were passing over. Swooping down on the Indian villages like a hawk on a field mouse's run, he would grab little children in his cruel talons and carry them off to his island aerie. The Indians called him Wompsikuck,[1] the Great White Eagle.

Year after year Wompsikuck terrorized the Cape tribes, leaving a trail of desolated wigwams and sorrowing families in his wake. No warrior had ever been quick-handed enough to sink a tomahawk into his brain; no bow arm had ever been strong enough to send a death-dealing arrow through the thick armor of feathers into his heart. Many a young man and woman bore to their graves the scars of the horrible lacerations made by his beak and claws when in sheer desperation they had tried to save their little ones.

One spring day when the herring run was on, Maushope was down in the brook with all of the other men from the village throwing out the silvery fish to the women on the bank, while his little girl contentedly played among the shell heaps behind his wigwam. Suddenly, the evil shadow of Old Wompsikuck swept down over them, and the shrieking swish of his great wings ripped through the air. Like every Indian child on the Cape, his little girl had grown up with the fear of that shadow in her soul and knew the sinister meaning of that sound. She scuttled for the wigwam door like a frightened quail, but before she half reached it, the talons of the fierce Wompsikuck closed around her, and she was swept off her feet in a smother of feathers and dust. As the great bird rose again above the roofs of the village with Nishkenon dangling under his huge body like a herring in the claws of a fish hawk, she looked down straight through the smoke hole into her father's wigwam.

Maushope stood aghast. He could not believe that Kiehtan, their own special guardian and benefactor, would knowingly let this terrible thing happen to his chosen favorites. Surely something must be wrong. Perhaps the cunning, old bird had watched his chance and slipped behind the back of the god while he was intent on helping his people with the herring catch. Whatever the reason, standing there whimpering like some frightened, old woman would not save his child from a terrible death nor call the god's attention to her danger. He would take the trail of the Great White Eagle until one of them lay dead.

Chanting a prayer to the Great Spirit, he took out of his medicine bundle his wonderful magic moccasins, fashioned of softest, tanned doeskin and worked with mystical figures in purple wampum which gave them supernatural power. Nishkenon's mother, first purifying her hands in sacred incense smoke from dried sweet grass laid on the hearth fire, reverently laced them securely to his feet. She then selected a choice leaf of his consecrated tobacco and tucked it into the tobacco pouch hanging at the back of his neck. Before the village had recovered from its confusion, Maushope was headed into the forest in the direction that the great White Eagle had taken.

Wearing the moccasins which gave him mile-long strides to every step, Maushope soon left far behind the waters of Cummaquid,[2] where the village of Mattakeese lay. Wakeby saw him pass like a shadow. The valleys of Cotuit and Poponesset looked with wonder on his flight. As he raced across the Cape, he never took his eyes off his quarry except to watch out not to splash into some pond hole or trout stream and thereby get the magic washed from his feet. He leaped the great marshlands of Menauhant and Succanesset at a single bound, and at last the bold headlands of the Isle of Capoge across the Sound loomed dimly on his sight. He could see the glistening white spread of the wings of Wompsikuck, circling high in the sunlit sky above him.

The magic of his moccasins had proven strong thus far, but would it carry him over the turbulent waters of Vineyard Sound? Too well he knew that a touch of running water would disperse all of their wonderful power. Great beads of sweat stood out on his forehead as he strode out on Nobska Head and measured the distance across to West Chop with his eye. It was a mighty leap, such as no Indian Paw Waw, be his medicine ever so powerful, had ever dreamed of before. If Kiehtan's face were turned away from him now, it meant the end of the trail.

But this was no time for useless questioning. Maushope pulled tightly the lacings of his moccasins and grimly shifted his weapons so they would be ready for instant use should he gain the farther shore. He chose a great rock lying at the water's edge from which to make the leap. The tense muscles of his sinewy legs knotted like whip cords as he crouched for the spring. Then, like a bronze arrow shot from a giant bowstring, his lithe body straightened out into the curve of a huge arc. It glistened higher and higher into the cool air over the Sound until he could look straight down into mid channel. Swinging himself into position as he neared the sandy bluffs, he landed high and dry on the island's shore.

There was no more doubt in his heart about Kiehtan. The Great Spirit was surely with him. As he circled south around the bend of Menemsha Bight, Old Maushope begged his magic moccasins for one more burst of speed. The sun was now riding low in the west over Naushon. Silhouetted above it, against the darkening sky was the Great White Eagle, his wings already set for the landing.

Maushope met Wompsikuck as he landed. His blood curdling "Wooach! Ha! Ha! Wooach!" rent the echoes of the cliffs. The swish of his swinging tomahawk sung through the air as it crashed into the skull of the bewildered bird. So swift and sure was the blow that Wompsikuck toppled over with not so much as a death flurry.

When Maushope rolled the ugly carcass away, there lay his little Nishkenon, unconscious, covered with feathers and blood, but still alive. He gathered her up tenderly in his strong arms and forgetful of magic or moccasins waded waist deep into the waters of the Sound to bathe her forehead and face and cleanse her little body from the blood and filth of the great bird. As he worked, he murmured into her ears the pet names she had heard so often around their wigwam fire in far away Mattakeese. He called her his little Wequashim, the moonlight of his heart; his beautiful clinging vine Weenomis; he pleaded with her to come back from the Spirit Land and be again his own Nepum,[3] the summer of his old age. At last the intensity of her father's love penetrated her numbed senses, and she opened her eyes and smiled.

As they climbed back up the headland, every gully and crevice was oozing with the lifeblood of the huge eagle, painting the cliffs as it ran. The Indians say that those red streaks which may be seen to this day on the face of Gay Head are the blood stains from Old Wompsikuck.

Once up the cliffs, Maushope made medicine over the body of his slain enemy. With his enemy lying dead at his feet and his little girl safe by his side, gratitude filled his heart to overflowing. Not only was his own little daughter alive and safe in his arms but also nevermore would this fierce marauder harass the tribes of his people. Kiehtan, the good god of his fathers, had listened to his prayers and watched over his footsteps. To him was due the thanks for victory.

He took the consecrated tobacco from his pouch very reverently. He crumbled it in his hand and tamped it into his red stone pipe with proper ceremony. Chanting the ancient fire ritual, he lit the fragrant weed with new fire struck from his fire stone. A slender column of mist-like incense ascended straight toward heaven on still air, bearing with it Maushope's message of thanksgiving to the Great Spirit.

The gentle southwest wind, the Sowwanishen[4] of the Indians, caught it as it rose and wafted it across the water of the Sound. The south shore of the Cape from Cuttyhunk to Monomoyick was soon blanketed under its mantle. It silently stole up the valley of Cotuit and filtered through the tall pines until the Lake of Wakeby was covered with another lake of mist. Creeping onward across the Cape, it broke over Shoot Flying Hill and slid down the northern slopes to the waters of Cummaquid.

In the Indian village of Mattakeese the women were still bewailing the loss of the little Nishkenon. The warriors stood about in silent groups stoically speculating on the outcome of Old Maushope's pursuit of the terrible Wompsikuck. The twilight shadows drew out from the forest and lengthened across the clearing. Almost imperceptibly at first, a smoky haze began to drift in between the lodges. It filled the air about them with vapory softness, enveloped the clearing, the wigwams, and the Indians themselves, in its silent, intangible shroud.

There was no mistaking this sign. It could mean but one thing. It was the smoke from Maushope's sacred tobacco. Never was known such rejoicing among the Cape Indians as when Maushope and his little girl passed through the villages on their homeward way. The magic of his moccasins had been lost when he waded into the waters of the Sound, so they were long on the shadowy trail and shining canoe streams before they saw their own tasseled cornfields again. When at last they strode into the Mattakeese clearing with the claws of the great White Eagle rattling at Maushope's belt, the whole tribe made high holiday to bid them welcome.

It was then that she was christened Nishkenon, meaning in the musical tongue of the Cape Cod Indians, The Little Rain, or as we say it, The Afternoon Fog.

Nishkenon's tale was done. She drew the youngsters about her and showed them the scars where the cruel claws of Wompsikuck had sunk into her tender flesh as he bore her away. She traced with her finger the dark, red mark on her skin that would not wash away, where his blood had trickled down over her as she lay under him as he fell before her father's tomahawk. She laughed as she told them of the long fasts and solemn rituals her father had to perform before he could get back the scattered magic of his moccasins.

Long after the coming of the white men when the old Indian women saw the mists come drifting in around their lodges, they would gather the children to them and laughingly say, "Look! Look! Nishkenon! Nishkenon! Here comes Old Maushope's Smoke!"[5]

Notes

1. Nickerson spelled the name of the Great White Eagle "Wampsikuck" in one version and "Wompsikuck" in the other. I have followed "Wompsikuck" since Roger Williams, *A Key into the Language of America*, ed. John J. Teunissen and Evelyn J. Hinz (Detroit: Wayne State University Press, 1973) shows an eagle to be "Wompissacuk" (163).
2. For interest in tribal origin of the place names, the location by county and the translation, see John C. Huden, *Indian Place Names of New England* (New York: Museum of the American Indian, Heye Foundation, 1962). Occasionally, Nickerson's spelling varies from the current spelling of a place. When I have reason to believe that his spelling of the word had some common usage, I have left it as in the example of "Poponesset" which is currently spelled "Popponessett."

3. "Summer" according to Williams is "Neepun" (144).
4. I have changed the spelling to conform to Williams (160-61). Williams explains that this wind brings the warmest climate and that they believe their gods chiefly dwell in the Southwest and that the souls of all their great men and women go there.
5. See William S. Simmons, *Spirit of the New England Tribes: Indian History and Folklore, 1620-1984* (Hanover: University Press of New England, 1986), 204-6 for the account that is most similar to Nickerson's. Simmons notes that Timothy Alden ("Memorabilia of Yarmouth, 1797," *Collections of the Massachusetts Historical Society* [Boston: Samuel Hall, 1798], 5: 54-60) first mentioned the legend of a giant cannibal bird, a version of which was recorded anonymously in 1915 in *Cape Cod Magazine* 1, no. 1 (1915): 15-16, entitled, "How the Fogs Came to the Cape." The anonymous account is significantly different from Nickerson's. There are no magic moccasins; the child is a male of sixteen years who dies before the Great Devil Bird is killed. The conclusion with "Here comes Old Manshope's Smoke!" is the same, except for the spelling of the giant's name.

V

Native American History and Genealogy

The Praying Indians of Lower Cape Cod

The Old Sagamore: Mattaquason of Monomoyick

Micah Rafe, Indian Man: Last Full Blood on Lower Cape Cod

U nquestionably, Nickerson's greatest contribution to Native American scholarship is in this section on Native American history and genealogy, especially his articles, "The Old Sagamore—Mattaquason of Monomoyick" and "Micah Rafe—Indian Man: Last Full Blood on Lower Cape Cod," which are only a sampling of similar research that is housed in the Cape Cod National Seashore, South Wellfleet, Massachusetts. See pages 23-24 for his Thanksgiving Day 1954 letter to his nephew describing his papers on the Lower Cape Cod Indians. I know of no other work that parallels his Native American genealogy on Lower Cape Cod.

The Praying Indians of Lower Cape Cod

Nickerson left about seventy notes for "The Praying Indians of Lower Cape Cod." I have silently and freely edited this article, adding additional notes. Almost all of Nickerson's quotations in this article are paraphrases (occasionally with factual errors), making a silent editorial practice necessary to avoid numerous, awkward editorial notes. Since the quality varies significantly from the articles published in the Bulletin of the Massachusetts *Archeological Society, I assume it is a rough draft. A very brief account, drawn from this article and carrying the title "The 'Praying Indians,'" appeared on 11 December 1958 in the* Cape Codder.

The term "Lower Cape Cod" refers to that neck of the woods stretching roughly from Bass River to the tip of the Cape. Bass River has from time immemorial always been recognized by the natives, whether of European or American descent, as the natural dividing line between the Upper and Lower Cape.

Very little directly pertaining to the religious beliefs of the Cape Cod Indians has been left on record, but it goes without saying that their gods differed little from those of their brethren of southeastern Massachusetts. Their two principal deities were Kiehtan, their good god, and Hobamoke, the evil one, who seems to have been a sort of twin brother to the Christian devil, himself. Kiehtan, spelled Kichtan, Kehtean, Ketan, Kuttan, and various other ways in the early writings, who most nearly resembled the beneficent God of the Englishmen, took good care of them in a rather limited manner as far as his powers and prerogatives permitted. But with old Hobbamock (spelled many ways such as Hobbamok, Hobbamoqui, Hobomoke, Hobbamocko), it was different.

He had to be watched out for in every way, given suitable gifts, and appeased at every turn, or his evil nose would get out of joint, and the poor Indian would suffer. Practically every one of the numerous taboos observed by the Native Americans was to guard against incurring the ill will of old Hobbamock. Hence, the prince of evil became their most feared and most potent deity, whose ministers on earth were everywhere and who was even more powerful than their good god Kiehtan.[1]

The Indians' ideas of their gods have been recorded by several writers. Edward Winslow, who came over on the *Mayflower*, visited among them soon after the Landing, and was a keen observer, has this to say, "For as they conceive of many Divine Powers: so of one, whom they call Kiehtan, to be the principal and maker of all the rest; and to be made by none. 'He,' say they, 'created the heavens, earth, sea, and all creatures contained therein.' Also that he made one man and one woman; of whom they, and we, and all mankind came: but how they became so far dispersed, that know they not."[2]

There was no Sachem before him who dwelt above in the heavens where all good men go when they die to see their friends and have their full of good things. His habitation lies far to the westward, wither the bad men go as well as the good. But when the bad men knock at his door, Kiehtan "bids them, *Quatchet*, that is to say, 'Walk abroad! for there is no place for such.' So they wander in restless want and penury."[3]

None of the Indians had ever seen Kiehtan, but the old men tell them of him. They believe his power to be good, and they endeavor to propitiate him so that he will give them plentiful harvests and victory over their enemies. In order to do this, they sing, dance, feast, give thanks, hang garlands, and other things in his memory.[4]

Winslow says, also, that the word Kiehtan had reference, he thinks, to antiquity for Chise is an old man and Kiehchise, a man that exceedeth in age,[5] in other words, The Old Man. He spent one very enjoyable night in the wigwam of Sachem Corbitant during which they discussed this and many other related subjects. Corbitant, who never trusted the white man nor joined their congregations, said that the same Power that we call GOD, they called Kietitan.[6]

Wood, in his *New England's Prospect*, also says that Ketan is their good god to whom they sacrifice after their garners are full with a good crop.[7] And Roger Williams tells us that after death the souls of all men and women went to the house of Kautantowwit, the Great Southwest God where the great and good had hopes as the Turks have of carnal joys. But the murderers, thieves, and liars wander restless abroad.[8]

No doubt the above descriptions come as near as possible to expressing the Cape Cod Indians' ideas of his good god Kiehtan in the days before the advent of the white man. Perhaps, it is a little colored by the attempts of the early writers to see in the Indian Kiehtan a deity similar to their own. Although the Indians acknowledged him as the oldest of their gods and the creator of all things, they were still a little skeptical as to his supreme power when matched against the wiles and witchcraft of old Hobbamock.

Of old Hobbamock, Winslow says that another Power they worship, called Hobbamock and to the northward, Hobbamoqui, who seems to be the Devil. They call on him to cure their wounds and diseases, believing he sent such ills because he was angry with them and would help them if they properly call on him. On the other hand, if Kiehtan sent them a mortal wound or incurable disease because he was displeased, believing it useless to try to appease his anger, they somewhat doubt if he is simply good.[9]

Hobbamock's representatives among the Indians were known to the Lower Cape tribes as Paw Waws. This word is found in the early records in a number of different spellings, such as Pow Wow, Powah, Powach, Pau Wau, etc., but according to the Apostle Eliot and the celebrated Indian fighter, Captain Benjamin Church, it meant a witch, wizard, or magician, no matter in what shape it appeared.

In curing the sick, the Paw Waw called directly on the Devil, himself, and if it were a wound, an invisible spirit, perhaps an eagle or a snake sitting on his shoulder, licked the wound and sucked out the evil. In extremely difficult cases, the Paw Waw would promise the Devil many skins, kettles, hatchets, beads, knives, and other valuables if he would come and help him out. The Paw Waw was also sometimes called in at childbirth, but usually the Indian women had little trouble, sometimes going out in their canoes in cold weather with their infants three days old.[10]

Daniel Gookin, who left much information concerning the New England Indians, says, "There are among them certain men and women, whom they call powows. These are partly wizards and witches, holding familiarity with Satan, that evil one; and partly are physicians, and make use, at least in show, of herbs and roots, for curing the sick and diseased."[11]

Passaconaway, the great Medicine Man of the Merrimac Country, was said to be able to make water burn, the rocks move, the trees dance, and even to be able to change himself into a flaming man. In the dead of winter, he could burn a tree to ashes and then by putting the ashes into the water make a green leaf grow out of it.[12] No wonder the Cape Cod Indians hinted that their evil god Hobbamock lived somewhere to the northward of Plymouth.

Thanks to Champlain, who visited the Monomoyicks at Stage Harbor in Chatham in 1606, we have an eye-witness description of the Paw Waws of the Lower Cape at that period. Speaking of the Indians there, he says, "There are, however, among them some persons who, as they say, are in concert with the Devil, in whom they have great faith. They tell them all that is to happen to them, but in so doing lie for the most part. Sometimes they succeed in hitting the mark very well, and tell them things similar to those which actually happen to them. For this reason, they have faith in them, as if they were prophets; while they are only impostors. . . . "[13] Up at the northwest corner of Little Bay in South Orleans is a little tidal cove, which to this day goes by the name of Paw Waw's Pond, a memorial to the Paw Waws of the Lower Cape.

For some twenty years or more after the Landing, little attempt was made by the colonists to impose their own form of religion on the natives. This was undoubtedly due in great part to their own bitter struggle for bare survival and their very superficial contacts with the Indians. As soon as they began to push out into the wilderness from behind their stockades at Plymouth and Boston, however, missionaries to the Indians began to appear among them, who, on their own initiative or under the sponsorship of the Society for the Propagation of the Gospel among the Indians, began the attempt to Christianize them.

This Society was incorporated in England in 1649, thanks largely to the efforts of Edward Winslow, who while in London on important business for the Plymouth and Massachusetts Bay Colonies published his "The Glorious Progress of the Gospel among the Indians." This publication contained excerpts from the letters of the Reverend John Eliot telling of his success among the Naticks and from Governor Thomas Mayhew of Martha's Vineyard, a devoted worker on the Islands.[14] The Society collected funds from every parish in England and even some from the struggling colonies. These monies were spent through Indian Commissioners in the new settlements with the avowed purpose "to incite the natives of the country to the knowledge and obedience of the only true God and Saviour of mankind, and the Christian faith."[15] It is from the reports made from time to time to the Society that we are indebted for most of what we know today concerning the Praying Indians of Lower Cape Cod.

Among the religious leaders who devoted their lives to the betterment of the natives in southeastern Massachusetts, the best known is John Eliot of Roxbury, who was called the Apostle to the Indians and whose influence was felt even among the Cape Cod Indians. But on the Cape itself, none was more dearly beloved or held in higher esteem than Richard Bourne of Sandwich, Old Mr. Bourne, as the Indians affectionately called him. His colleagues, Captain Thomas Tupper and Anthony Besse, worked with great success among the Herring River Indians around the Head of Buzzard's Bay and Manomet; while on the Islands, the Mayhews of the Vineyard covered both that Island and Nantucket.

The Reverend John Cotton, the pastor at Plymouth, preached to both the Cape and Island Indians in their own tongue and assisted greatly in bringing them into the fold. And last, but by no means least, was the Reverend Samuel Treat of Eastham, to whom the organization of the congregations of the Praying Indians on the Lower Cape is directly attributable.

There does not appear to have been much systematic effort made toward Christianizing the Lower Cape Indians until the pastorate of the Eastham Church was taken over by Treat in 1672. Up to that time, except for an occasional visit to their villages by such recognized religious leaders as the Apostle Eliot, the Reverend John Cotton, or the Reverend Bourne, the Indians below Bass River were left pretty much under the influence of their ancient Paw Waws. No doubt, this was due, as had been the case with Plymouth and Boston at an earlier date, to the fact that up to the time of Treat's arrival Eastham was still a struggling frontier town plumped down in the wilderness.

It is said that when Eliot first came down to the Cape to preach to the Indians that he had considerable difficulty because of the difference between their dialect and that of the Naticks near Boston with which he was familiar. He was bothered also by the opposition of some of the Indian leaders, a certain Sachem Jehu promising to bring his men into a meeting and then coming by himself and so late that it upset the service. One very aged Indian told Eliot that this same doctrine had been taught long ago by the crew of a French ship wrecked on Cape Cod before the white settlers ever came.[16] Another wanted to know why, if it were so important that the Indians be converted to the white man's religion, they had been allowed to go their own way untroubled for all these years.

The resident minister at Yarmouth is said to have attempted to continue the work started by Eliot. Meanwhile, Captain Tupper and Besse were working untiringly among the Herring River Indians, confining their effort mainly to the Manomet Country with headquarters at the ancient Commassakumkanit of the Indians at what is now Bournedale. Besse continued his work for many years, and the Tuppers, father, son, grandson, and great-grandson, devoted their lives to the welfare of the Indians for more than 150 years.

By 1658, Bourne[17] was deeply engaged among the great body of Indians on the Cape proper who had as yet seen the Light but faintly. No Indian preacher, not even the Apostle Eliot himself, was held in higher

ORDINATION of RICHARD BOURNE BY JOHN ELIOT AND JOHN COTTON, MASHPEE, 1670.

The New England Historical and Genealogical Register, 62 (1908): facing 139.

esteem among the Indians, and no man, white or red, ever questioned his integrity. Frequent references are made in the ancient records to the important part he played in seeing that the Indians got their just and legal rights in the disposition of their lands to the whites and in the making of their wills.[18] While his name is usually associated with the Mashpee Church and Reservation which he founded and which still survives, it was his untiring zeal and devotion to the cause of the Indians which laid the groundwork for the organizations which the Reverend Samuel Treat was to build up on the Lower Cape.

In the year 1670, the Reverend John Cotton of the First Church at Plymouth made the following entry on the Church records: "In this yeare, 70: Mr Richard Bourne of Sandwich sent to the chh for messengers to take notice of the fittnesse of sundry Indians to gather into a chh, at Mashpau, the Pastor, Elder & Secretary Morton were sent thither, Elders & messengers of many other ches were there also, the Indians after confessions &c were gathered into a chh, Mr Bourne chosen &

Mashpee's Old Indian Meetinghouse before restoration. Courtesy of the Mashpee Archives.

ordained their Pastor, all the ches present approoving thereoff. old Mr Eliot & our Pastor laid on hands."[19]

This was, as far as is known, the first formal organization of an Indian Church on Cape Cod—two years before Treat took up his ministry at Eastham and five years before the outbreak of King Philip's War. The Mashpee Church was the parent of the Praying Indians on Cape Cod, and Old Mr. Bourne may well be said to have been their godfather. He died in 1685, but the Mashpee Indian Meeting House still stands as a monument to his life-long devotion.

When the Reverend Treat[20] came to the Lower Cape in 1672 to take up his pastorate in Eastham, the tension in the relations between the Colonists and the Indians of southeastern Massachusetts was at the breaking point. The settlements were expanding by leaps and bounds, and the hunting grounds of the Indians were as rapidly diminishing. The old generation of Plymouth men had given way to a younger and more progressive type whose great ambition was to acquire more land. Sachem Massasoit, the Pilgrim's friend, had gone to his Happy Hunting Ground, and his son and successor, King Philip, would have none of the white man's ways.

The Praying Indians, under the careful guidance of their spiritual leaders, were attempting to adapt themselves to the ways of the newcomers but with indifferent success. The illegal sale of rum went merrily on, and the physical and moral stamina of the natives became so low that the birth rate fell away to almost nothing. Notwithstanding all this, there is plenty of evidence that the Indians on the Cape were treated far better than in any other section of New England, with the exception of Roger Williams' Providence Plantation, and when King Philip's War came, it paid off in big dividends.

Philip canvassed the Cape and the Islands persistently, using every wile of his strong personality to break down the loyalty of the Indians to their white brethren. He openly boasted that while the Praying Indians had adopted the laws and religion of the hated white men and might, therefore, be subject to the Colony courts, neither he nor his men had ever been Praying Indians and hence were subject to no one but their own Head Men and Sachems. Fortunately, for the colonists, he met with no success whatever among the tribes on the Lower Cape.

It was into this critical period that Samuel Treat was thrust when he accepted the pastorate of the frontier town of Eastham. He was the son of Governor Robert Treat of Connecticut and was born in Wethersfield on September 3, 1648. He was graduated from Harvard in 1669 and in 1672 was ordained as a Minister of the Gospel. He began his ministry at Eastham that same year and remained there until his death in 1717. On March 16, 1674, when he was twenty-six years old, he married Elizabeth Mayo, daughter of Captain Samuel and Tamson (Lumpkin) Mayo.[21]

The Reverend Samuel Treat consecrated his life to the Indians of the Lower Cape. He learned to speak their tongue, translated the Confession of Faith into the Nawset language, taught them to read and write in both Indian and English, and under his tutelage they became school teachers, justices of the peace, ministers of the Gospel, and respected citizens among the settlers. They learned to apply the code of the white men's law to their own civil affairs and administered it with wisdom and simple justice.

At the beginning of his labors among the Indians, Treat was aided greatly by the Reverend John Cotton of the First Church of Plymouth, one of the ministers who had "laid on hands" at the ordination of Richard Bourne as the pastor of the Mashpee Church in 1670. He had been very active in the Indian field for a number of years, preaching to Mayhew's Indians at Chappaquidick on Martha's Vineyard as early as 1666 and two years later holding a service at the lodge of Sachem Josiah Wampatuck near Titicut.

In the year 1672, the same year in which Treat took up his pastoral duties at Eastham, Cotton recorded in his diary, under date of July 25, that on that day he held a religious service with the Indians at Nawset, preaching to them in their own tongue. No doubt he initiated the new minister into some of the intricacies of the Nawset language while introducing him to the members of his new Indian congregation.

He was again at Nawset on June 18 in the summer of 1678, when eighty Indians attended his meeting. Undoubtedly, this was held in the wigwam of the Sachem at Potanumicut, near the head of Potanumicut Salt Water Pond in South Orleans, now known as Arey's Pond, which had become the headquarters of the tribe and where their first Meeting House was erected a few years later. In August he held another Indian meeting at Nobscusset, which was probably attended by the Praying Indians from Mattakeese and Satucket as well.[22]

In a report to the Society for the Propagation of the Gospel among the Indians, Bourne stated that on September 1, 1674, there were four hundred and ninety-seven Praying Indians in the Plymouth Colony, composed of three hundred and nine adults and one hundred and eighty-eight young men and maidens. One hundred and forty-two of these could read the Indian language; seventy-two could write it, and nine could read English.

He gave the number attending services on the Lower Cape as follows: At Nawset and Potanumicut, which apparently took in all of what is now Eastham and Orleans, there were forty-four; at Meeshawn and Punonakanit [also spelled Ponanakanet], meaning Truro and Wellfleet, there were seventy-two; Monomoyick, which covered all of Chatham, East Harwich, South Harwich, and Harwich Port, totalled seventy-one; and at "Sawkatucket" [also Sauquatucket], now Brewster, "Nobsquassit" [also Nobscusset], now East Dennis, "Mattakeese," now Yarmouth, and "Weequakut," Barnstable, there were one hundred and twenty-two. This made a grand total for the whole Lower Cape, including Yarmouth and part of Barnstable, of three hundred and nine Praying Indians in 1674,[23] the year before the outbreak of King Philip's War. Every religious leader was doing his utmost to hold the Indians in line against the day when it was certain the blow would fall. But no one, not even the Indian missionaries themselves, knew whether their influence would be strong enough to hold back the Praying Indians from joining King Philip.

In the spring of 1675, Cotton made a last swing around the Cape, preaching to Treat's Indians at Nawset on the 18th of March and on the next day to a gathering at Nobscusset.[24] In the July following, the tomahawk struck, but the Praying Indians of Cape Cod proved loyal to their religious leaders. All through the bitter days which followed, the restraining influence of these men of God held them back. In the spring of 1676, when the fortunes of war were going against the whites, if the thousand warriors on the Cape and the Islands had thrown in their lot with Philip, the pioneer settlements along the Cape would have become scenes of massacre and devastation. There were six hundred warriors in Bourne's territory alone,[25] and it was owing to the honesty and Christian philanthropy of him and his colleagues that Amos Otis was able to say that Richard Bourne did more to defend the Colonies at this critical time by his moral power over the Indians than did General Bradford at the head of his armies.

Eliot's Praying Indians were removed from Natick and the surrounding towns and placed on Deer Island in Boston Harbor for their own protection. Those around Plymouth and the outlying districts segregated on Clark's Island. But on the Lower Cape, the Indians remained in their own villages, and there is not on record one single case of treachery or violence. As a matter of fact, many of the Cape Indians enlisted in the Old Colony forces and gave invaluable aid as scouts and rangers. The Reverend John Cotton records that on the 18th of July, 1675, he met with a company of Cape Cod Indians in Plymouth who came to do service in the war against Philip and that on the 31st, nearly 40 Cape Indians went forth against Philip.[26]

When King Philip's War was finally over, Treat continued his activity in his field and by 1682 is said to have had five-hundred Praying Indians under his parochial charge. This was probably the high tide of their religious activity. The fate of Philip's followers had brought home to them beyond the question of a doubt that only two courses now lay open to them, conversion to Christianity or extermination.

At this period the Indian villages of the Lower Cape were still populous and prosperous. They were well governed by their Sachems and Head Men and by an exceptional group of white missionaries who guided them in both their moral and civil affairs. Their religious congregations were centered in their six principal villages. There was one at Eastham, the original Nawset, Treat's home town, which was really the parochial center for all Praying Indians of the Lower Cape and outlived all others. Farther down the Cape at Wellfleet was the Punonakanit congregation and another at Meeshawn in Truro, the ancient Pamet of the Indians. Over in Chatham stood the Monomoyick Indian Meeting House at the Head of Long Cove, and a fifth was at Sauquatucket around the headwaters of Stony Brook in High Brewster. There was a sixth which originally gathered at Nobscusset in Dennis but soon amalgamated with the Sauquatucket congregation in Brewster.

There was also a religious Indian center at Mattakeese in Yarmouth, which cannot, strictly speaking, be considered a part of the Lower Cape group, but which, in its last days after the remnant of the tribe had been moved over to the Indian Town Reservation on the west shore of Bass River in South Yarmouth and had its own Meeting House there, became a sort of half-way house in the westward migration during the final breakdown of the Lower Cape tribes.

Treat trained four of his leading Indians to be religious leaders in their own villages and to read his sermons in their own language, while he, himself, preached to them all collectively once every four weeks. Besides this, he also appointed Indian school teachers to teach their red brethren the three R's and instructed several of their Head Men until they were able to take up the legal duties of Justices of the Peace. These Indians were all men of a high order of intelligence as indicated by their petitions and agreements in the old archives, which in most cases were exceptionally well executed and usually signed in their own handwriting.

On the fly leaf of Justice Sewall's Account Book is an undated notation, apparently made about 1682, in which he names Lawrence Jeffery [also spelled Jeffryes] and Daniel Quequanset [also spelled Quequaquonset] as the Indian Justices at Potanumicut [also spelled Potanummacut and Portanimicut], in Treat's bailiwick.[27] Quequequanset was one of the Head Men of the Potanumicuts and a member of the family who lived near Quanset Pond in South Orleans and gave the Pond its name.[28] Lawrence Jeffery, more commonly known as Old Lawrence, was a prominent Nawset Sachem and the last of the so-called Ancient Indians. He lived until June 14, 1729, and was nearly a hundred years old at his death.[29] At the same time, Hercules and Richard Hantum were the Indian Justices at Satucket in Brewster.[30]

In 1685 we get another report on the Praying Indians on the Lower Cape by Governor Thomas Hinckley. He said that the Indians, commonly called the Praying Indians, who frequent these public meetings to worship God together at Pamet, Billingsgate, and Nawset numbered two hundred and sixty-four, and he named Great Tom as the religious leader at Nawset.[31] Great Tom, otherwise known as Minister Tom, Mister Tom, and Tom Coshanag, by which name Treat referred to him in 1683, continued to be the Indian Minister there until his death in 1719. He was a grandson of Sagamore Mattaquason of Monomoyick, as was his brother John Cussen, the Monomoyick Indian Minister. Their mother was the Old Sagamore's daughter known to the whites as Cussen's Squaw, and no doubt Coshanag, by which name Great Tom was sometimes known, was the Indian form of the word which the English commonly spelled Cussen. He founded the prominent Tom family of Potanumicut, of which his son John Tom, who also became a minister of the Gospel, was the best known.

Governor Hinckley also reported that Pamet was destitute of a minister since the death of Potonomotuck, "a prudent, sober man, which is much lamented," and that the Indians there were very desirous of having a new preacher. Potonomotuck was also known as Mr. John and was the progenitor of the family which later appears on the records by the name of Tonomotuck. He controlled most of the lands from Pamet to Provincetown and may have been the same "Indian of Pamet" to whom the Pilgrims returned "double the value" for the seed corn they took from Cornhill soon after the Landing.

Hinckley goes on to say that Indian Nicholas was the minister at Monomoyick, where there were one hundred and fifteen Praying Indians. Nicholas was sometimes known as Nick the Indian and was probably of the family of Sachem Nickanoose of Nantucket, whose son Captain Jeethrow lived at Monomoyick and probably married into the Monomoyick Tribe. The Nantucket Indians had from earliest time been under the religious leadership of the Mayhews of Martha's Vineyard.

The Nobscusset and Sauquatucket congregation had now amalgamated into one, with headquarters at Satucket in Brewster, and could muster 171 members. Manasses, the Satucket Indian minister, was a noted warrior and something of a wolf hunter as well. Mark Snow, the Town Clerk of Eastham, records that on April 22, 1690, "menases Indian brought to me four young wolves which he sayeth he lately caught about the Cleft Pond."[32] Manasses was also a member of Gorham's Rangers in the expedition against the French and Indians of Canada in 1697, as was certified by their commander, Captain Jonathan Gorham.[33]

The Hinckley report also mentioned that at Mattakeese Jeremy Robin was the Indian minister with seventy Indians in his flock. He was the husband of Aquanetva, the daughter of Sachem Nepoyetan, and their son Little Robin became one of the Head Men at Satucket. Aquanetva's sister Manatotomuske married Indian Ralph and their great-grandson Micah Ralph, better known as Micah Rafe, was the last full-blooded Indian on the Lower Cape.

The Praying Indian towns on the Lower Cape, including Mattakeese at Yarmouth, now mustered 560 Christians, and Hinckley added that besides that there were three times as many boys and girls under twelve years of age who attended the meetings. In the whole Colony at this time, there were 1439. But he commented mournfully that a great obstruction in bringing them to civility is their appetite for rum and the English furnishing it to them.

Many of the Indians of the Lower Cape were finding it difficult to support themselves, and procreation slowed significantly. Rum was a great disrupter, and there were bootleggers then as now, although the Colony passed stringent laws prohibiting sale of liquor to the Indians. It was not until the death of Treat some thirty years later that the full effects of it became apparent.

The same year that Hinckley turned in the above report saw the death of the well-beloved Old Mr. Bourne on the 17th of August 1685. His death left the Reverend Treat of Eastham the ranking white minister to the Indians and the only one still active in the religious field on the Lower Cape.

In the year 1691, the first grant was made to them for the erection of an English-built Meeting House. So far as I know, all the religious meetings held among them up to this date had been in the lodge of their Head Men or Sachems. Neither then nor at any later date as long as there was the least semblance of any tribal organization could these Indians be induced to join with the white men in the Meeting Houses of the settlers.

On the 20th of May 1691, the Town of Eastham voted as follows: "The towne have granted liberty to larrance Indian in the behalfe of himselfe and the other of the Indians at pottanumaquitt to sett up a meeting house on the Townes ground near the head of potanumaquit salt water pond for the Indians to meet on the Lords Day and other publick meeting dayes so long as they shall uphold and improve it for that goodly and commendable use of aforesaid and if they doe neglect or desist from the improving of it for that and use of aforesaid they shal no longer have the liberty of aforesaid, but it shal return and remaine the townes as before."[34]

Eight days later the Selectmen of the Town laid out the lot for the new Meeting House "on the western side of the Cartway that goes to potanomaquit near the head of the salt water pond." It measured six rods on the roadway and was five rods in depth.[35] On it the Meeting House was built that same summer and became known as the First Potanumicut Indian Meeting House to distinguish it from its successor which was built some time later on another lot. It stood on the north side of what is now known as Arey's Pond in South Orleans, the Potanumicut Saltwater Pond of our forefathers, across the road and about southeast from the residence of the late Frank Gould. At that period, the road or cartway between Eastham and Chatham lay much farther east than at present, so that the Meeting House was west instead of east of it. Many Indian skeletons have been exhumed in this area, the Indians following the custom of the whites and using their churchyards as burial grounds.

The Meeting House was doubtless patterned after the one erected in 1688 on Burial Hill in Bournedale by Justice Sewall for the Herring River Indians and which he describes as "a convenient comfortable meeting house for the natives at Sandwich, 24 ft. long—18 broad with two galleries—L30."[36] It was clap-boarded on the outside, ceiled on the inside and well filled with shavings between clap-boards and ceiling to keep out the cold. It must have been quite an imposing structure in the eyes of the Indians.

It is probable that the Monomoyick Meeting House was built soon after. William C. Smith, the Chatham historian, says it was built about 1691 and stood until about 1730.[37] It stood on the south side of Queen Anne's Road about southeast from the present East Harwich United Methodist Church, near the head of Muddy Cove of which Smith speaks, or as it was later known, Long Cove. This was the Monomoyick River of the Indians and their headquarters in ancient days.

There is no known record of a first Satucket Indian Meeting House, although Josiah Paine always referred to the one which stood at Pleasant Lake as the "last one." If there were one in the days of Manasses, the wolf hunter, it is logical to suppose it would have stood near his lodge which was in the village of the Sauquatuckets around the headwaters of Stony Brook in Brewster, the Sauquatucket River of the Indians.

As far as we know, neither the Meeshawn nor the Punonakanit congregations ever attempted to erect English-built Meeting Houses in their respective localities at Truro and Wellfleet. In their last days they joined their Nawset brethren in the First Potanumicut Indian Meeting House at South Orleans.

Two years after the erection of the Potanumicut Meeting House, that is, August 23, 1693, Treat described the work he was doing among the Indians in a letter to Increase Mather of Boston. " . . . I have, from time to time, imparted the gospel of our Lord Jesus Christ in their own language, and I truly hope not without success; and yet I continue in the same service, earnestly imploring, . . . a more plentiful down pouring of the spirit from on high among them. . . . They have four distinct assemblies, in four villages, belonging to our township; in which four assemblies they have four teachers, of their own choice. . . . These Indian teachers repair to my house once a week, to be further instructed, *pro modulo meo*, in the concernments proper for their service and station. . . . There are in the four abovesaid villages four schoolmasters, . . . who teach their youth to read and write their own language."[38] Treat adds that they have six magistrates.

The four villages which he mentions were Potanumicut at South Orleans where Tom Coshanag was the minister; Meeshawn and

Punonakanit, that is Truro and Wellfleet as of today, both now apparently under one head at Pamet with Samuel Munsha as minister; Monomoyick at Chatham where John Cussen was the minister; and Satucket at Brewster where Manasses still preached the word of God. Treat had translated the "Confession of Faith" into the Nawset tongue and had it printed. He "visited them often in their wigwams, associated with them in all kindness and affability, and joined in their festivals. In return, the natives regarded him as their friend, venerated him as their religious teacher; and loved him as their father."[39]

It will be seen that since the report of Governor Hinckley in 1685, a new Indian minister, Samuel Munsha by name, had been installed in the Pamet Indian parish, which now took in both Meeshawn and Punonakanit, succeeding old Potanumatock, who died just previous to the Governor's report. Munsha was of the Menekish or Munchase family of whom William Menekish, who lived near Boat Meadow Creek and was probably the father of Samuel Munsha, was perhaps the best known.[40] It is also noted that John Cussen, the grandson of Sagamore Mattaquason and brother of Great Tom of Potanumicut, was now the minister of Monomoyick in place of Indian Nick.[41] But Manasses still carried on at Satucket.

At this period, about 1693, Treat had five-hundred and five Praying Indians under his charge in his four Indian villages, the largest single group anywhere in southeastern Massachusetts. Old Mr. Bourne's Indians at Mashpee and the adjoining Upper Cape Towns, now under the supervision of the Reverend Rowland Cotton of Sandwich, had dwindled to two hundred and fourteen. Captain Tupper's Herring River congregation, which took in all the Indians around the head of Buzzard's Bay and Manomet, totalled 180. The Reverend John Cotton of Plymouth, whose Indian parish now embraced all the old Indian lands from Natick to Sakonnet and back to the eastern seaboard, could muster only 500 in all that area.[42]

Five years later, a survey of the Cape Cod Indians was made for the Society for the Propagation of the Gospel among the Indians by the Reverend Grindall Rawson and the Reverend Samuel Danforth of Taunton, two men eminently well fitted for this work, inasmuch as they could talk to the Indians in their own tongue and were experienced investigators. In their report, which was dated the 12th of July 1696, they stated that they found twenty-two families of Praying Indians at Potanumicut, where Tom Coshanag was still the minister as well as the schoolteacher. He had a Native American named Moses assisting him as he was getting well advanced in years. At Satucket, where Manasses was still minister, they reported fourteen families, with Joshua Hantum as chief Head Man. The Nobscusset congregation was now joined with them, Hantum being a descendant of old Sachem Mashantampaine of Nobscusset, retaining the Hantum part of the old Sachem's name. They also stated that Treat reported to them that "at Eastham, Harwich, East Harbor, Billingsgate and Monomoy," there were 500 Indians and that almost every head of a family could read the scriptures.[43]

Shortly after Rawson and Danforth had completed their survey, a group of Potanumicuts living on the southern part of the Reservation made a demand of Old Lawrence to give them a deed to a plot of land on Sampson's Island, in Little Bay, which they and their fathers had purchased years ago from his father, Sachem Sampson, for the use of the ministry. Sampson's Island, early known as Squonicot, had been deeded to the Sachem in 1665 by the Town of Eastham in exchange for his quarter right of drift whales found upon the shores in the lower part of Old Eastham, now Wellfleet.[44]

In a letter dated June 13, 1698, signed by Jacob Jeffery, who later became the Potanumicut Indian minister, Thomas Francis, Jabez Jacob, Isaac George, Judah George, and Moses Jeffery, Power of Attorney was given to Jeremiah Ralph and Quequaquonset, two of the Head Men of the Potanumicuts, to receive legal deeds and exchange said land.[45] Although there is no evidence to show how and when the deed was recovered and the exchange made, future events make it evident that this was in preparation for moving the Indian Meeting House off the Town's land and re-erecting it on a more convenient site on the Indian lands.

Very shortly thereafter, it was moved to the little knoll in South Orleans, where Arthur L. Sparrow[46] subsequently built his residence, which was much nearer the then center of Indian population in Potanumicut. Here it stood, with the Indian graves rapidly gathering around it, until it dropped to decay and the last Indian had gone from the land of his fathers. Its worn doorstone, over which the moccassined feet of so many Praying Indians once trod, long did duty as a doorstep for the South Orleans Post Office.

Ever since the merger of the Plymouth Colony with that of the Massachusetts Bay, the Indians of the Lower Cape had been getting more and more dissatisfied with the manner in which their civil affairs were handled. As early as 1694, a petition was sent to the General Court asking that the "body of laws whereby the sd Indians were governed in the time when Plimouth Colony was a distinct Govt." be revived, and asking that some discreet person be appointed to sit with them in their Courts. It was signed by Old Lawrence of Nawset, Hercules of Satucket, and Sachem John Quason Towsowet of Monomoy and was in "behalf of all the Indians in and about the towns of Yarmouth, Manamoy and

Eastham and the adjacent places thereabout." As a result, the Court appointed Shearjashub Bourne, Captain Thomas Tupper, and Jonathan Sparrow to have the inspection of the Indians in their respective Plantations.[47]

In 1703, the same trouble arose again. Another petition was presented, dated May 20, over the signatures of Old Lawrence, Quequaquonset, Richard Attamon, and John Tom, son of Great Tom the minister, for the Potanumicuts; Joshua Hantum and Lusty Tom, another son of Great Tom, for Satucket; and Joseph Quason, son of Sachem John Quason Towsowet and grandson of Sagamore Mattaquason, for the Monomoyicks.

They asked for a revival of the ancient methods of enforcing civil order established by the English Government at Plymouth under which they had sat formerly. They stated that they had voluntarily submitted to the royal authority of the English Crown, had abandoned all their "old pagan idolatries, superstitions and methods of government" which they entertained before the coming of the whites, and had lived in amity and friendship with the settlers.

Now, however, with no one to oversee their courts and instruct them in judicial procedure, they feared that immorality, irreligion, ancient idolatry, and customs would return upon them like a flood.[48] Their case was presented to the Legislature by their trusted friend, Colonel John Thacher, who explained that formerly the Indians had chosen their own magistrates, constables, and grand jurymen and had regulated their own civil affairs under a small body of laws drawn up by Hinckley "agreeably to our Plymouth laws." These they put into their own language and enforced in their own Courts which were held at Potanumicut for the Lower Cape.

He stated that as long as they were supervised by the Commissioners appointed by the Governor all went well, but of late years, under the new Governor of the Province of the Massachusetts Bay, no new Commissioners had been appointed, and no expenses allowed for the time and travel of the old ones. The Indians had become dissatisfied with their own Justices and their rulings, and their Government was dwindled to nothing, and vice was increasing among them.[49]

Treat was now getting to be an old man. Old Mr. Bourne had long since gone to his reward. The *Mayflower* Pilgrims who settled the Lower Cape who had treated the Indians with decency and justice had given way to another generation who, in general, despised the now broken and beggarly Indians and thought only of getting hold of their lands as speedily as possible. The simple laws of the Old Colony had been superseded by the more complex and onerous system of the Massachusetts Bay

Province, and the Head Men among the Indians saw only too plainly the down hill road into which their nation was slipping.

Two sweeping sales of Indian lands to the whites in 1711 left only small detached reservations and individually held parcels in the hands of the Native Americans. A small group of Monomoyicks still clung to their ancient tribal lands on the north bank of the old Monomoyick River; a few straggling Satuckets were clustered about the headwater ponds of old Sauquatucket River and the Head of Long Pond; and on the Potanumicut Reservation there was a rapidly diminishing band recruited from all the Lower Cape tribes but led by a group of able and conscientious Head Men who were endeavoring in every way to hold the remnant of their nation together.

It was a sad day for the Praying Indians of the Lower Cape when their staunch friend and beloved Pastor, the Reverend Samuel Treat of Eastham, passed away. For almost fifty years he had served both his white and his red parishes with honor and distinction. He died in the midst of a terrible blizzard which was known for a century on Cape Cod as the Great Snow. So great was the love the Indians bore him that they requested the privilege of digging through the snow and bearing his body to its last resting place. He was buried in the Old Eastham Burying Ground on the north shore of Town Cove, and the following was inscribed on his headstone:

"Here Lyes Interred ye Body of ye Late Learned & Rev'd Samuel Treat ye Pious and Faithful Pastor of This Church Who After a very Zealous discharge of His Ministry For Ye Space of 45 Years and a Laborious Travel For Ye Souls Of Ye Natives Fell Asleep in Christ March Ye 18 1716-17 In Ye 69 Year of His Age."[50]

Treat was the last white missionary to the Indians of the Lower Cape, and from this time on, their decline was very rapid. Great Tom, the Potanumicut Indian minister and schoolmaster, who had worked hand in hand with Treat since 1685, died about two years later.[51] The good work was continued by Great Tom's friend and neighbor Jabez Jacob, who had been one of the signers of the letter demanding the deed to the ministerial land on Sampson's Island. In a deed given to Samuel Mayo in February 1719, Jacob calls himself, "I Jabez Jacob of Harwich Indian Minister" and names his wife Betty.[52] No doubt he had been serving in this capacity under the tutelage of Great Tom and Treat for some time.

After the death of Jabez Jacob in 1720,[53] the church duties were taken over by John Tom, a son of the late Great Tom, who kept them going until his death. John Tom, without question, was the strongest character among the Potanumicuts in the last days of the Nawset Tribe. He was not only a Minister of the Gospel, a Justice of the Peace, and one of the so-called Privileged Indians but also a horticulturist of no average ability. At his death, his homestead and orchard were valued at L400., and his Bible and books at L6.[54]

He and his wife Martha, who probably belonged to the family of Old Pompmo the Medicine Man, lived near Fort Hill on Little Bay. He is frequently referred to in the early records as "Clark" and as "Minister Tom." He must have been well past middle age when he took up the work as Indian Minister. His death occurred in the spring of 1730, between the 10th of April and the 20th of May.[55]

The Monomoyick Indian Meeting House at the Head of Long Cove was closed about the time of John Tom's death. It appears that the Monomoyicks were never over enthusiastic about the white man's God, and it is likely their Indian Pastor John Cussen was dead before this date. Cussen was over seventy in April 1720, according to his own statement, when he testified in a controversy concerning gifts of land made by his grandfather, Sagamore Mattaquason, in 1670 to his children, one of whom was John's mother, Cussen's Squaw. In this deposition, he told how "Old Mr. Bourne" was present and had written the deed of gift.[56]

The Satucket Indian Meeting House now stood near the Head of Long Pond in Pleasant Lake on John Sequattom's Farm, between Seymour's and Hinckley's Ponds. It was located at the foot of the high hill southwest of Seymour's. John Sequattom died in 1743 and was probably buried on his farm near the old Meeting House;[57] he was the last of the Sauquatucket Indians to be recognized as such. There is no record that the Meeting House was ever used again after his death.

The Truro and Wellfleet congregations were pretty well scattered by now, the few families left in these ancient Indian villages coming to the Potanumicut Indian Meeting House in South Orleans to satisfy their needs for communion with the white man's God. Even the Potanumicut church was hard put to keep its doors open, not because of the lack of faith among its red members but simply because there were not many Indians left on the Lower Cape. Potanumicut at this period was what Mashpee became a little later, a haven for all the remnants of the Lower Cape tribes.

After John Tom's death in 1730, there seems to have been no one among the Potanumicut Indians capable of filling the vacant pulpit. As far as the records show, the next Minister was an Indian named Joseph Briant from Mashpee, perhaps a brother of the noted Mashpee Indian Minister Solomon Briant. Joseph Briant not only took up the religious work at Potanumicut but also looked after the Indian Town Parish at South Yarmouth until his death in 1759.

On the 31st of May 1759, Mr. Joseph Crocker notified the Commissioners for Indian Affairs that "Joseph Bryant (Pastor of the Indian Chh at Portnumicut and Indian Town in Yarmouth) died at Portnumicut on Thursday the 26th of April last. And as the Indians were well united in him, and as he was of a sober good conversation and one that seemed disposed to do all the good he could among them and as (by reason of the smallness of their number) it is feared they never will be resettled again and yet cannot be prevailed with to join with the English Assemblies, it must be accounted a great loss to them. This I thot proper to communicate to your Hnrs." Mr. Crocker also stated that there was due to Joseph Bryant for his salary "from the first of November last to the time of his death" the sum of L3-16-11, which covered about a five month's period.[58] A bronze tablet in the churchyard of the Indian Meeting House in Mashpee states that Joseph Briant was a Minister there, as well as at Potanumicut, where he died.

After his death, it was very difficult to find anyone qualified to go on with the work on the Lower Cape, but finally John Ralph, a member of the noted Ralph family of Potanumicut and a descendant of Ralph and Manatotomuskie of Nobscusset and of Sachem Iyanno as well, was prevailed upon to take up the work.

In June 1762, the Reverend Ezra Stiles of Connecticut visited Potanumicut and reported that the Indian minister there was John Ralph and gave a list of his parishioners. He found eight heads of families with wives and children, eight men with no wives, three widows with children, and ten widows with no children, the eldest of whom was Sarah Cuzzens, aged about 82. Stiles commented that he was told that "forty years ago at a wedding were counted seven score Indians at Potonumecut."[59]

The following year, an epidemic of smallpox struck the Lower Cape, and Bangs wrote that only five Indians were left alive in Eastham.[60] Eastham at that date did not include Potanumicut, but it did take in everything below the present town of Orleans. In 1765, the Reverend James Freeman stated that the Indians in Harwich numbered 95, most of whom were at Potanumicut,[61] which at that time was included in the township of Harwich.

On the 7th of December 1765, the Praying Indians of Indian Town in South Yarmouth presented the following petition to the Commissioners for Indian Affairs: " . . . The pettition of us the Subscribers Indians of Yarmouth Humbly Showeth. That whereas Mr. John Ralph who is ordained over the Indians at potenomecot has Come once a month ever since he has been ordained over the Indians and Preached among us which is considerable charge to him and we are poorly and not able to make him any satisfaction and his salary is small and he cannot continue to come to preach to us once a month as he has done with out he has some allowance for such extraordinary travel and if he dont come and preach to us we can have no preaching—humbly pray that you—consider our case and the said Mr. Ralph by making him some allowance for the time past that he has come and preached among us as also to allow him something more for the future by making some addition to his salary—to enable him to come and preach to us . . . "[62]

This petition was signed by fourteen of the Indian Town Indians, many of whom had been former residents of Potanumicut and the Lower Cape villages. It is doubtful if their petition was ever put into effect, because the following year, smallpox again devastated the Lower Cape. Thomas Freeman,[63] who was their legal Guardian at that time, went to a smallpox grave, himself, and John Ralph was appointed Justice of the Peace for the Indians in his place.[64] Only six wigwams were left in Indian Town, and the following year, 1767, they came over to Potanumicut once a month to worship at John Ralph's Meeting House, which was now the only Indian Meeting House left standing on the whole Cape below Mashpee.[65]

This was the last mention of organized activity among the Praying Indians on the Lower Cape. John Ralph died some time before 1788, because on September 8 of that year, his nearest living heir, his daughter Sarah Cowet of Mashpee, quit claim to her right in her late brother's land at Potanumicut,[66] the description of which shows that it was the minister's old houselot near the site of the Potanumicut Indian Meeting House in South Orleans. Undoubtedly, his remains lie in the Indian burying ground which surrounded it.

John Ralph is reputed to have been a very industrious and well-educated Indian and to have lived in the fashion of his white neighbors. He was somewhat of a farmer as well as a crack whaleman, from which he earned a good livelihood. Although he was a little addicted to liquor, himself, he pleaded with his brethren to curtail the immoderate use of it.

The Potanumicut Indian Meeting House must have closed its doors with the passing of John Ralph, shortly before 1788. No other Indian Meeting House on the Cape, with the exception of that at Mashpee, could boast anything like such a history. Not only had it been the recognized center for the Praying Indians of the Lower Cape but also had had for nearly a century an unbroken succession of Indian ministers, all of whom but one, Joseph Briant, had been natives of the place.

The last Indian had disappeared from the town of Wellfleet by 1770, when agents were appointed to take care of the Indian lands.[67] In Truro, only one family was left in 1792, where an old lady could still remember when there were so many little Indian children in the school that they used to "crow over 'em" (the white children).[68] After another smallpox epidemic in 1779, out of sixteen Indians still living at Indian Town in South Yarmouth, only five were left alive,[69] and by 1797, only one wigwam was left and that occupied by an Indian woman and a Black man.[70]

"In 1792, according to statistics given, `but few Indians remained in Barnstable County, except at Mashpee where were about eighty families, not more than forty or fifty individuals of unmixed blood.'"[71] At Potanumicut, the tribe had dwindled to five souls, and at Satucket, only one or two still clung to the soil, while below these once populous villages, not one Native American was left on the whole Lower Cape. By 1807, the Mashpee Indian Church was the only surviving Indian Church on Cape Cod, and the greater part of its congregation was already interracial.

Except for a few solitary individuals still clinging to their native soil at Potanumicut, Monomoyick, and Satucket, the last remnants of the Lower Cape tribes, degraded by rum and decimated by the inroads of smallpox, had long since filtered westward into the Mashpee Reservation. Here, around the old Mashpee Meeting House where, in better days, Old Mr. Bourne and the Apostle Eliot were wont to gather their Praying Indians by the hundreds, they made their final stand. Such was the havoc which less than 150 years of close contact with English civilization had wrought among the Cape Cod Indians.

Micah Rafe, the last full-blooded Indian on the Lower Cape, died at Askaonkton on the north bank of the old Monomoyick River in East Harwich in 1816. His wife Hosey, the great-granddaughter of Sagamore Mattaquason of Monomoyick, had died several years earlier. They were both members of the East Harwich Methodist Church. Bess Tobey of Eastham, half-Indian who died in 1821, was the last Praying Indian of record on the Lower Cape.[72]

As early as November 15, 1775, Bess Tobey was mentioned in the will of Joshua Hopkins of Eastham as "my Negro Woman Bess." She was then about forty years old and greatly beloved by him and his family. He gave her her freedom and the privilege of living in his "dwelling Dureing Her single Life," besides providing for her maintenance when "she is not able to maintain her self."[73] One of Mr. Hopkins' descendants still cherishes the quaint, old bottle which Bess, the last slave in the Hopkins family, used for their daily tot of rum.

Joshua Hopkins was the grandson of Giles Hopkins who came over on the *Mayflower* and bought the land on which Joshua lived of the Nawset Sachems. Bess Tobey was the last of the blood of the Nawset Sachems through the daughter of Sachem John Sipson, Hosey (Sipson) Tobey. By the peculiar irony of fate, she was granted her freedom from slavery and provided for in her old age by the grandson of the pioneer who bought his land of her grandfather.

That she was well thought of in the community, as well as by the Hopkins family, is attested by her baptism into the white Church by the Reverend Jonathan Bascom on November 3, 1805, when she was about sixty-five years old, and her admittance to full membership the same day.[74] She received her baptism at the Old Pochey Meeting House in East Orleans, which at that time was the South Parish Church of Eastham, and which is still standing. In the Bill of Mortality for the year 1821, this entry is found among the records of deaths: "Bess Tobey 85."[75] Thus came to a close the long story of the Praying Indians of Lower Cape Cod.

A few, musty records filed away and forgotten in the ancient archives, three or four rough fieldstones on the slope of a little knoll marking as many Indian graves around the site of the Last Potanumicut Indian Meeting House, a scarcely decipherable tribute carved on the headstone of their beloved white Pastor, Samuel Treat, and a worn doorstone trodden under the heel of the white man's foot—these are all that remain to remind us of a day when hundreds of devout Praying Indians gathered in their wigwams or in their English-built Indian Meeting Houses to learn the Word of the white man's God.

Notes

1. See "The Indian Pantheon" and "Shamanism" in William S. Simmons, *Spirit of the New England Tribes: Indian History and Folklore, 1620-1894* (Hanover: University Press of New England, 1986), 38-45.
2. Edward Winslow, *Good News from New England, The Story of the Pilgrim Fathers, 1606-1623 A.D.; as told by Themselves, their Friends, and their Enemies*, edited by Edward Arber (Boston: Houghton, Mifflin and Co., 1897), 582.
3. Ibid.
4. Ibid.
5. Ibid.
6. Ibid., 558.
7. William Wood, *New England's Prospect*, edited by Alden T. Vaughan (Amherst: University of Massachusetts Press, 1977), 100.
8. Roger Williams, *A Key into the Language of America*, edited by John J. Teunissen and Evelyn J. Hinz (Detroit: Wayne State University Press, 1973), 190, 194.
9. Winslow, *Good News*, 583.
10. Ibid., 584-85.

11. Daniel Gookin, "Gookin's Historical Collections," *Collections of the Massachusetts Historical Society For the Year 1792* (Boston: Munroe and Francis, 1806), 1: 154.

12. Wood, *New England's Prospect,* 100-1. Also see "Shamanistic Feats" in Simmons, *Spirit of the New England Tribes,* 60-64.

13. W. L. Grant, ed. *Voyages of Samuel de Champlain 1604-1618* (New York: Charles Scribner's Sons, 1907), 96.

14. Winslow Warren, "Edward Winslow," *The Mayflower Descendant* 5 (1903): 231.

15. Frederick Freeman, *The History of Cape Cod: The Annals of Barnstable County and its Several Towns* (Yarmouth Port: Parnassus Imprints, 1869), vol. 1: 201.

16. Charles F. Swift, *History of Old Yarmouth* (Yarmouth Port: the author, 1884), 38-39.

17. For folklore on Richard Bourne, see Simmons, *Spirit of the New England Tribes,* 85-88. Also see Elizabeth Reynard, *The Narrow Land: Folk Chronicles of Old Cape Cod* (Chatham: The Chatham Historical Society, Inc., 1978), 79-85. Both tell how the cranberry came to Cape Cod from heaven in the beak of a dove that fed Bourne while he argued with the devil.

18. State of Massachusetts, Massachusetts Superior Court of Judicature, 13717, "ould Mr. Bourne."

19. George Ernest Bowman, "Plymouth First Church Records," *The Mayflower Descendant* 4 (1902): 215-16.

20. For an account of Reverend Treat, see Reynard, *The Narrow Land,* 85-90.

21. These are W. Sears Nickerson's grandparents eight generations back ("Eastham Vital Records," *The Mayflower Descendant* 8 (1906): 243. Freeman, *The History of Cape Cod,* has Elizabeth the daughter of Rev. John Mayo (1: 350).

22. John Cotton Jr., "Diary of Preaching to the Indians on Martha's Vineyard," unpublished manuscript, Collections of the Massachusetts Historical Society, Boston, Massachusetts.

23. Gookin, "Gookin's Historical Collections," 1: 197-98.

24. Cotton, *Diary of Preaching to the Indians.*

25. Charles F. Swift, *Genealogical Notes of Barnstable Families, Being a Reprint of the Amos Otis Papers* (Barnstable: F. B. and F. P. Goss, 1888); 1: 106-7.

26. Cotton, *Diary of Preaching to the Indians.*

27. "Sewall's Account Book," in *A Genealogist's Letter-Book: Correspondence of Amos Otis Relative to Colonial Ancestry,* book 2, edited by C. W. Swift and A. L. Kelley (Yartmouthport, Massachusetts: "The Register" Press, 1913).

28. Barnstable County, Barnstable Probate Records, 4: 180.

29. State of Massachusetts, Massachusetts Superior Court of Judicature 11575.

30. "Sewall's Account Book."

31. "Thomas Hinckley to William Stoughton and Joseph Dudley," in *Collections of the Massachusetts Historical Society for the Year 1861* (Boston: John Wilson and Son), 5: 132-34.

32. Eastham Town Records 1650-1705, 1.
33. Massachusetts State Archives, 30: 500c.
34. Eastham Town Records, Ear Marks 1642-1770, Meetings 1630-1705.
35. Ibid.
36. Nathan Henry Chamberlain, ed., *Samuel Sewall and the World He Lived In* (Boston: De Wolfe, Fiske and Co., 1898), 131.
37. William C. Smith, *A History of Chatham Massachusetts* (Chatham: The Chatham Historical Society, Inc.), 265-66. Nickerson's father often pointed out to him the spot where it stood and where his father, who was born in 1808, could remember seeing the Indian graves.
38. "A Description and History of Eastham, in the County of Barnstabe. September. 1802," *Collections of the Massachusetts Historical Society* (Boston: Johnson Reprint Corporation, 1802), 8: 171-72. I have changed the spelling to current usage.
39. Frederick Freeman, *The History of Cape Cod: The Annals of the Thirteen Towns of Barnstable County* (Boston: the author, 1862), 2: 373.
40. Town of Plymouth, Massachusetts, Plymouth Colony Records, 8: 155.
41. State of Massachusetts, Massachusetts Superior Court of Judicature 15919.
42. Freeman, *The History of Cape Cod* (1862), 1: 687.
43. Josiah Paine, *A History of Harwich, Barnstable County, Massachusetts, 1620-1800: Including the Early History of That Part Now Brewster, With Some Account of its Indian Inhabitants* (Yarmouthport, Massachusetts: Parnassus Imprints, 1971), 401.
44. Ibid., 402.
45. Ibid.
46. Elredge Sparrow, who resided in this house which is on Route 28, about one mile south of the now South Orleans Post Office, understood that there was where this house is a small lean-to where the Indians worshipped.
47. Massachusetts State Archives, 30: 353.
48. Ibid., 491.
49. Ibid.
50. Nickerson copied the lines from the original headstone which was set up at the head of Treat's grave in Cove Burying Ground in Eastham (site of original Congregational church in Eastham) but which has since been replaced by a new marker. I have not been able to verify the exactness of his copy. Reynard in *The Narrow Land* has a copy of the epitaph, but it is in modern English. The new marker very simply reads, "Rev Samuel Treat/Died/Mar. 18, 1716/Aged 69 years." On the back of the stone is "Erected By/Olive, Mercy, & Lucia/Sisters of William E. Knowles."
51. Mayo Papers, 7: 83, Stanley W. Smith Collection, Sturgis Library, Barnstable, Massachusetts.
52. Ibid.
53. Ibid., 85.
54. Paine, *A History of Harwich*, 406.
55. Ibid.
56. Massachusetts Superior Court of Judicature 15919.

57. Barnstable Probate Records, Vol. VI, 353.
58. Stanley W. Smith Collection, Sturgis Library, Barnstable, Massachusetts.
59. Paine, *A History of Harwich*, 411.
60. Mary Rogers Bangs, *Old Cape Cod The Land: The Men The Sea* (Boston: Houghton Mifflin Co., 1920), 89.
61. Paine, *A History of Harwich*, 411.
62. Stanley W. Smith Collection, Sturgis Library, Barnstable, Massachusetts.
63. Freeman is Nickerson's great-great-grandfather.
64. Paine, *A History of Harwich*, 411.
65. Ibid.
66. Eldridge F. Small Papers, Stanley W. Smith Collection, Sturgis Library, Barnstable, Massachusetts. On 7 September 1788, Sarah Cowet sold land to Reuben Eldredge, and on 8 September 1788, Cowet sold land to Samuel Higgins.
67. Freeman, *The History of Cape Cod*, (1862) 2: 663.
68. Bangs, *Old Cape Cod The Land*, 89.
69. Timothy Alden, "Memorabilia of Yarmouth," *Collections of the Massachusetts Historical Society* (Boston: Samuel Hall, 1798), 5: 55.
70. Swift, *Genealogical Notes of Barnstable Families*, 171.
71. Freeman, *The History of Cape Cod*, 2: 558.
72. George Ernest Bowman, "Barnstable, Mass., Vital Records," *The Mayflower Descendant*, 25: 130.
73. George Ernest Bowman, "The Will of Joshua Hopkins," *The Mayflower Descendant* (Boston: Massachusetts Society of Mayflower Descendants, 1918), 20: 67-69.
74. Stanley W. Smith, "Records of the First Church in Orleans, Formerly the First Church in Easham, Mass.," *The Mayflower Descendant* (Boston: Massachusetts Society of Mayflower Descendants, 1912), 14: 55.
75. "Bill of Mortality in the South Parish of Eastham 1772-1828," *The Mayflower Descendant* (Boston: Massachusetts Society of Mayflower Descendants, 1907), 9: 37.

The Old Sagamore: Mattaquason of Monomoyick

Nickerson had two articles published in a scholarly journal, the Bulletin of the Massachusetts Archaeological Society; "The Old Sagamore" was published in July 1958 and "Micah Rafe" in January 1961. Since Nickerson saw these two articles as completed and since the Bulletin is available to scholars, I have decided to reprint the two pieces as they appeared. Reflecting the period in which the two articles were written, the language is occasionally pejorative to both African Americans and Native Americans. Believing that the two articles should be reprinted as they originally appeared, I have made no changes. All of the other pieces in the book have been rewritten or edited with an eye to tone and diction. I have not changed punctuation or endnote form to current usage. I have added in brackets after endnotes any appropriate corrections of factual errors and further information for greater ease in locating sources.

Foreword

The life of Mattaquason of Monomoyick, "The Old Sagamore" as he was familiarly known on the elbow of Cape Cod where he lived, covered an extremely interesting and difficult period in our early colonial history. He was born while yet the impact of white civilization had made no impression on the lives and customs of his people. He lived well into that period following King Philip's War which saw his tribe being reduced to almost abject slavery and its corn lands and camp sites fast becoming the farms and villages of the hated white men.

It is possible that he was old enough to remember Gosnold's *Concord* as she nosed along the Back Side of Cape Cod. It is quite certain that he witnessed the bloody fight on the shores of Stage Harbor in Chatham between his own tribesmen and the men of Sieur de Champlain. He must have known the bitter hatred stirred up by the kidnapping of his neighbors at Nawset by the slave stealing Captain Hunt; and he undoubtedly joined with savage joy in the retaliatory vengeance meted out to later shipwrecked crews as they were passed along from tribe to tribe for slow torture.

It is highly probable that he was one of the war party which ambushed Captain Dermer on the shores of Pleasant Bay, perhaps even its leader; and he unquestionably watched the *Mayflower* turn on her heel off his own Monomoyick the following year to carry the Pilgrims to Plymouth Rock and the Landing. Very likely he joined the Nawsets in their dawn attack on the Pilgrim bivouac on the Eastham shore a few days later, and it is certain he witnessed the first white settlement on the Lower Cape when the Pilgrim pioneers pushed down into the wilderness and cleared a site for their future town of Eastham. In a short twenty years he was to see the white men's cabins go up alongside his own wigwam at Monomoyick in Chatham.

That part of Cape Cod extending from Bass River to the tip at Provincetown has always been known in the vernacular as the Lower Cape. The Indians who inhabited it at the coming of the white man fall naturally into three main groups or tribes, as the word tribe has been commonly applied by Cape historians. They were the Nawsets, comprising the whole territory below Boat Meadow and Town Cove; the Sauquatuckets, embracing most of what is now the town of Brewster, part of Dennis, and a small section of Harwich; and the Monomoyicks, inhabiting the whole outer elbow of Cape Cod, including the whole town of Chatham, the eastern and southern parts of Harwich, and the greater part of Orleans, as the town boundaries stand today.

When the Pilgrims landed at Provincetown in 1620, and started their search for a suitable site for their settlement, the first Indians they encountered were the Nawsets. The Nawset sachem Aspinet was then the senior sagamore on the Lower Cape and could muster a hundred warriors. In 1621, when the little Billington boy strayed away from the Plymouth stockade, and wandered off into the woods, the Indians who found him took him to Sachem Aspinet's village at Nawset. He was kindly treated; and, when the Plymouth men came down by boat to take him off, they too were received in a friendly manner and the boy turned over to them unharmed. Shortly after this the Nawsets joined with many of the neighboring tribes in making a treaty with the whites, and it seemed that the bloody war hatchet of the Lower Cape Indians, which had so long been turned in righteous wrath against each and every white man who ventured to land on their shores, was at last to be buried.

The old injustices rankled, however. Two years later Aspinet joined the Massachusetts Bay Indians in a conspiracy to wipe out the white settlements; but, thanks to the prompt action of Captain Myles Standish and his little force of rangers, the plot was nipped in the bud and the ringleaders either killed or driven into hiding; where, it is said, many of them died of disease and starvation. Among the latter was Sachem Aspinet of Nawset; and while it is hard for me to believe that his tribesmen would allow their sachem to crawl off into the swamps and die because he attempted to rid their country of the detested whites, it is certain that he did drop completely out of the sight and knowledge of the colonists. If he ever showed himself again it was under another name, which is not at all unlikely.

The sachem of the Monomoyicks was not among the signers of the treaty of 1621, nor was he implicated in the conspiracy of 1623, as far as the records show. Consequently his tribe escaped the general demoralization which befell those whose sachems were either dead or driven into hiding. With the downfall of Aspinet the Nawsets never again raised the tomahawk against the whites, and their supremacy among the Lower Cape Indians was broken forever. From that day forward the leadership passed into the hands of the Monomoyick sachemry.

Whatever may have been the standing of the sachem of the Monomoyicks previous to 1623, it is certain that very little of importance in Indian affairs transpired on the Lower Cape for the next fifty years without his advice and consent. By the time of the so-called Nawset Purchase by the Plymouth men in 1643 Mattaquason of Monomoyick was firmly established as the great sachem of the Lower Cape tribes, and on the confirmation deed his name not only heads the list of Indian signatories but is the only one accorded the title of Sagamore. From that date on he was truly The Old Sagamore.

The Old Sagamore's Tribe

The Monomoyicks, like all the Cape Indians, took their name from the locality in which they had their head village. Strictly speaking, Monomoyick applied only to the lands bordering on the bay and river of that name. Pleasant Bay, on the elbow of Cape Cod, and now almost landlocked by the townships of Chatham, Harwich, and Orleans, was their Monomoyick Bay; and Long Cove or Muddy River as it is sometimes called, emptying into the Bay at its southwest corner under the Wading Place Bridge, was their Monomoyick River.

Here around the Head of the Bay, and across Monomesset Neck to Crow's Pond and Ryder's Cove, was their headquarters. Their kitchen middens still mark their camp sites from Wequasset at Round Cove along the shore of Askaonkton, their wading place, and up the River to Popomosset cowet's bound at its head. The grass still grows a little greener on their old corn lands around the headwaters of Ryder's Cove and Crow's Pond.[1]

The territory over which their Sachem held sway in his best years stretched far beyond the confines of his head village. From Allen's Harbor in Harwich Port eastward until it rounded the elbow of the Cape at Monomoy Point and followed the Back Side north to Pochet in East Orleans the Land of the Monomoyicks knew no bounds but the open sea. Its northern limits were marked roughly by the height of land running inland across Pochet between Meeting House Pond and Town Cove; and from the Cove out through Boat Meadow, the Onoskoteesit of the Indians, to the North Shore of the Cape. Turning westward along the Cape Cod Bay shore to Namskaket, an ill defined line running from the Head of Skaket south through the Cliff Pond Valley to the east end of Long Pond formed its westerly bounds, and continued on through the Grassy Pond back to Allen's Harbor again.

Of course, before the coming of the white men, the limits of the Indian tribal lands were never definitely fixed by metes and bounds. A height of land, a river valley, a string of ponds, or some such natural landmark was recognized as bounding the corn lands or hunting grounds of a certain tribe, and honored as such by its neighbors. Thus the high land of Pochet—spelled Pochey in the early records, and pronounced as it was spelled—meant literally The Dividing Place in the Indian tongue.[2]

Because of its semi-isolated situation the Monomoyick country was among the last of the Cape lands to be settled by the whites. Consequently, and because of the strong position held by its Sagamore among the Indians, it held its people together long after both the Nawsets and the Sauquatuckets, its nearest neighbors, had ceased to exist as tribal entities.

Champlain, who visited there in 1606 and spent several weeks in Stage Harbor, Chatham, gives us a vivid eye-witness account of Indian life while yet uncontaminated by white civilization. He describes the men as healthy, clean-limbed, and finely developed, and the women well proportioned and good looking. He pictures their comfortable, round-topped wigwams surrounded by fields of corn, beans, squashes, and tobacco, and he tells of their corn-barns dug into the sandy hillsides for storing their winter supplies—all in all presenting an air of general well-being and Indian abundance.

Both Champlain and Gosnold testify that the native dugout canoes were so well designed that on different occasions, when it was too dangerous to send the ships' boat in over the Bars, the Monomoyicks launched their own canoes through the surf and came off to the ships to trade. Their bows and arrows were no less skillfully made. Champlain records that during the fight with them at Stage Harbor an Indian dog jumped a Frenchman, and both dog and man were shot through by one Indian arrow.[3]

This period was undoubtedly the high water mark of Indian culture on Cape Cod. After Champlain's visit, which ended in bloodshed and death on both sides, there followed years of treachery and kidnaping on the part of the whites, and bloody retaliation by the Indians. The Monomoyicks never again regained that feeling of security which their semi-isolation had given them, and their almost peaceful development came to an abrupt end. Then came the terrible plague which wiped out whole villages around Massachusetts Bay and down the Cape, leaving scarcely enough alive in others to bury the dead. But for this tragic visitation it is a question whether the Pilgrims could have established a beachhead, so great was the hatred of the Indians toward all white men.

This then was the setting in the Monomoyick Country when the stork dropped little Mattaquason down through the smoke hole of his mother's wigwam sometime close to the year 1600. Up to this time no white man's ship had ever crossed the Bars and no white man's foot trod the soil of the Land of the Monomoyicks, so far as history records.

The Old Sagamore Himself

I reckon the approximate date of Mattaquason's birth as circa 1600 for the following reasons—In 1720 John Cussens, the Monomoyick Indian minister, a grandson of The Old Sagamore, testified under oath that he, Cussens, was then about seventy years old.[4] This would fix his birth around 1650, and there is reason to believe that Tom Coshanag, the Potanomacut Indian minister, was an older brother. John's mother was a daughter of Mattaquason, known to the whites as Cussen's Squaw; and it is reasonable to suppose that she must have been born around 1625 or before to have certainly had a son born by 1650, and probably another before that time.

We also find that Mattaquason's son, Sachem John Quason Towsowet, was selling land in his own name before 1663.[5] It is certain he would not have been doing this until he had passed his majority, and probably not until quite some time after, if he followed the usual Indian custom, his father being still alive and in his prime.

Again we find that Joseph, the fourth son of Sachem John Quason Towsowet, was of legal age by 1680,[6] which automatically sets his birth back before 1660; and he certainly had three brothers older than he, and possibly a fourth as well as sisters who may have been older. Therefore it would seem that their father, Sachem John, must of necessity have been born well back toward 1625, and perhaps much earlier.

In the course of research on the lives of hundreds of Cape Cod Indians it has been my experience that their birth dates almost invariably prove to have been earlier than the scattered records of their activities have at first led me to suppose. Therefore, taking all the known facts into consideration, I do not hesitate to fix The Old Sagamore's birth as early as 1600, possibly earlier, and his marriage circa 1620, or before.

It is highly probable that as a little black-eyed papoose he gazed with boyish wonder at the strange dress and fearful shooting-irons of Champlain's men as they made a landing in Stage Harbor in 1606. This would be his first close-up experience with white men, and it must have left an indelible scar on his young memory when the bloody fight which ensued left three Frenchmen dead on the shore and half a dozen Monomoyick scalps dangling at the belt of Sacondon, Champlain's Tarratine Indian guide, when they sailed away.

It was only five years later that Captain Harlow swept down the coast from Monhegan to The Vineyard, kidnaping the natives as he went; followed in 1614 by the notorious Captain Hunt, one of the famous Captain John Smith's men, who enticed seven of the neighboring Nawsets on board and then sailed away with them to be disposed of in the Malaga slave markets.[7]

Mattaquason was now a grown boy, and it is probable that some of Hunt's Nawset victims were his own kith and kin. Squanto, who later was to prove such an invaluable friend to the Pilgrims, and be the means of making peace between them and the Monomoyicks, was also among the natives whom Hunt took at Plymouth in the same raid. He somehow managed to escape the slave dealers, work his way into England and from there returned again to his native land.[8]

It is likely that the young Mattaquason entered with zest into the retaliatory torture of the unfortunate white crews wrecked on the Cape in the years which followed.[9] But we have no actual record of the contact of his tribe with the white men again until the year 1619, the very next year before the landing of the Pilgrims.

In the summer of 1619 Captain Thomas Dermer arrived on the coast of New England, bringing Squanto back and setting him ashore among his friends. Dermer then rounded the Cape and ran down the Back Side until he was off Pleasant Bay, where he brought his ship to anchor. At the head of a boat's crew he went in over the Bar and made a landing "in Manmock", as he spelled it. So far as the records show this was the first white man ever to land on the shores of the Bay.

The Monomoyicks ambushed the landing party, took Dermer prisoner, and came very near to wiping out his boat's crew. His men finally freed him by paying a handsome ransom in hatchets; whereupon he made a surprise counter attack on the Indians and succeeded in capturing their "Chief Sachem himself", as Dermer puts it. Before he would give the sachem up he got back all his hatchets and a canoe load of corn in the bargain. But he was so sorely wounded that he was thankful to get back aboard his ship alive.[10]

It is entirely possible that the "Chief Sachem" who was leading the war party of Monomoyicks was young Mattaquason himself. He would have been in his twenties by this date; and, if his father was dead, as I suspect, would have been at the head of his warriors. No mention of his father has ever come to my notice, either by name or inference, in the early records of the Colonists; and later I will relate an incident which leads me to believe that Mattaquason's father died while his son was still in his minority. In any event, it would be a safe bet that the young sachem would have been one of the war-party.

The next year was 1620 and the beginning of a new era, not only in the life of The Old Sagamore, but in the world as well. On the afternoon of November 19 young Mattaquason and his red brethren watched the *Mayflower* with her shipload of Pilgrim passengers turn on her heel off Monomoyick and head back for the landing at Plymouth.[11] He could not have even dreamed that on that little ship was a company of English men and women who would soon become his neighbors and friends, and that it was but the advance guard of unnumbered hundreds who, even in his own lifetime, would almost sweep his nation from the face of the earth.

Mattaquason had been reared in a school of treachery and bloodshed associated with the white men, and hatred toward them. It is not unnatural to suppose that he added his war-whoop to the blood curdling "Wooach! Wooach!" of the Indians who filled the jackets of the Pilgrims with their arrows a few days later on the Eastham shore.[12] But the winter passed; the *Mayflower* company established their beachhead at Plymouth; and when, in the summer of 1621, their little Billington boy strayed away into the woods and was picked up by the Indians he was carried to the village of the Nawsets and kindly treated.

While the rescue boat was lying offshore waiting for Sachem Aspinet to arrive with the lost boy, only two Indians were allowed on board the Pilgrims' shallop. One of them was "of Manamoick" they say, and it is unlikely he would have been accorded that honor unless he had been a man of some prominence in the tribe. This is the first recorded contact of the Plymouth men with a Monomoyick, and it may have been Mattaquason himself who was the Indian of Monomoyick.[13]

The next year, in November of 1622, Governor Bradford found his way into Monomoyick Bay itself in command of the little ship *Swan*, with Indian Squanto as guide and peacemaker. He was on a corn buying expedition, and after Squanto with some difficulty had convinced the Monomoyicks that the Pilgrims were neither kidnapers nor plunderers, he and his men were invited ashore to a feast of "venison and other victuals . . . in great abundance", as he describes it. While the peace pipe went the rounds Bradford bargained for eight hogsheads of corn and beans to be delivered on board the *Swan*, which goes to show that the Indians around Pleasant Bay were no mean farmers.

He was about ready to sail for home when Squanto was suddenly stricken down with a fever that soon ended in death. On his death bed he entreated the Governor to pray that he might go to the white man's heaven, and undoubtedly the Pilgrims gave him as nearly as was possible a white man's burial.[14] Of course his death occurred at the Monomoyick head village where the *Swan* lay at anchor. About one hundred and fifty years later an Indian skeleton was washed out of a hill between the Head of the Bay and Crow's Pond. It bore every evidence of having been buried at a very early date, but not in the usual Indian fashion, and may well have been the remains of Squanto.[15]

The visit of the Governor of Plymouth and the death of Squanto were important events in the early life of Mattaquason. Although no written treaty was ever signed by him with the Plymouth men it is a matter of record that in the Indian plot to wipe out the whites the following year the sachem of Monomoyick was almost the only leading Indian from Boston to Provincetown not implicated in the conspiracy.

Later in that same winter Governor Bradford again came in contact with two of The Old Sagamore's men. This time he was on still another corn buying expedition and an overnight guest at the lodge of Sachem Caunacum at Manomet, near the present village of Bournedale on the Cape Cod Canal. It was a bitter cold night, and Caunacum and his guests were about ready to turn in when in stalked two runners from the Sagamore of the Monomoyicks, forty miles away down the Cape. "Having set aside their bows and quivers they sat down by the fire and took a pipe of tobacco," as Bradford describes it, neither speaking nor being questioned until they were warmed and refreshed. "At last they looked toward Caunacum and one of them made a short speech and delivered a present to him from his Sachem which was a basket of tobacco and many beads." After this courteous formality the runners proceeded to deliver the message from their Chief

Hobomok, who was Bradford's interpreter since the death of Squanto, translated as the runners went along.

It seems that a powerful Powaw, or Medicine Man, of the Monomoyicks had killed a man from another tribe in an argument over a game of chance, to which the Indians were inveterate addicts. The tribe to which the murdered man belonged was much stronger than the Monomoyicks, and threatened war on them unless they put their Powaw to death. All of Caunacum's men then expressed their opinions as to what should be done in the matter, and it was finally decided that "it was better one should die than many," since the Powaw deserved it and the others were innocent.[16] All this was of especial interest to the Governor, he having been the guest of the Monomoyick Sagamore such a short time before.

Sachem Caunacum seems to have been a sort of Elder Statesman to the Cape tribes at this period, and it is my opinion that the reason the Monomoyick Sagamore sent his runners to him through the January night may have been because Mattaquason's father was dead, and he was just entering upon the responsibilities of his sachemship, being then only about twenty years old. This was a life or death matter, fraught with great danger to his tribe, and he therefore sought the advice and counsel of a more experienced and powerful leader.

The very next Spring the Indian conspiracy to wipe out the whites came to an ignominious end; and Caunacum himself, along with Iyanno of Cummaquid, Aspinet of Nawset, and other powerful chieftains went down to defeat and death. The Sagamore of the Monomoyicks, however, came through unscathed; perhaps because of his very youth, perhaps because of the unwritten bond between him and Governor Bradford of Plymouth.

In the Spring of 1626 the ship *Sparrow Hawk*, out of England for Virginia, struck on the outer bar of Monomoyick Bay in a storm, pounded over into the deep water inside, and had to be beached to keep her from sinking. Some of the Indians who came off in their canoes could speak English and offered to send runners to Plymouth to ask for aid. When Governor Bradford heard that the wreck lay in the "harbour that lyes about the middle of Manamoyacke Bay" he knew exactly where she was, having been in the harbor himself in 1622 with Squanto as pilot.

He came down by boat to Namskaket, portaged his supplies of spikes, oakum and pitch across the Cape to the head of Arey's Pond, reloaded his goods into the canoes of the Indians, and paddled down the Bay to the stranded ship. He and his men patched up the leaking *Sparrow Hawk* and got her ready for sea again, but another easterly caught her before she got clear of the harbor and piled her up again for good and all. The shifting sands soon buried the hulk; but many years later it washed out again, and today is safely moored in Pilgrim Hall, Plymouth, the only transatlantic liner of the *Mayflower* period in existence.

By the time of the wreck of the *Sparrow Hawk* in 1626 Mattaquason was undoubtedly married and the father of at least two children. There can be no question but that he took an active part in all these activities, and not only saw the little ship, but trod her decks. It would be interesting to know who it was among his men that spoke in English to the shipwrecked party.

Thus, for the first few years after the settlement at Plymouth, the Pilgrims were in almost constant and peaceful contact with the Monomoyick Indians and their Sagamore.

In 1643 a company of Plymouth men, headed by Thomas Prence who later became Governor of the Old Colony, purchased a large tract of land of the Indians on the Lower Cape. It became known as the Nawset Purchase, and originally extended "between sea and sea—from the bounds—at Nameskaket to the Herring Brook at Billingsgate."[17] The following year a settlement was begun at Nawset, which later became the township of Eastham.

The confirmation deed of the Nawset Purchase also included Pochet Island, which Mattaquason had reserved out of the original sale, as well as other additions made since the original purchase in 1643. It lists the moose-skins, hatchets, etc., which were paid, and states that the Monomoyick lands sold to the "purchasers of Eastham by Mattaquason" extended as far north as "Onoskotiset called by the English Boat Meadow."[18] Boat Meadow lies on the present line between the towns of Eastham and Orleans.

This deed was signed by the "ancient Indians" who made the original sale, or their legal heirs. "SAGAMORE OF MONOMOITT MAT-TAQUASON" heads the list of signatories, and is the only one accorded the title of sagamore. By this sale he alienated his claim to all the lands north of the south line of the Purchase; that is, north of a line extending from Namskaket across the Cape to Keskegansett, the tide-water pond north of Sampson's Neck in South Orleans. At about the same time he set aside the ancient Atacospa, the Neck in South Orleans stretching down to Little Bay between Arey's Pond and Pleasant Bay, as a home for the remnants of the fast dwindling Nawsets and other tribes of the Lower Cape. This tract became known to the Indians as Potanomicut, a name still in common use among the whites in the boyhood of this writer.

The right of The Old Sagamore to dispose of lands far outside of these bounds was recognized at a much earlier date, however. When Governor Prence decided to purchase the Province Lands at the tip of the Cape in

1679 from Sachem Sampson, he found that Peter and Joshua, two Indians of Pamet, had already bought some of it by "purchase from John Quason by consent and order from his father Mattaquason Sachem" in 1654.[19] Governor Prence recognized the validity of this prior sale, and proceeded to make a satisfactory adjustment with Peter and Joshua to clear the title.

"About the year 1655" according to the Plymouth Colony records "William Nickerson—entered into a bargain with Mattaquason the Sachem of Monomoit" concerning large tracts of land in the present towns of Chatham and Harwich.[20] There is a tradition that while the bargain was being made The Old Sagamore retired to his wigwam to await a sign. If a bear should come prowling around within the next few days the deal would be off, but if a deer showed up it would be a sign that all was well. It must have been a deer which turned the scales because that bargain stood for nearly twenty years between the red man and the white, with never a scrap of paper passed between them.

The Old Colony government had made it a misdemeanor for any one to purchase Indian lands without its consent. In actual practice this gave an absolute monopoly to the real estate dealers among the Plymouth men, of whom Nickerson was not one. He ignored the law, arguing that the land belonged to the Indians to dispose of as they saw fit. He paid The Old Sagamore "a shallop, ten coats of trucking cloth, six kettles, twelve axes, forty shillings in wampum, a hat, and twelve shillings in money" on the deal,[21] but the sachem was shrewd enough not to get tangled up with the government by setting his hand to any deed.

The dispute between the government and Nickerson dragged on. He was fined five pounds for every acre he had bargained for, and when he did not appear to pay his fine nor answer the charges against him he was disfranchised as a citizen. In the meantime, to show his contempt for the land laws, he deeded a tract of fifty acres out of "the lands that I purchased of ye Indian Sagamore at Monomoy" to his daughter Elizabeth Eldredge on June 15, 1662.[22] Of course he had no legal title to it whatsoever; nevertheless this same deed was held valid by the Colony Court twenty years later; and, so far as I know, was the first deed ever given by one white person to another in the town of Chatham.

In 1664 The Old Sagamore and his son, Sachem John Quason Towsowet, together with William Nickerson appeared at the Plymouth court where the whole matter was threshed out. The outcome was that Nickerson was allowed one hundred acres out of the thousands he had bargained for, and the balance was granted to various men who stood close to the Colonial government. Eventually Nickerson and his children made satisfactory adjustments with these men and got legal possession of the greater part of the original purchase, except for a large tract on the west shore of Pleasant Bay. This writer was bred and born on this debatable West Shore land, thanks to a romance which fused the bad blood engendered between William Nickerson and Josiah Cook, to whom this tract was granted by the government. Cook was allowed to buy it of Pompmo, a Nawset Indian, evidently as a gesture of rebuke to Mattaquason for making a bargain without the consent of the Plymouth men, but a third generation Nickerson-Cook wedding finally settled the dispute.[23]

The same year in which Nickerson got his grant from the Colony for his first one hundred acres he moved in and cleared land for his homestead at the head of Ryder's Cove in Chathamport. Tradition says that the wigwam of The Old Sagamore stood a short distance north from the cabin of the pioneer. The site of the white man's house is well authenticated;[24] and it is certain that there was an Indian campsite just to the north of it on the banks of the Cove and across to Crow's Pond. Here these two rugged old men lived side by side in peace and amity despite the wranglings of the Colony court.

The Old Sagamore was still in possession of most of the Monomoyick tribal lands in Chatham and Harwich. In the year 1670 he gave Cotchpinecote Neck, now Old Harbor in North Chatham, to his daughter Sarah, the wife of Maskuck, by a deed of gift. According to Menekish, an Indian living on the Neck, "The ould sachem of Monemoy called Mattaquason—gave to his daughter Sarah Quason a piece of land called Cochpinecate neck—and ould Mr. Bourne the minister—made a writing of it."[25] Mattaquason's grandson, the Indian minister John Cussen, corroborated Menekish's statement, and added that he very well knew old Mattaquason—sachem of Monemoy."[26] Old Mr. Bourne was Richard Bourne, the noted and well-beloved missionary to the Indians, whose justice and fair dealing was never questioned by white man or red.

Another of The Old Sagamore's daughters, known as Cussen's Squaw, the mother of John Cussen the minister, had already been allotted the upland at Tom's Neck, where Chatham Light now stands. It is referred to in the Plymouth Records as "Tom's neck that is in the possession of ye Sagamore's daughter that was Cussen's Squa."[27] Still another daughter, Old Skinnecut's Wife, was in possession of the neck in South Harwich east of the pond which still goes by the name of Skinnecut's Pond.[28]

The Old Sagamore was evidently doing his best to provide for his three daughters before commencing to actually deed any land to the whites. He knew that upon his death whatever remained of the tribal lands would automatically revert to his one and only son, Sachem John Quason Towsowet.

The Plymouth Records show that at the March court of 1672 William Nickerson sued The Old Sagamore for withholding the deed to his Monomoyick lands.[29] It is my opinion that this was simply a test case, agreed to beforehand by both parties, in order to bring to a head the haggling of the court and clear the title while yet both parties were alive. All this time, since the bargain of 1656, neither Mattaquason nor the Plymouth men to whom the court had made the grants had ever given Nickerson a deed of any sort.

Both Mattaquason and the pioneer were now getting to be old men. They were very nearly of an age, both now around seventy.[30] Both knew that their generation was fast giving way to a new influx of land-grabbers whose only interest in the Indian was to quash his title to his land. Tension between the settlers and the natives, which was soon to break out into King Philip's bloody war, was fast building up.

As a result of this suit Mattaquason, together with his son, Sachem John Quason Towsowet, gave his first deed to William Nickerson. It was dated June 19, 1672, and conveyed a great tract in Chatham to the first settler. It was bounded on the east by a line running from Pimpnuet, the Step Stones Meadow, to the head of the Oyster Pond; and westerly by a range from the head of old Monomoyick River near the East Harwich Meeting House to Mashpoxet, now Taylor's Pond in South Chatham. It included Nickerson's original homestead lot of an hundred acres, and the farms he had already set out to his sons and daughters. In addition it included also the Neck lying between the Oyster Pond and Stage Harbor, which was described as follows: "our neck—called Saquanset beginning at a Rock—at the head of the—oyster pond, ranging—easterly—crosse the uplant to—the syde of a cove or River called Naxtouweest—." This Naxtouweeset is now the Mill Pond, and its outlet under the bridge is just a short distance from the scene of Champlain's fight with the Monomoyicks in 1606. Nickerson paid The Old Sagamore two four-year-old steers, one cow and calf, and two bushels of Indian corn for Saquanset shortly before the deed was drawn.[31]

In addition to all the trade goods, wampum, cash and cattle already paid to The Old Sagamore, the pioneer was also required to pay "ninety pounds in current New England pay" to the speculators, to whom the Colony had granted most of his original purchase.

On the 29th of March, 1678/9, another large tract was deeded to Nickerson, including all the land west of his 1672 line up to what is now approximately the Harwich-Chatham town line. It read in part: "All—our land—that lyeth westward of ye former lands purchased to a creek called by ye Indians Maspatuxet, by ye English—Reed River—northerly—straight to a pond & over ye end of ye pond—to ye highway and then—easterly as ye highway rangeth to a tree where Indian popamosset cowet's Bound is & and so to ye Muddy Cove &—to my former Bounds—forst purchased of Mattaquason and John Quason, sachems of Monamoy."³²

While the above deed was signed by John Quason alone there is evidence that The Old Sagamore was still alive, although very aged, and that he gave his approval and consent.

The last sale of land in his lifetime was that of August 16, 1682, comprising meadow at the Step Stones and at Tom's Neck. The Step Stones is called Pamuet in this deed, evidently just another spelling of the Pimpnuet of the 1672 deed. It also states that the upland on Tom's Neck "is in ye possession of ye Sagamore's daughter that was Cousins Squa, ye upland ye Sagamore did give his daughter & he did give his son John Quason alias Towsowet to dispose of the meadow which Mattaquason and John Quason have sold unto William Nicarson senr of Monamoy-."³³

From the wording of the above deed it seems certain that The Old Sagamore was alive as late as the middle of August, 1682; and Mr. William Smith, in his excellent History of Chatham, expresses the same opinion, referring to the same document. This last sale left practically nothing within the present limits of the town of Chatham in the hands of the Indians with the exception of the upland at Tom's Neck, still in the possession of Mattaquason's daughter, Cussen's Squaw; and Cotchpinecote Neck, which he had deeded to his daughter Sarah, the wife of Maskuck.

Before another year had rolled around The Old Sagamore had gone to the Happy Hunting Grounds of his fathers, soon to be followed into The Great Beyond by the old pioneer with whom his life had been so inextricably mixed. On the 25th of September, 1683, *Young* John Quason, Mattaquason's grandson, was required to acknowledge a transfer of land formerly made by his father Sachem John Quason Towsowet,³⁴ something which had never been required during the lifetime of The Old Sagamore. It is my studied opinion that Mattaquason had passed away since August 16th of the previous year.

I suppose The Old Sagamore and the old pioneer sleep their last sleep on the knoll overlooking the homestead of the first settler and the campsite of the old Indian. A stone marks the grave of the white man, but this hill was a Monomoyick burying ground long before the first white man ever landed on our shores.

The Old Sagamore's Descendants

The name of the wife of The Old Sagamore has never come to my knowledge; but four of his children, one son and three daughters, are mentioned in existing records, and probably constitute all that ever arrived at legal age. They were:

> Sachem John Quason Towsowet
> Cussen's Squaw
> Old Skinnecut's Wife
> Sarah, the wife of Maskuck

After the death of The Old Sagamore, about 1683, the disintegration of his family was swift and complete. His only son, Sachem John Quason Towsowet, who took over the affairs of the sachemry, lived only a little over ten years; and by the time of his death the greater part of the tribal lands of any value had been alienated, his children scattered, and most of the dignity and prerogatives which went with the title of sachem sadly dimmed. Sachem John's eldest son, known to the whites as *Young* John Quason, who was the rightful heir to the honors of the sachemry, never even lived on the Monomoyick lands, and was very rarely accorded the title of Sachem.

Sarah's great granddaughter, Hosey Ralph, who died in 1800 at Askaonkton on the north bank of the old Monomoyick River in East Harwich, just above the Indians' ancient Wading Place, was not only the last survivor of The Old Sagamore's line on the Monomoyick tribal lands, but the last full-blooded Indian *woman* on Lower Cape Cod.

The Family of Sachem John Quason Towsowet

The Old Sagamore's Only Son

The only known son of The Old Sagamore was known to the whites as Sachem John Quason, alias Towsowet, and he must have been born circa 1630 or earlier; for, by 1654, he was disposing of land in his own name with the consent of his father, as I have previously shown. It was not customary among the Lower Cape Indians to assume such responsibility until some time after reaching their majority. The Chatham historian, Mr. William C. Smith, has conjectured that his wife's name may have been Bappanum, but I have never found anything to corroborate this. However the names of eight of his children still stand on the records: John, Josephus, Samuel, Joseph, Jeremiah, Sarah, Betty, and Wahenanun.

Sachem John was alive on September 5, 1694, when he signed a petition to the General Court concerning the revival of the "Body of Laws whereby the Indians were governed in the time when Plymouth Colony was a distinct Gov't."[35] Apparently he was dead before March 25,

1696/7, when four of his sons deeded a tract of land at Askaonkton to Captain Jethro without his acknowledgment, which most certainly would have been required had he been alive.[36] About fifteen years after his death his surviving children all set their hands to a blanket sale of the remaining Monomoyick lands, reserving only a small tract on the north bank of Monomoyick River at Askaonkton, and another on the west side of Round Cove at Wequasset. They also reserved the right to peel bark from the cedar trees and gather sedge for their wigwams anywhere on the deeded land.

This deed was dated May 18, 1711, and became known as the Quason Purchase, or Sixteen Share Propriety Deed, sixteen being the number of white partners sponsoring the deal and dividing the property. It covered a great part of the present town of Harwich, and embraced all the unsold Indian lands from Chatham bounds west to the Herring River, and north to the Sipson-Quason Line running east from Long Pond to Round Cove. Most of it was woodland and commons, the valuable farm lands having already been taken over by the whites. The sons and daughters of the Sachem signed in the following order, each by mark: John Quason, Josephus Quason, Sam Quason, Joseph Quason, Sarah Pompmano, Betty Nopie, Wahenanun. Another son, "Jeremiah Quason, late deceased," was mentioned in the deed, and Little James, the husband of Wahenanun, signed with her.[37] Undoubtedly they signed in the order of their ages, as was the custom; i.e., John as the oldest son, and Sarah Pompmano the eldest daughter.

JOHN, the eldest son, known as "Young John Quason", must have been born as early as 1650, for his younger brother Joseph, the fourth son, was of age by 1680. Young John, as I have said, never lived on the land of the Monomoyicks, but made his home at Indian Town on the west shore of the Bass River in South Yarmouth. He died between 1727 and 1734.[38] His wife's name does not appear in the records, but he left a son Amos, who was in Captain Richard Bourne's Company in the Expedition against the French in 1725.[39] This son Amos also lived at Indian Town, and probably married his cousin Rebecca, the daughter of his uncle John.[40] She was dead in 1738, when he married Mercy Ned.[41] There is no record of any children.

JOSEPHUS, the second son, also lived in Indian Town. He had children living in 1697,[42] but there is no further record of them. He was dead before 1733.[43]

SAMUEL, the third son, married Hannah Attamon of Potanomicut,[44] where he made his home some part of the time. He died in 1717.[45] His son David left no children,[46] but his daughter Betty, who married Joshua Ralph and died before 1744 left a son Joshua.[47] It is probable that

Samuel was also the father of John and Samuel, the latter of whom is referred to in 1762 as Sachem of Monomoy at the age of 62.

JOSEPH, the fourth son, must have been born about 1660, as he was of age by 1680.[48] He died between 1714 and 1725. It is probable his wife was a daughter of Sachem Nickanoose of Nantucket, and that Joseph and Deborah, who later appear at South Harwich, were their children. Deborah married Sam Robin in 1709 and died about 1730, leaving a son called Ebenezer Quason of whom nothing further is known.[49]

JEREMIAH, who is mentioned in the Quason Purchase Deed of 1711 as "late deceased", was evidently dead before 1697,[50] leaving no record of wife or children.

SARAH POMPMANO, the eldest daughter, was undoubtedly named for her father's sister, Sarah; who in turn may have been named after the pioneer William Nickerson's daughter, Sarah. Evidently her husband, Peter Pompmano, was already dead when she signed the Purchase Deed in 1711, as his name does not appear along with hers. It is possible that he was a grandson of that Peksuot whom Captain Miles Standish slew with his own knife, as Longfellow so graphically describes.[51] Sarah died after 1711,[52] leaving no record of children; but Lois Pompmore, who was found dead in "a field—in a cold and frosty time" on Christmas day, 1790,[53] was undoubtedly one of her descendants.

BETTY NOPIE, the second daughter, was apparently a widow by 1711. A Betty Nopie, who married a Ned on the 20th of February, 1724,[54] was probably her daughter. This Betty Ned was alive and a widow November 7, 1758, when she was appointed Guardian of her son David, then nineteen years old.[55] The son David married Sarah Ralph, February 20, 1761,[56] and had one son alive in 1762.[57]

WAHENANUN, who with her husband, Little James, signed the Quason Purchase Deed in 1711, and stuck to her Indian name to the last, was the youngest daughter. She is the only Monomoyick Indian woman of whose Indian name I have documentary proof. She was married to Little James whose Indian name was Namisto, before 1694[58] and their wigwam stood at Wequasset on the west shore of Round Cove in East Harwich. She died between 1711 and 1714, her husband outliving her by some fifteen years.[59] Their only known child, Isaac James, known to my people who were his neighbors as "Isaac Jeems", was the last "wigwam Indian" on the Monomoyick lands. His Indian house, covered with cedar bark and thatched with sedge, which his mother had reserved the right to gather when she signed the Purchase Deed, stood at the tidewater terminus of the old Sipson-Quason Line, as his mother's had before him.[60]

Isaac Jeems' only son, also named Isaac James, died of yellow fever at Castle Island in Boston Harbor in 1746, while in the service of the Colonial Army in the old French Wars.[61] Isaac Jeems himself lived until about 1789,[62] and so far as I know was the last full-blooded *male* descendant of The Old Sagamore on the ancestral lands. Isaac was the great-grandson of Mattaquason, but his cousin Hosey Ralph, The Old Sagamore's great-great-granddaughter, who lived nearby at Askaonkton, outlived him by eleven years.

My great grandfather Elnathan Eldredge, Jr., bought the old Indian's property after his death,[63] and I was born within a stone's throw of his old campsite, which still goes by the name of "Isaac Jeems' Wigwam" in my family. Isaac Jeems' death brings the book of records on the Family of SACHEM JOHN QUASON TOWSOWET to a close.

The Family of Cussen's Squaw

The Old Sagamore's Daughter

The Old Sagamore's daughter, known as Cussen's Squaw in the records, must have been born by 1630, for her son John Cussen testified in 1720 that he was then seventy years old,[64] and it is very probable that Tom Coshanag, the Potanomicut Indian minister who was apparently older than John, was also her son. She and her family lived on Tom's Neck, between the Lighthouse and Stage Harbor, on the land set off to her by her father before his death.

Her son John Cussen became the Monomoyick Indian minister as early as 1697, and died after 1720 when their Meeting House was closed.[65] He left no children of record. If Tom Coshanag, or Minister Tom as he was sometimes known, was also her son, his descendants were pretty well scattered by 1750, leaving no identifiable grandchildren of Cussen's Squaw.[66]

Her husband's name in its various forms may have been an abbreviation of the name of Chief Tooken-cosen, who was very prominent on the Cape about this period. She was alive as late as 1682,[67] and perhaps much later.

The Family of Old Skinnecut's Wife

The Old Sagamore's Daughter

We know that Old Skinnecut's wife was the daughter of The Old Sagamore through the testimony of her son John Skinnecut, Jr., that he was given land at South Harwich in 1680 by his grandfather Mattaquason.[68] To have had a son of legal age by 1680 she must have been born circa 1640 or earlier. She and her husband, Old Skinnecut, lived near the pond in South Harwich which still bears his name, Skinnecut's Pond. She was probably dead by 1692, and her husband by 1701.[69] Their only known child, the son John Skinnecut, Jr., was alive as late as 1730.[70] He never lived on his father's land, and left no record of wife or children.

The Family of Sarah, Wife of Maskuck

The Old Sagamore's Daughter

I have reserved until last the family record of Sarah, the wife of Maskuck, alias Stephen, because of its outstanding place in the story of The Old Sagamore. It was Sarah's great granddaughter, Hosey (Stephen) Ralph, who was the last of Mattaquason's blood descendants to live on the tribal lands, as well as the last full-blooded Indian woman on Lower Cape Cod.

Sarah lived on Cotchpinecote Neck at Old Harbor, in North Chatham, on land which was hers by deed of gift from her father. She and her husband were both dead by 1689;[71] and their three sons, Doggamus, Richard Stephen, and Mortaquit alias Stephen, who lived on the Neck, were all dead before 1720.[72] Doggamus had a son named Peter Doggamus who was a noted warrior against the French and Indians from 1710 until 1750,[73] but left no children of record. Richard Stephen had a son Simon who was alive in 1737.[74]

Mortaquit alias Stephen, Sarah's youngest son, who was born about 1670 and lived until nearly 1720,[75] left a son Stephen Stephen, alias Stephen Mortaquit, who married Sarah Jethro before 1720.[76] Her father was Captain Jethro, a noted Nantucket Indian Captain,[77] who probably married into the Quason family; and who eventually settled down in the Monomoyick Country at the Head of the Bay at Askaonkton, which became known to the whites as Cap'n Jeethro's Farm.

Stephen Stephen built his lodge on his wife's father's land and started raising a family.[78] But he died in the terrible small-pox epidemic of 1730, leaving his widow with four minor boys, John, David, Stephen and Samuel, and a baby girl named Hosey. Richard Knowles became administrator of Stephen Stephen's estate and guardian of the four boys.[79] The name of the baby girl does not appear in the guardianship papers, perhaps because she was just another Indian girl with no legal standing, or possibly she was yet unborn. But that she was one of the family is abundantly attested by later events.

Three of the sons disappear from the records after the appointment of their guardian in 1731. But David, the second son, who must have been quite a lad at the time of his father's death, killed another Indian in 1736 and was committed to jail. In 1737 while awaiting trial he broke jail, was recaptured the following year, and in 1739 was tried, convicted of manslaughter, branded, and sold as a slave.[80]

This simmers the record of all the known descendants of The Old Sagamore down to this one little fatherless Indian girl named Hosey Stephen, his great-great-granddaughter. In order to keep the record straight, here is her line of descent: The Old Sagamore's daughter Sarah married Maskuck alias Stephen; their son Mortaquit alias Stephen had a son called Stephen Stephen alias Stephen Mortaquit who married Sarah Jethro; little Hosey Stephen was their daughter, and thus the great-great-granddaughter of Mattaquason.

Hosey was presumably born about 1730, the year of her father's death, and was brought up at Askaonkton by her widowed mother. On the 9th of June, 1753, her intentions of marriage to Micah Ralph were filed with the Town Clerk of Chatham.[81] I have never found a record of their marriage, but it may exist in some Church Record of the time, and I have little doubt they were legally married.

In 1772 her husband Micah Ralph petitioned the Court for a legalization of her lands, stating that she was the granddaughter of Captain Jethro, and fixing her identity as the daughter of Stephen Stephen and his wife Sarah (Jethro) Stephen.[82]

Hosey and her husband lived the last of their days in an English frame house at Askaonkton, on the north bank of Long Cove in East Harwich, just above the ancient Monomoyick River Wading Place of their forefathers. The site is well known to me and to many others whose people were their neighbors. My people remembered Hosey as a short, soft spoken, kindly Indian woman, hospitable and highly respected in the neighborhood. She was not only the last surviving heir to the property of her grandfather which was known as "Cap'n Jeethro's Farm", but by reversion to all the existing rights and reservations in the Monomoyick lands, of her great-great-grandfather, The Old Sagamore.

She and her husband were both full-blooded Indians, although Micah was not a Monomoyick. Micah's father, who was also named Micah Ralph, was a Potanomicut Indian, and died in service in the French and Indian Wars about 1748.[83] Micah's grandfather, Jeremiah Ralph, was one of the so-called Privileged Indians, and a Head Man in the Potanomicut Tribe in South Orleans, where Micah was born.[84] He was presumably the son of Sachem Ralph of Nobscusset and his wife Manatotomuske, daughter of Sachem Nepoyetan of Mattakeese.[85] Thus

Micah was almost certainly a descendant of Sachem Iyanno of Cummaquid, whom Nepoyetan succeeded.

My grandfather, who lived until I was a grown boy, knew Micah well. He was known locally as Micah Rafe, the Indian corruption of the word Ralph. My great-grandfather, and my great-great-grandfather, whose papers and accounts are among my prized possessions, had many business transactions with him. They show that he was very meticulous in squaring his debts, and that he wrote a clear and extremely legible hand.

Hosey Ralph made her will on the 12th of October, 1798, leaving the enjoyment of all her property to her "beloved husband Micah Ralph", and naming him sole executor. Her will was brought to probate March 29, 1800, and it is likely she died shortly before that date.[86] Sixteen years later, on the 18th of March, 1816, her husband's will was probated,[87] when he must have been nearly ninety years old. He and Hosey were buried side by side in the fields a short distance north of their house, at Askaonkton.

The death of Hosey (Stephen) Ralph brought to a close the two hundred year record of the family of The Old Sagamore. If any of his blood goes on today, as well it may and probably does, its identity is long since lost in the mixed blood of the Mashpee or the Gay Head Indians. But from the birth of Mattaquason, about the year 1600, until the death of his great-great-granddaughter Hosey Ralph in 1800 the Indian blood ran pure through every generation, and can be identified through all these years by documentary evidence still in existence.

In no other Indian family on the Lower Cape can any like genealogical continuity be absolutely proven by the records. In no other instance is the history of the ruling house so truly that of the tribe. That of the Monomoyicks begins with the birth of The Old Sagamore and ends with the death of his great-great-granddaughter.

Notes

1. In 1622 Governor Bradford was in "Manamoyack Bay" on a corn buying expedition, followed in 1626 by his relief of the shipwrecked *Sparrow Hawk* at "Manamoyake Bay", which identifies it as Pleasant Bay. See his history of Plimoth Plantation, cited hereafter as *The Bradford History*. [William Bradford, *Bradford's History "Of Plimoth Plantation"* (Boston: Wright and Potter Printing Co., 1899), 262.]

   Monomoyick River and Askaonkton are found in a deed dated March 25 from John, Josephus, Samuel, and Joseph, grandsons of the Old Sagamore, to Captain Joshua Jethro. Mass. State Archives XXVIII-618/9. Monomesset Neck, now Eastward Ho Golf Links, is given in a deed dated October 13, 1702 from William Nickerson the Second to his son William.

Wequasset is still in use for the Round Cove area. "Indian popamosset cowet's Bound" is named in a deed dated March 29, 1678/9 from John Quason to William Nickerson, the Pioneer, and was approximately the same as the Harwich-Chatham bound standing today, just east of the East Harwich Meeting House.

The first white settlement in Chatham was at the head of Ryder's Cove, and went by the name of Monomoyick until incorporated as the town of Chatham.

2. See "Poshee—it divides" in the *Natick Indian Language Dictionary*.
3. Voyages of Sieur de Champlain, and Histoire de la Nouvelle France, for Champlain. [*Voyages of Samuel de Champlain 1604-1618*, edited by W. L. Grant (New York: Charles Scribner's Sons, 1907), 95-100. This note would have been better placed after the preceding paragraph which corresponds more directly to the material in Champlain.] Archer's and Brereton's Narratives for Gosnold. [Gabriel Archer and John Brereton, *The Gosnold Discoveries . . . in the North Part of Virginia, 1602 Now Cape Cod and the Islands, Massachusetts*, ed. Lincoln A. Dexter (Sturbridge: Plaza Printing, 1982), 18-19. The material here corresponds to the preceding paragraph.]
4. "John Cousins, Indian Minister", testimony April 1, 1720. Mass. Superior Court of Judicature 15919. Cited hereafter as Mass. Sup. Crt. Jud.
5. He sold a tract in Province Lands to Joshua and Peter prior to 1654, from copy of indenture in my Collection. Also land "toward Monomoy" to William Chase about 1653, Stanley W. Smith Collection X-15. [The copied deed of the William Chase acknowledgment, dated 25 September 1683, is in the Sturgis Public Library, Barnstable, Massachusetts. John Quason acknowledges a transaction his father made thirty years before.]
6. Mattaquason deeded land to grandson Joseph about 1680, so he must have been of legal age. Mass. Sup. Crt. Jud. 299776. In the Quason Purchase deed he was the fourth of his brothers to sign. Ibid 144324.
7. *General History of New England*, by Captain John Smith. [Captain John Smith, *A Description of New England* (Boston: William Veazie, 1865), 65-66. The number is twenty-seven, not seven ("betrayed twenty feauen of thefe poore innocent foules, which he fould in Spaine for flaues").]
8. Squanto was brought back by Captain Thomas Dermer. See Dermer's letter to Purchas, New York Historical Society.
9. Both *The Bradford History* and *Mourt's Relation* tell of the shipwrecks. [*Mourt's Relation*, ed. Dwight B. Heath (Chester: The Globe Pequot Press, 1963).]
10. See Dermer's letter to Purchas.
11. *The Mayflower* was turned back by head winds and shoals off Chatham.
12. See *The Bradford History* and *Mourt's Relation*.
13. Ibid.
14. See The Bradford History [155].
15. Description of Cape Cod, *Massachusetts Magazine* III-74ff.
16. From Edward Winslows, *Good News From New Engaland*. [See *The Story of*

the Pilgrim Fathers, 1606-1623 A.D.; as told by Themselves, their Friends, and their Enemies, ed. Edward Arber (Boston: Houghton, Mifflin and Co., 1897), 542.]

17. *History of Cape Cod,* Freeman, II-348, 349. [Frederick Freeman, *The History of Cape Cod: The Annals of The Thirteen Towns of Barnstable County* (Boston: George C. Rand and Avery, 1862), 2: 348-50. "The Court doth grant unto the Church of New Plymouth, or those that go to dwell at Nauset, all the tract of land lying between sea and sea, from the purchaser's bounds at Namskaket to the herring brook at Billingsgate. . . . "]

18. My Collection, photostat copy from Mass. Sup. Crt. Jud.

19. Photostat copy of the Indenture, in my Collection.

20. Plymouth Colony Records IV-162. [*Records of the Colony of New England,* ed. Nathaniel B. Shurtleff, M.D. Court orders: vol. 3, 1651-1661 (Boston: William White, 1855), 3: 162-63.]

21. *History of Chatham,* by William C. Smith, I-73. [William C. Smith, *A History of Chatham Massachusetts,* 4th ed. (Chatham: The Chatham Historical Society, Inc., 1992), 73. Smith also lists "twelve hoes, twelve knives."]

22. Ibid I-63. [It should read "ye lands that I purchased of ye Indian Sagamore Mattaquason at Manamoy." Also, the date should read, "ye fifteenth day of January in ye thirteenth year of ye Reign of our Sovereign Lord King Charles The Second & in the year of our Lord God one thousand six hundred and sixty-one" (62-63).]

23. From deed, Stanley W. Smith Collection, X-67.

24. William Nickerson's house stood about one hundred yards northwest of the Electric Light Co.'s Transformer in Chathamport.

25. Mass. Sup. Crt. Jud. 13717. Testimony of Menekish, Indian.

26. Ibid 15919. Testimony of John Cussen, Indian.

27. Plymouth Colony Deeds, V-508.

28. Proof that she was The Old Sagamore's daughter is found in the testimony of her son, John Skinnecut, Jr., that Mattaquason was his grandfather. Mass. Sup. Crt. Jud. 29776.

29. Plymouth Colony Records, VII-171. ["damage of two hundred pounds. . . . The jury find for the defendant."]

30. William Nickerson was born in 1604, in Norwich, England; The Old Sagamore circa 1600.

31. Plymouth Colony Deeds, III-251.

32. Plymouth Colony Deeds, V-463.

33. Ibid, V-508.

34. Stanley W. Smith Collection, X-15; Acknowledgment by Young John Quason of land transferred thirty years previously by his father to William Chase. [See editorial comment on note 5.]
    Also Mass. Sup. Crt. Jud. 14324; Deed Old Humphrey and his son Zackariah, Indians, to Caleb Lumbert land which they bought of "Sachem Mattaquason." They were required to procure "from Old John Quason and Young John Quason" a confirmation of the title.

35. Massachusetts State Archives XXX-353. ["Government"]
36. Ibid XXVIII-618/9. This was a tract in East Harwich north of Wading Place, which became known as "Cap'n Jeethrow's Farm."
37. Barnstable County Records, 6th Book, folio 38.
38. *Mayflower Descendant* VII-158, John Kenrick Papers: Deed to son Amos April 22, 1726/7, who sold the property Aug. 17, 1734 to Edward Kenrick and belonging "originally to my deceased father John Quason." ["Eastham and Orleans, Mass., Vital Records," volume 8, not volume 7: "originally the land of my Deceassed father John Quason now lawfully desending to me being the only son & heir of sd Deceased." Kenrick is spelled "Kendrick" and "Kenwrick."]
39. *History of Chatham*, Smith, 267.
40. *Mayflower Descendant* VII-158, John Kenrick Papers: Deed Oct. 15, 1733 to Edward Kenrick from "Amos Quason and Rebecka his wife." [Vol. 8, not 7.]
41. *History of Harwich*, Paine, 448. [Josiah Paine, *A History of Harwich: Barnstable County Massachusetts 1620-1800* (Rutland: The Tuttle Publishing Co., Inc., 1937).]
42. Stanley W. Smith Collection: Deed Sept. 7, 1697, to Thomas Atkins and Joseph Harding in which he reserved the right for himself and "his children now living" to plant and live on any part of the land.
43. Mayflower Descendant VII-158, John Kenrick Papers: April 22, 1733, Amos and Rebecka Quason quit claim to their reversionary rights in the reserved land of Josephus, who was now dead. [I am not satisfied that I have found Nickerson's reference. Volume 8, page 158 reads: on 15 October 1733 Amos and Rebecca Quasson "sell unto the sd Edward Kenwrick. . . . . all our Right. . . . . to all that thirty acres of land lying neer to the Mudy Cove River in harwich above sd which was the land of her the sd Rebecka Quasons father John Quason of sd harwich Deceast."]
44. Barnstable County Probate Records III-543: In the division of Samuel Quason's estate, May 21, 1721, his wife Hannah is called the daughter of "Attamon Chusick."
45. Barnstable County Probate Records III-507: Joshua Ralph, his son-in-law, was appointed administrator of his estate Jan. 23, 1717/8.
46. *History of Harwich*, Paine, 447: Sept. 6, 1735, his son David sold land to Thomas Clark which had been left him by his father Samuel Quason.
47. Stanley W. Smith Collection VIII-5, deed Oct. 13, 1735, "Joshua Ralph and bette his wife of Eastham, daughter of Samuel Quason of Chatham late deceased" to Thomas Clark. [Deed is in Sturgis Public Library.]
48. Mass. Sup. Crt. Jud. 299776, John Skinnecut testified that he and his cousin Joseph Quason were given land about 1680 by their grandfather Mattaquason. Hence they must have been of age by 1680.
49. On April 2, 1714, Joseph quit claim to land deeded to Papoos Francis by Isaac James, Barnstable County Deeds VII-60. In a controversy over his South Harwich land, 1724, it appears that he was dead, and that his daughter Deborah, the wife of Sam Robin, lived on the land with her son

Ebenezer Quason. She testified that her uncle was Paul Noose of Nantucket, Mass. Sup. Crt. Jud. 17882, 31347, 29308, 29776. Deborah's estate was settled April 5, 1731, with no mention of her son, *History of Harwich*, Paine, 438.

50. Mass. State Archives XXVIII-618/9, Jeremiah did not sign the deed when his brothers sold land to Captain Jethro, March 25, 1697, and was probably dead before that date.

51. Mass. Sup. Crt. Jud. 12967, John Sipson, Indian, 73 years old, testified that "old Pekswat" was the father of "Paupmonet", who was the father of Simon Pompmo. Simon Pompmo was the brother of Peter Pompmo, the husband of Sarah Quason.

52. She cannot be identified after the signing of the Purchase Deed, but there is reason to believe that she may have been the Sarah Quoy alias Cowet of later years.

53. Mass. Sup. Crt. Jud. 144584, "Inquisition taken at Eastham—before Benjamin Pepper Gentleman, one of the Coroners."

54. Eastham Records XBII-81, her husband was David Ned. [There is obviously an error in XBII; it was probably XVII; the records have been rebound and are no longer so numbered. The records do show that Bethia Nopie married David Ned 20 February 1733, not 1724 (Marriage Intentions 1716-35, page 109). Justice of the Peace Joseph Doane officiated.]

55. *History of Harwich*, Paine, 429. [Paine uses her full name, Bethiah Nopie.]

56. Ibid 429.

57. Ibid 410.

58. *History of Chatham*, Smith, 265. [She is listed as the eighth child; her name is spelled "Wawhanana."]

59. She signed the Purchase Deed of 1711, but in an exchange of her Wequasset land at Round Cove, March 26, 1714, between her husband Little James and Papoos Francis, her name does not appear and it is to be assumed that she was dead; Barnstable County Deeds, VII-60. Her husband was present at the inquest of "Larrance Jeffre" on June 14, 1729; Mass. Sup. Crt. Jud. 11575.

60. *History of Harwich*, Paine, 280, 420. The Sipson-Quason Line between the Quason Purchase and the Sipson Purchase, so-called, ran from the east end of Long Pond "southeast a little easterly to the Round Cove, a little distance from Isaac James his house."

61. Ibid 280, 420. He died in November or December, 1746.

62. Ibid. This agrees with tradition in my family.

63. Barnstable Records, Harwich Book, 11-19.

64. Mass. Sup. Crt. Jud. 15919: Testimony by John Cussen in April, 1720.

65. *History of Chatham*, Smith, 146: John Cussen, Indian Minister of Monomoyick.

66. Tom Coshanag, alias Minister Tom or Great Tom, had numerous descendants, but by the middle of the century they were either dead, scattered up the Cape or crossed with negro slaves.

67. Plymouth Colony Deeds, V-508; deed from Sachem John Quason and his father to William Nickerson August 16, 1682, states that Tom's Neck "is in ye possession of ye Sagamore's daughter that was Cousins Squa."

68. Mass. Sup. Crt. Jud. 29776: "John Skinnoquit" testified that his grandfather gave him land at South Harwich "about fifty years ago." This was on July 9, 1730.

69. Stanley W. Smith, Collection, Osborn Nickerson Papers: On June 1, 1692, her husband sold some of her land to Jeremiah Howes with no mention of her name in the transaction; and in 1701 her son John sold more of the same tract, with no mention of her husband's name, which would indicate that they were both dead.

70. See Note 68 above. He does not appear on the records after this date, to my knowledge.

71. Mass. Sup. Crt. Jud. 13780; William Nickerson, son of th[e] pioneer, bought land on Cotchpinecote Neck of Doggamus, Richard and Mortaquit on August 29, 1689; which indicates that both their father and mother were now dead.

72. Ibid: Testimony given April 21, 1720, shows that all three were dead.

73. Mass. State Archives, Vol. 73, folio 744: His petition to the Governor and Council in January 1750 states that he was "at ye reduction of Annapolis (in 1710)"—and in 1749 had just returned from being taken captive in 1745.

74. Mass. Historical Society, 81 J-12: A writ was served on Simon Stephen Sept. 24, 1737, by Samuel Knowles.

75. Mass. Sup. Crt. Jud. 15919, 13780, 163539: Testimony by several witnesses in 1720.

76. Barnstable Probate Records IV-51: He is named as her husband in the division of her father's estate, Jan. 14, 1723/4. By 1720 they had five children so must have been married by 1720.

77. Mass. State Archives XXV-5006: "Capt. Jethro an Indian under Maj. Church.["] Nantucket Historical Bulletin 3-128: Captain Jethro made complaint against his father Sachem Nickanoose.

78. *History of Chatham*, Smith, 266. [This note should have been placed after the date of his death. See note 79 which refers to the guardianship of his children. Smith lists a son Joshua, not John.]

79. Barnstable Probate Records IV-580, 581, 582, and V-53.

80. Mass. State Archives XXXI-228, 229.

81. Town Records, Chatham, Mass. See also Mayflower Descendant XIII-28.

82. Mass. State Archives XXXIII-622.

83. Barnstable County Probate Records VII-82 and VIII-452: Samuel Knowles was appointed administrator of his estate May 28, 1748. On June 29 his inventory showed "wages which was received of Brigd Waldo—Old Tenor 36.13.07."

84. Jeremiah Ralph was the third signer of the Privileged Indians' Agreement with the 17 proprietors of the Sipson Purchase, which took in much of South Orleans. Copy in my Collection.

85. Mass. Sup. Crt. Jud. 3491: Deed March 1, 1677, "Ralph Indian of Nobscusset—and Manatotomuske his wife daughter—of—Nepoyetan" to John Wing and John Dillingham.

Manatotomuske, her sisters Penasamuske and Aquanetva, and Wahenanum, the daughter of Sachem John Quason Towsowet, are the only Lower Cape Indian women of whose Indian names I have found documentary proof. There is no absolute proof that Sachem Ralph and his wife were the parents of Jeremiah Ralph, but a great deal of circumstantial evidence points that way.

86. Barnstable County Probate Records XXII-25.
87. Ibid XXXII-7.

Micah Rafe, Indian Man: Last Full Blood on Lower Cape Cod

See introductory note for "The Old Sagamore" for editorial practice for these two articles. "Micah Rafe" was published in the Bulletin of the Massachusetts Archaeological Society *in January 1961.*

Foreword

It is with mingled feelings of reverence and hesitation that I attempt the story of Micah Rafe, the last full blooded Indian on Lower Cape Cod; reverence, because he stands alone at the journey's end of his people; hesitation, because all we have learned about any Cape Cod Indian is, at best, but fragmentary and incomplete. The Indians kept no written records; and it is only from old deeds, old court records, and probate files that it is possible to fit their blood ties together. With this apology I offer what little I know about him so it will not be lost forever to lovers of things Indian and Cape Cod.

Following the old custom I define the Lower Cape as stretching easterly from Bass River to the tip of the Cape. Bass River has from time immemorial been a natural landmark dividing Cape Cod into the Upper and Lower Cape in the geography of the natives.

First let me set down what I learned by word of mouth from my grandfather Nickerson who could remember Micah Rafe. He told me time and again that Micah was the last full blooded Indian in the town of Harwich. Whether or not he heard this directly from the lips of the old Indian himself I cannot say, but he, his father and grandfather had every opportunity to know since all were born and grew up beside Micah in the

Micah Rafe's signature, with permission of the Massachusetts Archaeological Society.

little village of East Harwich. My grandmother too—her mother was a Wixon said to have been part Indian—as well as her grandfather, who kept a record of his dealings with Micah Rafe over a period of years, must have believed the same thing or she never would have let my father and grandfather pass it along to me so positively.

What was common knowledge to them, my people, came to me first hand along with great-great-grandfather's little hand-made account book in which he reckoned his debts and credits with Micah Rafe. Since that time I have devoted years of research into the lives of Lower Cape Indians and have never yet turned up anything among the ancient records to contradict what they told me. It is therefore my considered opinion that Micah Rafe was not only the last full blooded Indian in the town of Harwich, as my grandfather told me, but the last full blood on all of Lower Cape Cod as well.

His real name was Micah Ralph. That is the way he signed it himself, frequently adding "Indian Man" as if to let the world know he was not a half-breed. Among my treasured heirlooms is a document signed by him in 1780 when he was in the prime of life. His signature is a good one, the bold assured hand of a man accustomed to the use of ink and quill. Side by side with that of the white man who signed with him, Micah's needs no apology.[1]

He pronounced his surname Rafe, spoken to rhyme with safe. That is the way I learned it from the people who lived beside him and heard it from his own lips. It was always difficult for the Indians to get their tongues around the sound of the English L, as Edward Winslow found out soon after the *Mayflower* arrived. Even the great Massasoit himself called him Winsnow.[2] Ralph became Raf and then degenerated into Rafe. Ralph's Pond, which lay within the lands of Micah Rafe's grandfather, became Rafe's Pond and then in turn was corrupted into Race Pond which was easier to say. Thus it remains to this day with very few people knowing why.[3]

In this Paper I shall call him Micah Rafe because it is easier for me to think and speak of him in my mother tongue, and besides it will serve to distinguish him from his father whose name was also Micah Ralph.

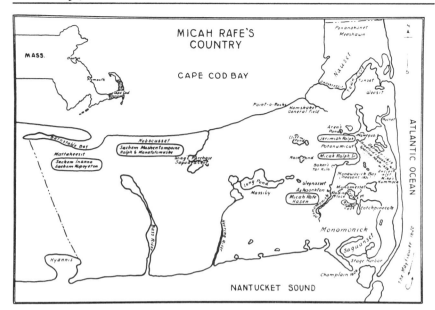

Micah Rafe's country. With permission of the Massachusetts Archaeological Society.

Micah Rafe and his squaw Hosey lived in a little house at Askaonkton on the north bank of old Monomoyick River in East Harwich.[4] My people, who also lived near, always called it Long Cove, which I suspect may have been a literal translation of its Indian name. On today's maps it is entered as Muddy River, but whatever its name, it is and always has been a charming little stream. In connection with Micah Rafe I like to think of it by its easy flowing Indian name. The spot where his house stood and which my grandfather pointed out to me was on the still unalienated lands of the Monomoyicks although Micah himself was not a Monomoyick. It was through his marriage with Hosey Stephen, the great-great-granddaughter of old Sagamore Mattaquason and the last surviving heir to his lands,[5] that he came to end his days in the Monomoyick Country.

Some of Micah's Ancestors

The Ralph blood ties stretched straight across the Cape to the North Shore sachems who welcomed our immigrant forefathers to their lands— Sachem Napoyetan, Sachem Mashantampaine, perhaps even to Iyanno of Cummaquid himself, that pleasant young sachem of whom one Pilgrim wrote that he was "personable, gentle, courteous and fair conditioned, about twenty-six years of age, and indeed not a savage at all except in his attire."

A few years later Sachem Iyanno was implicated in an ill-fated plot to wipe out the whites and is said to have hidden in dismal swamps and died miserably of starvation when it failed. That an able bodied young Indian with the whole of North America open before him and not over twenty-five armed white men on the whole coast from Canada to Florida should go off and starve to death even if his tribesmen would let him is hard for me to believe. It seems more likely he simply dropped out of sight until the disturbance was over and then reappeared under another name, of which the Indians always had plenty.

Be that as it may, when the purchase for the new towns of Yarmouth and Barnstable were being made not long after, we find that Napoyetan had become the sachem at Iyanno's town; and the old records show that in giving title he distinctly stated that these lands were his "own proper inheritance."[6] According to Cape Cod Indian custom "inheritance" came through heirship from the former sachem, and as Iyanno was the sachem before Napoyetan it is logical to conclude he was a son or brother.

Thirty-five years later, after Napoyetan had gone to the Happy Hunting Ground of his people,[7] his three daughters complained to the March Court of 1675 that John Wing the Quaker and Lieutenant John Dillingham were squatting illegally on their lands. They brought suit in the names of their husbands, recorded as Ralph of Nobscusset, the husband of Mana-toto-mus-ke; Sampson of Nobscusset, Pe-nasa-mus-ke's husband; and Robin of Mattakeesit, whose wife was Aqua-netva.

This introduces us to the great-grandparents of Micah Rafe—Ralph of Nobscusset and his wife Manatotomuske, the daughter of Napoyetan. It goes without saying that in those early days Ralph must have been a scion of royalty to have been married to an Indian princess, the daughter of a sachem. Besides being brothers and marrying sisters he and Sampson were sons of old Sachem Mashantampaine of Nobscusset, who was getting very aged and turning the responsibilities of his sachemry over to his sons. According to Indian custom the older was recognized as higher in rank, and as early as 1657 Sampson appears as sachem of Nobscusset in renewing their treaty with Plymouth and again in 1671 and 1674.[8] Ralph['s] name also often appears conjointly with that of his brother on the records.

Ralph is the first Indian with that name I have ever run across in the early records up to his day and one of the rare instances of an Indian family's replacing its name with one not found in the Bible. His wigwam undoubtedly stood near that of his father on the north side of Scargo

Lake, then known as Nobscusset Pond, in the present Dennis on land the old sachem had reserved when the bounds of the original Yarmouth were run out by Mr. Edward Winslow, Captain Myles Standish, and Mr. Edmond Freeman.[9] Probably Ralph, Sampson, and their father are buried with their squaws in the little Indian graveyard there—one of the very few enclosed and preserved on the Cape.

The complaint brought against Wing and Dillingham by the daughters of Sachem Napoyetan occurred just at the time of King Philip's War and was non-suited, but it was shown that John Wing the Quaker had already built a house on land never sold by their father.[10] An amicable settlement was finally made, however, and Wing and Dillingham acquired title to the disputed land by two deeds of like description, both dated the first of March, 1676. One deed ran from Robin of Mattakeesit and his wife Aquanetva, whose English name was Sarah; the other was from Ralph and Sampson of Nobscusset and their wives Manatotomuske and Penasamuske. The old Sachem Mashantampaine gave his consent to this last deed showing that he was still alive. It was witnessed by Indian Hercules, the Sauquatucket Indian Justice.[11]

This tract became known as Wing's Purchase, and the ranges were run out in the winter of 1678 by John and Thomas Freeman, two sons of Major John, together with Ralph and Sampson of Nobscusset and Robin of Mattakeesit. They blazed the trees on its boundaries across the Cape and back again; and to end all future controversy and make the title clear, the Indians gave possession "by turf and twig" in the good old Saxon manner. Thus the record remains to this day on the books.[12] The old Dillingham House in West Brewster still stands on the land the squatters liked so well.

Jeremiah Ralph, Micah's Grandfather

In the latter years of the sixteen hundreds the old town of Eastham embraced the neck of land in South Orleans stretching easterly between Arey's Pond on the north and the waters of Pleasant Bay on the south. At that period it was called Pota-numi-cut by the Indians whose grandfathers had known it as Ata-cospa. John and Tom Sipson, sons of Quan-tocka-mon, the last hereditary sachems of the once powerful Nawset Tribe,[13] were living on the south side of the river near the pond's outlet and were gathering around them the fast dwindling remnants of the Lower Cape Cod Indians into what was becoming known as the Potanumicut Tribe.

Through the excellent missionary work of Parson Samuel Treat of the Eastham parish, Potanumicut had become the center of the Christian

Indian activities as well as the seat of Indian government. Under his guidance they "sett up a Meeting House—near the Head of Potanumaquitt Salt water pond,"[14] now Arey's Pond, into which he could gather on occasion over five hundred Praying Indians, as they were called, although no Indian for another hundred years was ever persuaded to cross the threshold of a white man's church. The Parson made a practice of calling to his own house once a week "to be further instructed *pro modulo meo*"[15] his four regional Indian preachers; namely, Old Potanomatock from Meeshawn and Ponanakanet down the Cape; John Cussen from over at Monomoyick and his brother Tom Coshanag of the Potanumicut congregation—both of them grandsons of the Old Sagamore; and from Sauquatucket, Manasses the Wolf Hunter, a sharpshooter in Gorham's Rangers. What a sight it would be, could we turn back the years to peek into great-grandma Elizabeth's kitchen and see those four wise old Indians listening respectfully, as they are instructed in the Word of the white man's God *"pro modulo meo."*

Here also in the Potanumicut Indian Village we find Jeremiah Ralph, the grandfather of Micah Rafe, already a member of the Sachem's Council—or Head Men as the whites called them—and a leader among the Praying Indians. Though I have never yet dug up a document saying in so many words he was the son of Ralph of Nobscusset, my knowledge of Indian customs and the history of his own life leave no doubt whatever in my mind. To the best of my knowledge, he was the first Indian bearing the name of Ralph mentioned in the Lower Cape records after Ralph of Nobscusset. Unquestionably he was named Jeremiah for his uncle Jeremy Robin, the well known Indian minister of Mattakeesit, the husband of Manatotomuske's sister Aquanetva. His birth occurred somewhere about 1670-1675, which was during the child-birth period of Manatotomuske's life. His wigwam stood next to that of Sachem John Sipson into whose family he had almost certainly married. According to the prevailing custom of that day this could not have happened unless he himself had been of royal Indian blood. Neither would he have been made one of the Sachem's Council and presented hundreds of acres of land in the Sipson sachemry simply because of "love and good will," as the records state.

In an old Town Book under date of January 27, 1694, may still be found "The mark of the cattle of Jeremy Ralph, Indian of Eastham,"[16] Potanumicut, as I have said still lying within the jurisdiction of Eastham township. That he owned cattle with the rights to pasturage in the Commons of the settlers—General Fields as they were known—indicates that he was recognized as a man of substance and standing by his white neighbors; and his life history bears this out.

He and Que-que-quanset were given Power of Attorney in 1698 by several of their neighbors who spoke of them as their "Trusty and well-beloved friends."[17] Sachem John Sipson mentions "ye lands of jerimi Ralph on ye westerly side" of Seanascot Cedar Swamp in a deed to John Rogers in 1704[18] and simply "because of love and good Will" presented him in 1707 with 100 acres bordering on the shore of Cliff Pond from Flying Beach, the Poconepoys of the Indians, to Grassy Nook their Mornoomanset, and stretching southerly to Race Pond which still bears the Ralph family name in corrupted form.[19]

In the year 1711 the Potanumicut sachems with the consent of the tribe made a blanket sale of all their unsold Indian land south and west of South Orleans, which became known as The Seventeen Share or Sipson Purchase.[20] They reserved only a few acres on which to live and the privilege of peeling bark, cutting firewood, and certain other rights of value to the Indians. When the sachems a year later, without consulting the tribe at all, deeded these reserved privileges to the white proprietors, an immediate protest arose from the Head Men of the Potanumicuts.[21]

For an Indian to attempt the recovery of something already in the possession of a white man was no simple undertaking. This group, nevertheless, while agreeing that the sachems had made the original sale with the full consent of the tribe, claimed that it had never consented to the sale of the reserved rights and privileges. When the proprietors were finally forced to return 100 acres to the Indians in lieu of the reserved privileges, Jeremiah Ralph, together with Jabez Jacob, John Tom, Richard Attamon and Thomas Quanset signed the Agreement on behalf of the tribe on February 28, 1715.[22] In following out the lives of these five, known as the Privileged Indians, I have found that they were all extremely able and intelligent men. Three out of the five, even at that early date, signed the Agreement in their own handwriting, and in after years Jabez Jacob and John Tom became ministers of the Gospel.

Jeremiah's share in the allotted land, at least the greater part of it, never fell into the hands of the white men until long after the last Ralph was dead. Some of it bordered on what later became my father's cow pasture and in my boyhood went by the name of The Injin Land. Old men then living could remember when it was in fact Indian land, and the property was not sold until I was eleven years old.[23]

Besides having become a large land owner by 1720 Jeremiah appears to have been accepted by the white men as a full partner in the lucrative whale fishery. Among the names of such men as Edward and Joshua Bangs, John and Samuel Sears, David Smith and Benjamin Myrick when laying claim to a "larg whail fish which was on shore at or near a place called Green's Harbor," that of Jeremiah Rafe, Indian, stands out as an equal.[24] In 1723 he was chosen to serve on the Coroner's Jury at the drowning of Israel Moses in Eastham.[25] An interesting old account against "jerima raf," kept by Samuel Mayo between 1723 and 1725, lists powder and shot, shoes, even a house, and some wood. By December 31, 1725, he had nearly squared the debt, for we read "I Jeremiah Ralph Reconed with Samuel Mayo and to balance between us there remains due from me to sd Mayo fifteen shillings and three pence."[26] But as late as 1737 he is occasionally mentioned as though still alive and until 1738 his son Jeremiah continued to be referred to as Junior.[27] On April 3, 1738, a court paper concerning a Hallett family row over Yarmouth lands speaks of Jeremiah the younger without the title for the first time.[28] It is quite likely his father had passed away not long before that date.

Micah Rafe's Father, Micah Ralph

From testimony given in a Kenrick-Mayo boundary dispute we learn that Joshua and Jeremiah Ralph, Jr. were brothers, the sons of Jeremiah, Sr., Micah Rafe's grandfather. Joshua testified that he lived on the land where his father's wigwam stood—just below Arey's Pond—and that he and his brother Jeremiah dug a ditch and built a fence on the disputed fourteen acre lot which adjoined it.[29] But we have to wait for Jeremiah, Jr., to kill a man before we discover that they had a brother named Micah.[30] Had Jeremiah, Jr., set one more fence on debatable ground or fought another duel to the death we might now have a complete family tree of the Ralphs.

Joshua married Betty Quason, the granddaughter of Old Sagamore Mattaquason, and died before Apr. 5, 1748, when William Bourne of Barnstable was appointed administrator of his estate.[31] If Jeremiah, Jr., who was of age before 1719,[32] ever had a wife or children, I have never seen a record of it. On the 11th of November, 1732, when he brought his whaleboat in to the Point-o'-Rocks in Brewster and hauled her up for the winter just below John Freeman's warehouse, he was a boatsteerer in the employ of Captain Edmond Freeman.[33] Captain Freeman's boatsteerers were the pick of the whaleboatmen and sailed on a good lay. His credit stood high at the Freeman warehouse and although it was strictly against the law to sell liquor to the Indians, prohibition worked much the same in 1732 as it did a couple of hundred years later. Before he and his two shipmates, Jacob Jacob and Isaac Attaman, struck out across the Cape for Potanumicut and home, young Jeremiah bought a quart or more of rum; and as that rum was the immediate cause of putting on record the identity of Micah Ralph, Sr., Micah Rafe's father, here is a brief digest of the events which followed, taken directly from the Court records.[34]

As the Indians journeyed they drank, and according to Attaman—the only eye-witness—Jeremiah commenced to get quarrelsome, arguing angrily with Jacob about a loan he claimed to have made him. When they reached Flying Beach at the east end of Cliff Pond, they went down on the white sands to fight it out and "Jeremiah struck—Jacob down, who commenced to make a choking sound in his throat—and tried to crawl away." When Isaac remonstrated Jeremiah turned on him and beat him until he could scarcely stand, but he managed to drag Jacob off the beach and rushed to a neighboring house to "fech fire" as the record quaintly states. By the light of the fire they could see Jacob's "clothes was exceeding blody," and Jeremiah, sobered by the enormity of his act, said "he would go and call help to get Jacob home for he was afraid Jacob wold dy and he shold be hanged." Attaman said he too was afraid "Jacob wold dy before anybody came back—he bled so much." It was "neer day" before help came; and then into the little circle of firelight rode Micah Ralph, Sr., on horseback. After they failed to get him onto the horse because "he was too weak and faint and full of pain," Micah went back for more help and long after daylight "many Indians came with him and carried Jacob away."

Poor Jacob lingered on for only a few days. A Coroner's Jury, four of whom were Indians, decided that he came to his death "by a stab—in ye left side of his Brest a little belo his collar bone." It began to look as if Jeremiah's fear of being hanged might indeed come true. When the jury returned a verdict of manslaughter, his attorney, James Otis, moved that his client be given the benefit of clergy. The Good Book was placed in his hands, he read his "clergy" and was "branded on the brawn of his right thumb," after which by paying the costs of the court he was set free. In 1744 he enlisted in Captain Elisha Doane's Company for the siege of Louisburg, from which he never returned.

Micah Ralph, Sr., testified "that about eleven of the clock in the night after the eleventh day of November, 1732," his brother Jeremiah Ralph, Jr., came to his house and told him about the fight. Thus we learn without question that Micah Ralph, Sr., was the brother of Jeremiah Ralph, Jr., and therefore the son of the first Jeremiah Ralph. His wigwam stood a short distance north of Baker's Tar Kiln Meadow in South Orleans near the Second Potanumicut Indian Meeting House, which was on the little knoll where the residence of the late Arthur Sparrow now stands. Both were on part of his father Jeremiah's share of the Privileged Indians' lands. His house is definitely pinpointed in a deed from Edward Kenrick to his son Jonathan in 1739.[35]

After the active part Micah Ralph, Sr., took in bringing home his brother's victim and his straight-forward testimony in the trial which followed I have not found him mentioned again in the records except for the reference to his house until the year 1745. That was during the War of the Austrian Succession in Europe and the bloody hostilities which flared up as a result between the New England settlers and the French and Indians of Canada. Our Indians had always fought on the side of the New Englanders in these old wars with the French-Canadians and they now flocked to the colors in greater numbers than usual owing to the increasing difficulty of getting a living in the old Indian way. Micah Ralph, Sr., enlisted for service in the forces of Brigadier Waldo and was mustered into Gorham's Rangers, a company of Indian and white Cape Cod whaleboatmen, one of whom was my great-great-grandfather Stephen Nickerson. They were as tough a bunch of fighting men afloat or ashore as our modern Marines and had always been under the command of a Gorham since the days of King Philip's War in 1675.

Whether he was killed in action or died of camp fever, which was very prevalent among the troops, I have never learned; but his name appears next in 1748 on the Barnstable County Records which are fairly glutted with the accounts of army wages due to the estates of Indians who had given their lives under the English flag. From Potanumicut alone, now a part of Old Harwich, besides that of Micah Ralph, Sr., were listed the name of Nathan Quoy, William Ned, Isaac James, Jr., Eben Cowett, David Moses, and the two other Ralphs, Samuel and Joseph.

Letters of Administration and Power of Attorney were issued by the Court to Mr. Samuel Knowles on the 23rd of July, 1748, empowering him to collect and distribute the wages of Micah Ralph, Sr., and his buddies who failed to return. It would seem from the records that Mr. Knowles took good care of himself and his Court friends in the distribution. He charged five pounds apiece for his own "time and trouble in Gitting" every dead soldier['s] wages, the Registrar was allowed three pounds five shillings for jotting down the few brief words required by law for each one, and the Honorable Judge one pound apiece for sitting to hear the returns. Micah's inventory showed "wages which was received from Brigadier Waldo" amounting to thirty-six pounds ten shillings. What was left, "the Ballance due ye Estate," namely, twenty-seven pounds, five shillings and seven pence, was finally allotted to the widow "to support hirself and family and Small children."[36]

Micah Rafe Himself

One of these children was Micah Rafe, probably only a little papoose in his father's wigwam on the night his uncle Jeremiah came there for help after the fight at Cliff Pond. By the time of his father's death in

1748 he must have been a grown boy because on the 9th of July, 1753, he filed with the Chatham Town Clerk his intentions of marriage to Hosey Stephen.[37]

Before we take up the story of his own life, however, let us check back on his ancestry to see why there is every reason to believe he was a full blooded Indian. In the first place there can be no doubt at all that his great-great-grandparents, Napoyetan and Mashantampaine, and their squaws, as well as his great-grandparents, Ralph of Nobscusset and his wife Manatotomuske, were pure bloods. Of course that also certifies Jeremiah Ralph, his grandfather, and if, as I feel certain, Jeremiah married a daughter of the Sipson sachems before 1694, there can be little question of her descent, the Indians not having begun to cross with the Negroes until after that date. Micah himself would have known had there been the least taint in either his father or mother-or for that matter in that of his grandparents. Had they been of mixed blood, I am certain he would never have been so proud of himself as Indian Man nor have led my people, who knew him so well, to believe he was a full blood.

It may also be well to recall into what sort of Indian life he was born and in which he was destined to live. Since the death of Parson Treat the change in the Lower Cape Indians had been almost unbelievable. They loved and respected him so deeply that when he died during the Great Snow of 1717 they begged for the privilege of digging through the drifts and bearing his body to its grave. But with his restraining influence gone the sale of liquor increased by leaps and bounds, leading Governor Hinckley to comment that it "was a great obstruction in bringing them to civility" because of "their appetite for rum and the English selling it to them." The young women and the widows left by the inroads of rum and war intermarried more and more with the Negro slaves of the settlers. To distinguish them from the few remaining full blooded Indians their offspring became known locally as Negro-men and Negro-women, sometimes even as black-men or black-women.[38]

The old tribal rule of the sachems, guided by the voice of the people as expressed through their Councils, had broken up long ago. The ancient villages were becoming mostly deserted except for a few degenerate and squalid halfbreed beggars, despised by the whites and even unable to produce their own kind. The best of the survivors had trickled westward to Mashpee or on to Gay Head where their descendants may be found to this day. With the death of John Ralph, the last Potanumicut preacher, who I suspect was Micah's brother, Micah Rafe saw the closing forever of the last Indian Meeting House on Lower Cape Cod. In my boyhood its doorstone, worn smooth by the feet of hundreds of Praying

Micah Rafe's Ancestors 1595-1816

1

SACHEM IYANNO of Mattakeese, now Yarmouth. Born circa 1595. Wife unknown. Welcomed Pilgrims to his village in 1621 when 26 years old. May have been forefather of Micah Rafe. Said to have died in Indian up-rising in 1623, which I doubt.

2

SACHEM NEPOYETAN of Matta-keese. Born circa 1620? Wife unknown. In 1639 he was sachem over Iyanno's lands, "as his own proper inheritance," hence may have been son or brother. Dead before 1676.

3

MANATOTOMUSKE their daughter. Born before 1655. Of legal age by 1676. Married Ralph of Nobscusset. Died after 1680.

1

SACHEM MASHANTAMPAINE of Nobscusset, now Dennis. Born circa 1600? Wife unknown. Had two sons, Sampson and Ralph. Died after 1676.

2

RALPH of Nobscusset their son. Born before 1650. Younger brother of Sampson who succeeded his father as sachem. Married Manatotomuske. Died after 1680.

4-3

JEREMIAH RALPH of Potanumicut, now South Orleans, their son. Born circa 1670. I believe he married into the Sipson family of the Nawset sachemry. Distinguished as one of the tribal Head Men and of the Privileged Indians. Died circa 1735.

5-4

MICAH RALPH, Sr., of Potanumicut, their son. Born circa 1700. Wife unknown. Father of Micah Rafe. Soldier in Governor Shirley's War. Died or killed in the service. Estate settled 1748.

6-5

MICAH RAFE of Askaonkton, now part of East Harwich. Born circa 1730. Married Hosey Stephen. Lived and died just above the Wading Place, on north bank of old Monomoyick River. Last full blooded Indian on Lower Cape Cod. Left no descendants. Will probated 18 March 1816.

His Wife's Ancestors 1600-1800

1

The OLD SAGAMORE, Mattaquason of Monomoyick, now Chatham and East Harwich. Born circa 1600. Wife unknown. Headquarters around Head of Pleasant Bay, Crow's Pond and Ryder's Cove. Died 1682/1683.

────────────

2

SARAH MASKUCK of Cotchpinicut, now Old Harbor, Chatham, their daughter. Married Stephen, alias Maskuck before 1668. Both dead before 1689.

────────────

3

STEPHEN MORTAQUIT of Cotchpinicut, their son. Born circa, 1668. Wife unknown. Of age by 1689. Dead before 1720.

────────────

4

STEPHEN STEPHEN of Askaonkton, their son. Born by 1695. Married Sarah Jethro about 1715. Left her a widow with 6 small children when he died in small pox epidemic 1730.

1

SACHEM NICKANOOSE of Nantucket. Born by 1634. Wife unknown. The Great Sachem of Nantucket. Died circa 1677.

────────────

2

CAPTAIN JOSHUA JETHRO of Askaonkton. Born before 1654. I believe he married into the Quason family of the Monomoyick sachemry. Noted Indian captain in Gorham's Rangers under Maj. Benjamin Church. Died just before 17 May, 1722.

────────────

3

SARAH JETHRO of Askaonkton, their daughter. Born circa 1700. Married Stephen Stephen. Dead before 1755.

5-4

HOSEY STEPHEN of Askaonkton, their daughter. Born just before 1730. Married Micah Rafe 1753. Last descendant of The Old Sagamore on the Monomoyick tribal lands, and last full blooded Indian woman on the Lower Cape. Left no descendants. Will probated 29 March, 1800.

Indians, was doing duty as the doorstep to Squire John Kenrick's South Orleans Post Office.

By 1770, after the last Indian had disappeared from Wellfleet, the town disposed of its remaining Indian land.[39] Only one halfbreed family was left by 1792 in Truro where an old lady could remember when there were so many little Indian children in school that they used to "crow it" over the whites, as she put it.[40] By 1800 the old Potanumicut village had dwindled to four halfbreeds huddled in one wigwam and by the time of Micah's death in 1816 it could truly be said that the Lower Cape Indians had been wiped from the face of the earth.

Long before I ever saw a written record of either Micah Rafe or his wife Hosey I knew their names and where their house stood. She was remembered as very short of stature, industrious and hospitable, and noted for her cheerfulness and kindliness by her neighbors. The Stephen family to which she belonged was the last of Old Sagamore Mattaquason's blood to cling to the Monomoyick Country, and she was the last of her family. The line of her descent is fully documented, thanks to the squabbles of the white men over Indian lands. The Old Sagamore's daughter Sarah who married Stephen, alias Maskuck, about 1670[41] had three sons, one of whom named Stephen, alias Mortaquit, had a son Stephen Mortaquit, alias Stephen Stephen.[42] Stephen Stephen married Sarah Jethrow, the daughter of Captain Joshua Jethrow, before 1722[43] and died in the Indian plague of 1730,[44] leaving a number of small children, among whom was Hosey.

Hosey's maternal grandfather, Captain Joshua Jethrow, better known to the whites as Cap'n Jeethro, a noted Indian captain in the early French and Indian Wars, was the son of Sachem Nickanoose of Nantucket. Between 1690 and 1696 he led an Indian group in Gorham's Rangers under Major Benjamin Church against the French-Canadians in the Canadian Provinces.[45] It is likely he married into the Monomoyick Sachemry about this time because, when peace was declared we find that he was deeded land bordering the north bank of old Monomoyick River by the grandsons of Sagamore Mattauquason.[46] Here he settled down for life, evidently becoming as good a farmer as fighter because the hundred acre tract on which his wigwam stood and where Micah Rafe and Hosey were to end their days soon came to be known as Cap'n Jeethro's Farm. In order to establish beyond question that Micah actually lived where my people said he did, I have traced the history of Cap'n Jeethro's Farm from the date he bought it in 1697 until the death of Micah himself in 1816.

Joseph Nickerson, son of the pioneer William who settled the town of Chatham, bought a large tract and built a home on the north shore of old Monomoyick River, the dividing line between Chatham and Harwich. On the east it abutted Cap'n Jeethro's Farm as is shown by a deed to his son in 1709.[47] When the surviving heirs of the Old Sagamore sold what is practically now the whole town of Harwich to the sixteen white proprietors in 1711, they reserved out of it fifty acres adjoining "joshua Jethros his land next to ye Wading Place."[48]

After the old warrior went to his final Hunting Ground in 1722, his farm fell to his three children: a son Joshua; a daughter, the wife of Samuel Crook; and Hosey's mother Sarah, the wife of Stephen Stephen. A division of the property in 1724 gave the northerly two-thirds to the two daughters and the southerly third to the son Joshua.[49] Joshua's third embraced the spring and the gully where Micah Rafe[']s house later stood, undoubtedly the site of old Cap'n Jeethro's wigwam and his son Joshua's after him.

It is likely Hosey's mother died soon after Micah and Hosey were married in 1753 because in 1755 Micah wrote Judge Borne [Bourne] that he wished a division of the land on which he and Sam Crook lived—that is, the northerly two-thirds of the farm owned jointly by their wives. I have before me a copy of the reply the good Judge sent to Thomas Freeman, Justice of the Peace for the Indians and a great-grandfather of mine. It says in part: "If Sam'l continues obstinate he will expose himself to great charge and trouble, pray tell him so from me, and that this is not merely to friton him to his duty but he shall soon feel as well as fear, if he chooses it." A postscript adds that in case he stands out, "to sue him and then Ralph will have his own half and Sam's half for the charge of the bill."[50]

When young Joshua Jethro's wife Esther died the 22nd of March, 1744, one of the Coroner's Jury at the inquest was Micah's uncle Jeremiah Ralph—the same Jeremiah whose hand had been branded for the killing at Cliff Pond twelve years earlier.[51] Joshua himself probably died not long after 1757 because that year he was whaling out of Billingsgate with his brother-in-law, Sam Crook [52] and the following year his wigwam site turns up in the possession of Elisha Linnell, who transferred it to Nathan Young on the 17th of July, 1758.[53] On the 19th of November, 1760, he in turn deeded it to John Arey, from whom Micah Rafe bought it for twenty dollars March 13, 1769.[54] It is my guess Joshua had given Linnell a deed to it as security for a debt and that Micah finally had it deeded back to him with a clear title. After 1769 Micah and Hosey made their home on this coveted riverside site.

In 1772 Micah filed a petition with the General Court seeking to get the rights inherent in the original deed of 1697 from the Monomoyick sachems to Cap'n Joshua Jeethro. He stated that his wife, "hosea," was the Cap'n's granddaughter and now the only living heir.[55] The Courts' answer in 1774 was that Micah had rights to thirty acres, fifteen in his own name and fifteen in right of his wife and that "she hath in reversion a right to all of the said sixty acres."[56] This made them at last sole owners of the original Cap'n Jeethro's Farm on the old Monomoyick River at Askaonkton.

In Micah's day the mouth of the river lay open to Pleasant Bay, which once went by the same name as the river.[57] The ancient Wading Place Path of the Indians from Cotchpinicut in North Chatham on its way to Nauset and down the Cape crossed on the sands at the mouth of the river at Askaonkton just below the present Harwich-Chatham causeway on Route 28.[58] The causeway still goes by the name of Wading Place Bridge, a name I hope Cape Codders will never forget.

Then, as now, the river wound down between steep moss-covered banks, topped with wind-blown beach-plum trees and stippled with the bronze green of the savin. Lush sedges edged its shores save here and there where a sandy canoe-beach made a landing place. No earth-filled highway bridge shut out the flow of the harbor tides; since the days of the glacier the cold waters of the North Atlantic had poured in twice in every twenty-four hours to keep it sweet and clean.

The country roundabout Micah's house, stretching up river and over the hills around the Head of the Bay, was once the headquarters of the Monomoyick Tribe in the days when Hosey's great-great-grandfather Mattaquason was the Old Sagamore of all the Lower Cape Indians.[59] Over around Crow's Pond and Ryder's Cove in Chathamport the kitchen middens where their wigwams once stood may still be traced except where they have been carted away for building roads or obliterated by the inexorable hand of the archaeologist. Until the coming of the white man this was a favorite region with the Indians. Fish filled the streams; clams, quahogs, and oysters crowded the sands, and mouldering deer bones in the shell heaps bear witness that venison was plentiful. Fruitful cornfields, rich with fertilizer from the spring herring-run, stretched back from tide-water and vied with the bean, the squash, and tobacco. Veritably this was a land flowing with Indian milk and honey.

Micah's house cuddled into the bank a short distance up stream from the Wading Place, where the warmth of the winter's sun struck full upon it and the summer's sou'wester, called the Sowanisha by some Indians, swept cool across it down the valley of the Monomoyick. A boiling-spring of sweet water[60] bubbled up through the white sands at the foot of the bank, and a gully leading down to it from the housespot above still scores the face of the bank. Old deeds say that here "the creeturs" went down to drink, but countless generations of moccasined feet used that path long before the creatures of a white man ever saw it.

Many interesting Indian relics have been recovered from the site of his house. Skillfully wrought pottery work, implements of the chase, bones of the long extinct Great Auk, teeth of the bear, and bones of the deer and seal are mute reminders of a forgotten past. One of the most fascinating is an ancient bone comb something like those over which Spanish ladies draped their mantillas. About eight inches long by two wide and possibly an eighth of an inch thick, it was found buried six feet deep in ashes and charcoal.[61]

When my grandfather showed me this spot over sixty-five years ago—it is now 1960—it was marked simply by a slight dip in the ground perhaps ten feet across by three feet deep. This was before the archaeologists began their investigations. I was told Micah was no "wigwam Indian" but lived in an English-built house, framed, boarded, and shingled, with a smoke-hole in the roof. Probably he kept his fire Indian fashion on a hearth in the center of the floor under the smokehole. I never saw a scrap of brick, stone, or mortar there to indicate there was a chimney. The dip in the earth suggested that he may have had a little old round Cape Cod cellar laid up with logs.

The last "wigwam Indian" in these parts was Isaac James, better known to my people as Isaac *Jeems*, a cousin of Micah's wife Hosey, the son of Wa-he-na-nun and her husband Little James. His wigwam stood at Wequasset in East Harwich on the west side of Round Cove just above the Town Landing. It was Quanset-hut-shaped with a smoke-hole in the roof, framed with bent saplings, covered and lined with flag mats, and thatched with peeled cedar bark and rushes. Early settlers remarked that but for the smoke which couldn't get out and the fleas that didn't want to, these Indian houses were snugger and warmer than their own first cabins.

When Wahenanun, a granddaughter of The Old Sagamore, and her brothers made their blanket sale to the Harwich Proprietors in 1711, she reserved this campsite for herself and her heirs, together with the right to peel bark and gather flags and rushes from the neighboring cedar swamps.[62] Isaac's only child, a son, was a casualty in the old French and Indian Wars [63] and the property fell to Micah and Hosey after Isaac's death. They later sold it to my great-grandfather,[64] and the spot was still known as "Isaac Jeem's Wigwam" when I was born almost within a stone's throw of it.

Wahenanun, Isaac's mother, is one of the four Indian women on Lower Cape Cod of whom I have documentary proof as to what their menfolk called them in their native tongue around their own campfires. It is noteworthy that all four were closely linked with the life story of Micah Rafe: Manatotomuske, his great-grandmother; her two sisters,

Penasamuske and Aquanetva, alias Sarah; and his wife's cousin Wahenanun.[65] It seems a pity that out of the hundreds of sweet-sounding names of the Indian women and maidens only these four were saved in the records. Surely Indian Aquanetva sounds as well to the English ear as Hebrew Sarah.

From their doorway Micah and Hosey looked out on scenes rich in memories of their people. Tales of outstanding events in the lives of their forefathers had always been told and retold around the tribal campfires until they became unwritten Indian history, passed along by word of mouth from one generation to the next, just as my grandfather told me what he knew about Micah Rafe. I am sure these last Indians treasured in their hearts more Cape Cod Indian lore than we can ever learn from printed book and written record. Not far away over the hills lay Stage Harbor in Chatham, the Saquanset of the Indians, where the first blood of Hosey's people was spilled by the whites in 1606 when Champlain sailed away leaving half a dozen Monomoyicks and two of his own men dead on the shore. Downstream below the Wading Place was The Bay where Captain Thomas Dermer, the first white man of record to set foot on its shores, made a landing at "Manamock" in 1619 and was nearly wiped out by the Monomoyick sachem and his men, very likely Hosey's great-great-grandfather, the Old Sagamore himself. The very next year Mattaquason undoubtedly watched from the top of his Monamesset— the Great Point of today in Chathamport—as the Pilgrim's *Mayflower* turned on her heel off-shore and headed back for The Landing.

Two years later Squanto piloted Governor Bradford in over the Bars to "Manamoyack Bay" and up to the Monomoyick headquarters around its Head. Bradford tells us that the famous Indian fell sick and died there and was given a Christian burial, perhaps in the very burial ground in which Micah and Hosey sleep. When, in 1626, the little *Sparrow Hawk* pounded in over the Bars of the "blind harbour that lyes about the midle of Mana-moyake Bay," Bradford came down again, repaired the damages, bought corn for the half-starved passengers, and rounded up the seamen gone AWOL with the handsome Indian maidens. She was about ready to sail when another gale caught her and piled her up a total loss, directly across The Bay in sight of my boyhood home. She sanded up, the sedge grew over her, and the spot became known as The Old Ship Lot to the mowers. Eventually it fell into the possession of Micah Rafe and was known as Mike's Hummock.

There was no white settlement between Bass River and Eastham until 1664, when my immigrant ancestor William Nickerson came down over the Indian trail, later known as the Monomoyick Cartway, and built his cabin beside the wigwam of The Old Sagamore. Little could they have guessed that in so few years the house of the last Indian Man on the Lower Cape, just across the river to the north, would be standing alone among the homes of the English settlers. Among such surroundings Micah Rafe passed the evening of his life, a fit setting for the final days of the Last Indian.

Not long after Micah and Hosey were settled in their home on the old campsite by the river, Elnathan Eldredge married Dorothy Freeman and moved into his new house at Wequasset,[66] built on land which was deeded to one of her forefathers to square a debt of two pounds five shillings owed his father Major John Freeman by "Jno Quason of Monomoy, Indian Sachem Deceased."[67] This was Sachem John Quason Towsowet, son of the Old Sagamore, the father of Wahenanun, and brother of Hosey's great-grandmother Sarah Maskuck. Incidentally, this piece of land has never been owned to this day except by an Indian or my people.

After Elnathan's father, Ebenezer, a miller in Chathamport, died, Elnathan moved the mill across The Bay and set it up anew on top of the high hill just to the northeast of Round Cove. As a boy I played among its rotting timbers over a hundred years later, but its nether millstone which once ground Micah's corn still does duty on the very same spot as a doorstep to Wequasset Inn.

Elnathan was as good at bookkeeping as at grinding his grist, and I am proud that his hand-made account book in which he kept careful reckoning of his debts and credits with Micah Rafe was preserved and handed down to me, his great-great-grandson. From it we glean a little insight into the activities of the last old Indian. Elnathan, being a cobbler as well as a miller, made shoes for Micah and his household, together with leathern bands for his cattle which drank from the spring at the foot of the gully "where the creeturs go down to drink," according to the old deeds. Among the other items noted we find such articles as homespun cloth for the Indians' shirts and dresses, which must have come from the spinning wheel of great-great-grandma Dorothy.

Little if any cash passed between them for all this traffic. Sometimes the bill ran as high as thirty-five dollars old tenor—a lot of money in those days—but it was always paid. Credits, such as "reping an acre of rie" or "squawing hay from the flats" were common—perhaps from Micah's own Mike's Hummock down The Bay.[68] One account was squared by "One seduck which waid 3 pounds and a half" and another by "100 pomkings," showing that Cap'n Jeethro's farm was still living up to its name.

I can see them now: the dusty miller, blue-eyed, red-faced and huge of frame as were all the early Saxon Eldreds, one hand in the hopper and the other in the till, bartering with the shrewd, black-eyed old Indian who had learned long since to buy goods by the span of his own right hand rather than the short-thumbed span of the white man.

His family, besides Hosey and himself, consisted of Hannah Moses and her little boy Isaac born in their house, as both the Rafes were so careful to state in their wills. I am not certain Micah and his wife ever had any children of their own although the Rev. Mr. Stiles reported in 1762 that they may have had "perhaps two boys" living with them.[69] If this was true and these were their own, then they probably died before little Isaac Moses was born, because he was the only youngster there after 1770. Perhaps that was why they loved him so dearly even though he had a taint of black Moses blood in his veins.[70]

Micah Rafe owned several large tracts of land in the Harwiches, Orleans and Brewster. I have already mentioned the salt-marsh across The Bay from my boyhood home known as Mike's Hummock.[71] There was also a wood-lot near the head of Long Pond in East Harwich,[72] four acres "in the head of Skaket general field" where his grandfather Jeremiah used to pasture his cattle,[73] as well as his inherited rights in the Privileged Indian property, and through his wife all her reversionary rights to the remaining Monomoyick lands. After the death of Isaac James the Wequasset lot known as Isaac Jeem's Wigwam also fell to him along with Isaac's burial place.

Two moss-grown boulders beside the Wading Place Path, just over the hill to the northwest of the site of Isaac James's wigwam, marked his grave and undoubtedly that of his mother Wahenanun. In the top of the larger one were two curious cup-shaped holes which tradition said were the result of Indian squaws' pounding with pestles as they sat and grieved for their dead.[74] On my way to school along this Wading Place Path I often added my irreverent bit to the holes on that boulder, which then stood among a dozen or more old fieldstones marking the graves of as many Indians, covered today by the fallen leaves of three-quarters of a century.

On the 12th of October, 1798, Hosey made her will, making Micah sole executor and signing by mark. She left to her "Beloved husband, Micah Ralph" during his natural life the improvement of her "Estate, in lands or in any otherwise belonging or coming" to her. Immediately after his decease "all and every part—in any name or nature" was to go to "our beloved friend (born in our house) Isaac Moses, son of Hannah Moses, now and for a long time resident in our house." The will did not come to probate until nearly a year and a half later, on the 29th of March, 1800, and it is probable she lived until not long before that date.[75]

She was the last of The Old Sagamore's descendants to live on the
Monomoyick lands and the last full-blooded Indian woman on the whole
Lower Cape. Two other Indian women outlived her and are sometimes
referred to by historical writers as the "last Indians," but a careful checking of the records shows that neither was a full blood. Beck Crook of
Harwich, the last living heir to the ancient Sauquatucket tribal lands, is
said to have deplored her black skin but trusted God to make her soul
white.[76] Bess Tobey, a direct descendant of the Nawset sachems, was
named in the will of Joshua Hopkins in 1775 as "my Negro woman."[77]

Micah had already sold to Reuben Eldredge in 1793 his remaining
nine acres in the old Ralph land in South Orleans where his father's wigwam and the last Potanumicut Indian Meeting House once stood.[78] On
the 15th of April, 1810, shortly after Hosey died, my great-grandfather
Elnathan Eldredge, Jr., and his brother, sons of the miller, bought his
two-acre "Isaac Jeems's Wigwam" lot at Round Cove in East Harwich,
which had fallen to his wife by reversion on Isaac James' death.[79] Isaac
Moses witnessed Micah's signature to this deed and from this date all
legal papers signed by the old Indian were attested to by him. It is
noticeable, however, that while Micah frequently signed as "Micah
Rafe—Indian Man," Isaac Moses who had a streak of Negro blood never
spoke of himself as an Indian. Isaac lived until after 1738, was an excellent penman, and a violinist of local repute. The fieldstone marking his
grave and that of his wife Nancy alongside the Bay Road was still in place
within my memory.

Micah Rafe was getting along in years and even though Hannah
Moses and young Isaac made his last days as comfortable as they could,
he missed Hosey, who had kept his hearth fire burning for nearly half a
century. On the 7th of July, 1814, he made his will, bequeathing "unto
Isaac Moses—born in my house—all real and personal Estate," with the
request that he "support his mother Hannah Moses—during hir natural
life."[80] On the 10th of December that same year he disposed of part of
his Skaket General Field lot in Orleans to Henry Knowles.[81] The last
transaction of his life, so far as I know, was his sale on May 19, 1815, to
Ensign Nickerson of his salt-marsh known as Mike's Hummock near the
ancient entrance to Pleasant Bay, where the wreck of the Sparrow Hawk
still lay.[82]

Before another spring rolled around he too had gone the way of all his
race. When on the 18th of March, 1816, Isaac Moses presented for probate the "Will of Micah Ralph, late of Harwich" the last chapter of a long
life was closed.[83] Judging from the date of his marriage and other circumstances connected with his life, we know he must have been between
eighty and ninety years old.

Micah Rafe was laid away beside Hosey in the old Indian burying ground at Askaonkton on Cap'n Jeethro's Farm, on the west slope of the first hill on the north side of Bay Road going west from the Wading Place, not far from where they had lived so happily together. My brother Carroll's wife, Mrs. Emogene Nickerson, who was born and grew up almost within a stone's throw of both their house spot and burial place, could remember when their graves were mounded with fieldstones, among which, she said, the spring violets always grew larger and bluer.

Thus the story of Micah Rafe—Indian man comes to a close with no apologies for its errors or incompleteness. It is much less than I would like to give and infinitely less than he deserves. I offer it, however, as a small tribute to the memory of a fine old Red Man. It is my hope that some day my native town will feel moved to place a lasting marker on his moss-grown grave or at the site of his house at Askaonkton on the banks of the old Monomoyick.

It must be a solemn thought for a childless man to know that when his eyes close in death a chain of generations which began when man began is broken. How profoundly more so must it be to know, as Micah knew, that a race is dying with you.

Notes

1. A true copy of Micah Rafe's signature. [The petition or a copy of it is in the National Seashore Archives. Stanley W. Smith wrote Nickerson, February 17, 1933, "I was quite surprised to find our friend, Micah Ralph, popping up with a petition and it seemed to me, a very interesting one."]
2. *Good Newes From New England.* Edward Winslow. [Edward Winslow, *The Story of the Pilgrim Fathers, 1606-1623 A.D.: as told by Themselves, their friends, and their Enemies,* ed. Edward Arber (Boston: Houghton, Mifflin and Co., 1897), 550]
3. In 1798 "land—at Ralph's Pond." Division deed heirs of Moses Higgins. Stanley W. Smith Collection.
4. "northerly of Monomoyick River." Deed March 25, 1696/7 John, Josephus, Samuel, and Joseph Quason to Captain Joshua Jeethro. Photostat my Collection from original in *Mass. State Archives* XXXIII-618/90. Site of Micah's house 100 years later, whose wife was granddaughter of Captain Jeethro.
5. *Mass. Archaeological Society Bulletin.* July 1958. ["The Old Sagamore," 65.]
6. Freeman's *Cape Cod,* 1-161. [Frederick Freeman, *The History of Cape Cod: The Annals of the Thirteen Towns of Barnstable County* (Boston: W. H. Piper and Co., 1869), 1: 160, not 161.]
7. "Napoatan Indian Sachem, deceased," circa 1656 *Indian Wars of New England.* H. M. Sylvester. [Herbert Milton Sylvester, *Indian Wars of New*

England, 3 vols. (Boston: W. B. Clarke Co., 1910), 1: 78. The court date is 2 March 1674. The spelling of the name is "Napoitan."]

8. Swift's *Old Yarmouth,* 31. [Charles F. Swift, *History of Old Yarmouth* (Yarmouth Port: the Author, 1884), 30-31.] Also Freeman's *Cape Cod,* 1-158, 267, 278. [1: 266-67, 1: 277-78, 1: 155-59.]

9. Swift's *Old Yarmouth* 31 [30-31]. Also Freeman's *Cape Cod* 1-158.

10. "John Wing hath built, fenced—lands of Naipotan—not by him sold." *Indian Wars of New England.* H. M. Sylvester. [This is not a direct quotation, only the spirit of the complaint described on page 78.]

11. *Mass. Superior Court of Judicature* 4784, 3491.

12. *Plymouth Colony Deeds* 111-10.

13. "Sons of Quantockamon," *Plymouth Colony Records* V-150. [The records read, "Whereas John Gibson and Thomas Cloake, two Indians soe called, whoe are the reputed sones of Quantockamew, of Pottanumacutt"; later in same paragraph, "John Sibson and Tom."]

14. *Eastham Town Records,* no paging, 1648-1770.

15. In a letter from him to the Rev. Cotton Mather.

16. *Eastham Records* 1648-1770, no paging.

17. *History of Harwich,* 402. Paine. [Josiah Paine, *A History of Harwich: 1620-1800* (Rutland: The Tuttle Publishing Co., Inc., 1937). I also have seen from the Nickerson Collection a copy of the original "letter of Attorney" containing these quoted words which Paine acknowledges as his source.]

18. Original deed 26 April 1704. Stanley W. Smith Collection V-9. [In Sturgis Library, Barnstable, Massachusetts.]

19. Photostat of deed 25 October 1707. Mrs. Hodges Papers, Stanley W. Smith Collection.

20. *Mass. Superior Court of Judicature* 8331. Harwich Proprietors Records.

21. *Ibid. Court* 18544, *ibid.* Records.

22. *Ibid. Court* 15050. Agreement Seventeen Share Proprietors with the Privileged Indians.

23. Sold by Act of the *Mass. State Legislature* of 1891.

24. Testimony of Edward Winslow May 11, 1720. *Mass. Superior Court of Judicature* 14094.

25. *Ibid. Court* 15727. Israel Moses inquest February 2, 1723.

26. Stanley W. Smith Collection, Samuel Mayo Papers.

27. *History of Harwich,* 406. Paine. [On page 406 reference is made to Jeremiah Ralph witnessing a codicil, dated 1730; there is no mention of junior.]

28. "Jeremiah Ralph of full age." *Mass. Superior Court of Judicature* 46037.

29. Joshua Ralph's testimony. *Ibid. Court* 18384.

30. Micah testified "my brother Jeremiah Ralph Jr." *Ibid. Court* 35145.

31. *Barnstable Probate Records* 111-507.

32. "being of full age." *Mass. Superior Court of Judicature* 163481.

33. *Ibid. Court* testimony 34431, 35145.

34. *Mass. Superior Court of Judicature.* Most of the testimony and proceedings in 34431 and 35145.

35. "neer Micah Ralph's house," deed Edward Kenrick to son Jonathan 2 April 1739, also quit-claim from brothers Solomon and Thomas 23 October 1743/4. Stanley W. Smith Collection, Kenrick Papers.

36. "Micah Ralph Indian Man of Harwich lately died intestate." *Barnstable Probate Records* VII-82 and VIII-452/3. Soldier under Brig. Waldo, and settlement of his estate.

37. "Mikiah Ralph and Hose Stephens." Chatham Records, *Mayflower Descendant* XII-28.

38. Bess Tobey, granddaughter of Sachem John Sipson, was called "my Negro Woman" by Joshua Hopkins in his will, 1775.

39. Swift's *Old Yarmouth* 171. [It is not clear from reading this that *all* of the Indians disappeared or that *all* of the land was sold (170-71).]

40. Freeman's *Cape Cod* I-558. [This quotation is not in Freeman's work. It's in Mary Rogers Bangs, *Old Cape Cod The Land: The Men The Sea* (Boston: Houghton Mifflin Co., 1920). It states as many Indian children at school as whites, and the exact quotation is "crow over 'em" (89).]

41. John Cussens testified in 1720 that the Old Sagamore's daughter Sarah married "one Stephen about fifty years ago." *Mass. Superior Court of Judicature* 151919.

42. Stephen Stephen, alias Stephen Mortaquit's own testimony, *Ibid. Court* 151919, 13717, 163529.

43. Division of the Captain's estate. *Barnstable Probate Records* IV-51.

44. Appointment of guardian for children. *Ibid. Records* IV-580/1/2.

45. Mentioned in letter from Lieut. Col. Jno. Gorham to Major Wally, Commissioner for War, dated April 8, 1697. *Mayflower Descendant* VI-184.

46. Deed John, Joseph, Josephus and Samuel Quason to Captain Joshua Jethrow 25 March 1697, land at Askaonkton. Photostat my Collection from original *Mass. Archives* XXXIII-9.

47. "easterly to Joshua Jeethro's land." Deed Joseph Nickerson to son William 5 Nov. 1709. *Mayflower Descendant* VIII-156. [The deed reads "Jethrowes Land."]

48. From Harwich Proprietors' Records. *Mass. Superior Court of Judicature* 144324.

49. Division to Stephen Stephen and others. *Barnstable Probate Records* IV-51.

50. Letter Judge Sylvanus Bourne to Justice Freeman. Original in Stanley W. Smith Collection, facsimile my Collection.

51. Coroner's Inquest, *Mass. Superior Court of Judicature.*

52. Petition of the whalemen. *Mass. State Archives* XXXIII-299.

53. Deed Linnell to Young, *Mayflower Descendant* XVII-173/4.

54. Deed Arey to Micah Rafe, Stanley W. Smith Collection IX-170.

55. Petition to General Court by "Micah Ralph a poor Indian of Harwich." *Mass. State Archives* XXXIII-622.

56. The Court's answer. *Ibid. Court* XXX-624/626.

57. The Sparrow Hawk was wrecked "right before—Manamoyake Bay," Bradford's History of *"Plimoth Plantation"* 262, State edition.

58. "Joshua Jettiros land next to the Wading Place." Quason Reserve deed 7 April, 1712. *Mass. Superior Court of Judicature* 63888.
59. William Nickerson, my immigrant ancestor, built his cabin in 1664 near the wigwam of the Old Sagamore at "Monomoy." It was only a short distance south of where Micah's would stand 100 years later.
60. Cape Codders always called their cool, bubbling springs "boiling springs."
61. Cleon Crowell Collection, along with many other rare relics. [May 11, 1932, Nickerson wrote Crowell, from Florida, requesting that he draw a rough plot of the lay of the land where Micah's house stood. On May 23, 1932, Crowell sent a letter with the drawing. Crowell frequently wrote of his Indian relics. October 20, 1933, he wrote, "I've got an old, old, spoon that I dug out of Micah Ralph site, also a pair of small siccors [scissors] which has been through a fire. We found the bottom of an old skillet too. These pieces may be the *only ones* used by *Micah* & *Hosey* which we can look at today, who knows?"]
62. Deed Quason heirs to the Sixteen Share Proprietors. *Barnstable County Records* VI-38.
63. 1748 *Barnstable Probate Records* VII-82.
64. Deed Micah Ralph to Elnathan Eldredge, Jr., and brother Samuel. *Barnstable Registry of Deeds* Book 1-120. My great-great-grandmother Dorothy (Freeman) Eldredge, great-grandfather Elnathan Eldredge, Jr., grandmother Jane (Eldredge) Nickerson, my father Warren J. Nickerson and I, were all born on land adjoining Isaac Jeems's Wigwam.
65. My friend the late Wm. C. Smith in his *History of Chatham* mentioned that Wahenanun's mother, the wife of Sachem John Quason Towsowet, may have been named Bapanum, but gave no documentation.
66. They were married Oct. 13, 1770. *Harwich Vital Records*. [According to his source they were married 31 October, not 13 October.]
67. Original deed from Young John Quason, son of the sachem, to Thomas Freeman, Aug. 13, 1711. Stanley W. Smith Collection, E. F. Small Papers.
68. "Squawing" was granther's way of spelling *scowing*. The salt hay from the tidal marshes was brought off on wooden flatbottomed scows to cure in the mainland hayfields.
69. History of Harwich, Paine. [Actually, "sons," not "boys" (410).]
70. The Moses Indian family crossed blood very early with the Negro slaves. See my *Lower Cape Cod Indians, Book 2, The Nawsets*. [In National Seashore Archives.]
71. Original deed Micah Ralph to Ensign Nickerson 19 May 1815. Stanley W. Smith Collection, Osborn Nickerson Papers.
72. Deed Isaac Moses to Benjamin Eldredge 27 July, 1838 "formerly land of Micah Rafe's." *Barnstable Registry of Deeds* 111-86.
73. *Ibid. Registry* 1-24. Deed Micah Ralph to Henry Knowles 10 December 1814.
74. Archaeologists tell me these were holes in which the Indians polished their stone sinkers.
75. From Hosey's will. *Barnstable Probate Records* XXX-7 and XXII-25.

76. *History of Harwich*. Paine. [Paine says she was a pure blooded Indian, adding, "Often times in speaking of her loneliness, and the lowly condition of her race, she would brighten up, and express her feelings respecting her condition, and her full belief in the white man's God who, though 'she had a dark skin,' had power to make her soul as white as the snow flakes that fall from heaven" (445).]
77. My *Lower Cape Cod Indians, Book 2. The Nawsets*. [His source was probably "The Will of Joshua Hopkins," *The Mayflower Descendant* (Boston: Massachusetts Society of *Mayflower* Descendants, 1918), 20: 68.]
78. Original deed Micah Ralph to Reuben Eldredge 23 May 1793. Stanley W. Smith Collection X-35.
79. Deed Micah Ralph to Elnathan Eldredge, Jr., and his brother Samuel. *Barnstable Registry of Deeds*, Harwich Book 1-120.
80. Micah's will recorded, *Barnstable Probate Records* XXXII-7.
81. Deed Micah Ralph to Henry Knowles et. als. *Barnstable Registry of Deeds*, Orleans Book 1-24.
82. Original deed Micah Ralph to Ensign Nickerson. Stanley W. Smith Collection, Osborn Nickerson Papers.
83. Micah's will presented, *Barnstable Probate Records* XXX-7.

Bibliography

Alden, Timothy. "Memorabilia of Yarmouth." In *Collections of the Massachusetts Historical Society*, 5: 54-60. Boston: Samuel Hall, 1798.

Alden, Vaughan T. *New England Frontier: Puritans and Indians, 1620-1675*. Boston: Little, Brown and Company, 1965.

Archer, Gabriel and John Brereton. *The Gosnold Discoveries . . . in the North Part of Virginia, 1602 Now Cape Cod and the Islands, Massachusetts*. Edited by Lincoln A. Dexter. Sturbridge: Plaza Printing, 1982.

Arner, Robert D. "The Story of Hannah Duston: Cotton Mather to Thoreau." *American Transcendental Quarterly* (1973): 19-23.

Axtell, James. *Beyond 1492: Encounters in Colonial North America*. New York: Oxford University Press, 1992.

Bangs, Mary Rogers. *Old Cape Cod The Land: The Men The Sea*. Boston: Houghton Mifflin Co., 1920.

Belknap, Jeremy. *The History of New Hampshire*. Dover: S. C. Stevens and Ela and Wadleigh, 1831.

Bender, David L. and Bruno Leone, eds. *Christopher Columbus and His Legacy: Opposing Viewpoints*. San Diego: Greenhaven Press, Inc., 1992.

"Bill of Mortality in the South Parish of Eastham 1772-1828." *The Mayflower Descendant* 9 (1907): 36-39.

Bowman, George Ernest. "Barnstable, Mass., Vital Records." *The Mayflower Descendant* 25 (1923): 130.

———. "The Marriage of Edward Southworth and Alice Carpenter." *The Mayflower Descendant* 10 (1908): 1-2.

———. "The Mayflower Marriage Records at Leyden and Amsterdam." *The Mayflower Descendant* 22 (1920): 62-64.

―――. "Plymouth Colony Vital Records." *The Mayflower Descendant* 18 (1916): 68.

―――. "Plymouth First Church Records." *The Mayflower Descendant* 4 (1902): 212-17.

―――. "The Record of Governor Bradford's Baptism, on the Parish Register at Austerfield." *The Mayflower Descendant* 7 (1905): 65-66.

―――. "The Will of Joshua Hopkins." *The Mayflower Descendant* 20 (1918): 67-69.

Bradford, William. *Bradford's History "Of Plimoth Plantation."* Boston: Wright and Potter Printing Co., State Printers, 1899.

"The Captain of the *Mayflower*." *Cape Codder*, 2 October 1958.

Caverly, Robert B. *Heroism of Hannah Duston, together with the Indian Wars of New England*. Boston: B. B. Russell and Co., 1875.

Chamberlain, Rev. Nathan Henry, ed. *Samuel Sewall and the World He Lived In*. Boston: De Wolfe, Fiske and Co., 1898.

Chapman, Paul H. *Discovering Columbus*. Columbus, Georgia: ISAC Press, 1991.

Chase, George Wingate. *The History of Haverhill, Massachusetts*. Shelburne, Vermont: New England History Press for the Haverhill Historical Society, 1983.

Coleman, Emma Lewis. *New England Captives Carried to Canada: Between 1677 and 1760 During the French and Indian Wars*. 2 vols. Portland: The Southworth Press, 1925.

Cotton, John, Jr. "Diary of Preaching to the Indians on Martha's Vineyard." Collections of the Massachusetts Historical Society.

Crosby, Alfred W., Jr. *The Columbian Exchange: Biological and Cultural Consequences of 1492*. Westport: Greenwood Press, 1972.

Curry, Dorothy Neff. The Descendants of William Neff who Married Mary Corliss January 23, 1665 Haverhill, Massachusetts. Special Collections, Haverhill Public Library, Haverhill, Massachusetts.

"A Description and History of Eastham, in the County of Barnstable. September, 1802." In *Collections of the Massachusetts Historical Society*, 8: 154-86. Boston: Johnson Reprint Corporation, 1802.

The Duston-Dustin Family Thomas and Elizabeth (Wheeler) Duston and their Descendants. Compiled by The Duston-Dustin Family Association Genealogists. Special Collections, Haverhill Public Library, Haverhill, Massachusetts.

"Eastham and Orleans, Mass., Vital Records." *The Mayflower Descendant* 8 (1906): 243.

Eccles, W. J. *France in America*. New York: Harper Torchbooks, 1972.

Freeman, Frederick. *The History of Cape Cod: The Annals of Barnstable County and its Several Towns*. 2 vols. Yarmouth Port: Parnassus Imprints, 1965.

————. *The History of Cape Cod: The Annals of The Thirteen Towns of Barnstable County.* Boston: George C. Rand and Avery, 1862.

Freeman Genealogy. Boston: Franklin Press, Rand, Avery and Co., 1875.

"From 'Plymouth Colony Wills and Inventories,' vol. 3, part 1, pages 2-5." Bowman, George Ernest. "Alice (Carpenter) (Southworth) Bradford's Will and Inventory." *The Mayflower Descendant* 3 (1901): 144.

Fulke, Ed. "Success Story—1880-1952." *Daytona News Journal.* 12 October 1952.

Gathorne-Hardy, G. M. *The Norse Discoverers of America.* Oxford: Clarendon Press, 1970.

Gookin, Daniel. "Gookin's Historical Collections." In *Collections of the Massachusetts Historical Society for the Year 1792,* 1: 143-226. Boston: Munroe and Francis, 1806.

Grant, W. L., ed. *Voyages of Samuel de Champlain 1604-1618.* New York: Charles Scribner's Sons, 1907.

Gray, Edward F. *Leif Eriksson: Discoverer of America A.D. 1003.* New York: Kraus Reprint Co., 1972.

Green, Eugene and William L. Sachse. *Names of the Land: Cape Cod, Nantucket, Martha's Vineyard, and the Elizabeth Islands.* Chester: Globe Pequot Press, 1983.

Heath, Dwight B., ed. *Mourt's Relation A Journal of the Pilgrims at Plymouth.* Chester: Globe Pequot Press, 1963.

Holly, H. H. *Sparrow-Hawk A Seventeenth Century Vessel in Twentieth Century America.* Boston: The Nimrod Press, 1969.

Hovgaard, William. *The Voyages of the Norsemen to America.* New York: American Scandinavian Foundation, 1914.

"How the Fogs Came to the Cape." *Cape Cod Magazine* 1, no. 1 (1915): 15-16.

Huden, John C. *Indian Place Names of New England.* New York: Museum of the American Indian, Heye Foundation, 1962.

Hutchinson, J. R. "The *Mayflower,* Her Identity and Tonnage." In *The New England Historical and Genealogical Register.* 70: 337-42. Boston: The Society, 1916.

Lescarbot, Marc. *The History of New France.* Edited by W. L. Grant. 3 vols. Toronto: The Champlain Society, 1911.

Livermore, Charles W. and Leander Crosby. *The Ancient Wreck, Loss of the Sparrow-Hawk in 1626. Remarkable Preservation and Recent Discovery of the Wreck.* (Anonymous pamphlet.) Boston: Alfred Mudge and Son, 1865.

MacDonough, Rodney. "Phineas Pratt of Plymouth and Charlestown." *The Mayflower Descendant* 4 (1902): 87-98.

Marsden, R. G. "The *Mayflower*." *The Mayflower Descendant* 18 (1916): 1-13.

Mather, Cotton. *Magnalia Christi Americana*. 2 vols. Hartford: Roberts and Burr, 1820.

"The *Mayflower* Marriage Records at Leyden and Amsterdam." *The Mayflower Descendant* 9 (1907): 115-16.

Meinig, D. W. *The Shaping of America: A Geographical Perspective on 500 Years of History*. New Haven: Yale University Press, 1986.

"Micah Rafe." *Bulletin of the Massachusetts Archaeological Society* 22 (January 1961): 17-30.

Mirick, B. L. *History of Haverhill, Massachusetts*. Haverhill, 1832.

Moriarty, G. Andrews Jr. "Notes." *The New England Historical and Genealogical Register*. Boston: The Society, 1929, 83: 250-51.

Morse, Mary Harrower. "Murderess or Heroine?" *The New England Galaxy* 9, no. 4 (spring 1968): 40-5.

Munro, William Bennett. *Crusaders of New France*. New York: U.S. Publishers Association, Inc., 1918.

Nickerson, W. Sears. *The Bay - as I see it*. Published by his daughters, 1981.

———. *Land Ho! - 1620: A Seaman's Story of the Mayflower Her Construction, Her Navigation and Her First Landfall*. Boston: Houghton Mifflin Co., 1931.

———. "Land Ho! - 1620. Pilgrims' Progress Along the Backside of the Cape." *Cape Codder*, 30 May 1957.

———. "Micah Rafe." *Bulletin of the Massachusetts Archaeological Society* 22 (January 1961): 17-30.

———. "The Old Sagamore." *Bulletin of the Massachusetts Archaeological Society* 19 (July 1958): 53-68.

———. "That Bright Dawn When *Mayflower I* First Sighted Cape." *The Sunday Standard Times*.

———. "The Old Sagamore." *Bulletin of the Massachusetts Archaeological Society* 19 (July 1958): 53-68.

Otis, Amos, "An Account of the Discovery of an Ancient Ship on the Eastern Shore of Cape Cod." In *The New England Historical and Genealogical Register*. Boston: The Society, 1864.

Pagden, Anthony. *European Encounters With the New World: From Renaissance to Romanticism*. New Haven: Yale University Press, 1993.

Paine, Josiah. *A History of Harwich Barnstable County Massachusetts 1620-1800 Including The Early History of That Part Now Brewster, With Some Account of its Indian Inhabitants*. Yarmouthport, Massachusetts: Parnassus Imprints, 1971.

Parkman, Francis. *France and England in North America*. 2 vols. New York: The Library of America, 1983.

Plumb, Albert H. *William Bradford of Plymouth*. Boston: Gorham Press, 1920.

Quint, A. H., ed. *Journal of the Rev. John Pike of Dover, New Hampshire*. Collections of the Massachusetts Historical Society, September 1875.

Reeves, Arthur Middleton, ed. *The Finding of Wineland the Good: The History of the Icelandic Discovery of America*. New York: Burt Franklin, 1895.

Reynard, Elizabeth. *The Narrow Land: Folk Chronicles of Old Cape Cod*. Chatham: The Chatham Historical Society, Inc., 1985.

Rowlandson, Mary. *The Narrative of the Captivity and Restoration of Mrs. Mary Rowlandson*. Lancaster, Massachusetts, 1903.

Russell, Howard S. *Indian New England Before the Mayflower*. Hanover: University Press of New England, 1980.

Sale, Kirkpatrick. *The Conquest of Paradise: Christopher Columbus and the Columbian Legacy*. New York: Alfred A. Knopf, 1991.

Salisbury, Neal. *Manitou and Providence Indians, Europeans, and the Making of New England, 1500-1643*. New York: Oxford University Press, 1982.

Sibley, John Langdon. "William Vaughan and William Tufts Jr. at Louisburg, 1745." *New England History and General Register* 25: 376-99.

Simmons, William S. *Spirit of the New England Tribes: Indian History and Folklore, 1620-1984*. Hanover: University Press of New England, 1986.

Smith, Stanley W. "Records of the First Church in Orleans, Formerly the First Church in Eastham, Mass." *The Mayflower Descendant* 14 (1912): 53-56.

Smith, William C. *A History of Chatham Massachusetts*. 4th ed. Chatham: The Chatham Historical Society, Inc., 1992.

Smith, Captain John. *General History of New England: A Description of New England*. Boston: William Veazie, 1865.

"Somerset House Prerogative Court Records," *The Mayflower Descendant* 1 (1899): 230-31.

Sprague, Frank William. *Barnstable Gorhams: The Old House in which they lived, and Their Services in the Colonial Wars*. Boston: the author, 1896.

———. *Col. John Gorham's "Wast Book."* Boston: David Clapp and Son, 1898.

Stackpole, Everett, Lucien Thompson, and Winthrop Meserve. *The History of the Town of Durham, New Hampshire (Oyster River Plantation)*. Town of Durham, 1913.

Stannard, David E. *American Holocaust: Columbus and the Conquest of the New World*. New York: Oxford University Press, 1992.

Stratton, Eugene Aubrey. *Plymouth County Its History and People 1620-1691*. Salt Lake City: Ancestry Publishing, 1986.

Swift, Charles F. *Genealogical Notes of Barnstable Families, Being a Reprint of the Amos Otis Papers*. Barnstable: F. B. and F. P. Goss, 1888.

————. *History of Old Yarmouth*. Yarmouth Port: the author, 1884.

Sylvester, Herbert Milton. *Indian Wars of New England*. 3 vols. Boston: W. B. Clarke Co., 1910.

"Thomas Hinckley to William Stoughton and Joseph Dudley." In *Collections of the Massachusetts Historical Society*. Vol. 5. Boston: John Wilson and Son, 1861.

Thomas, M. Halsey. The Diary of Samuel Sewall 1674-1729. Vol. 1. New York: Farrar, Straus and Giroux, 1973.

Todd, Glenn. Introduction. In *Captivity Narrative of Hannah Duston related by Cotton Mather, John Greenleaf Whittier, Nathaniel Hawthorne, and Henry David Thoreau, four versions of events in 1697, interspersed with thirty-five wood-block prints by Richard Bosman*. San Francisco: Arion Press, 1987.

Ulrich, Laurel Thatcher. *Good Wives: Image and Reality in the Lives of Women in Northern New England 1650-1750*. New York: Alfred A. Knopf, 1982.

Vaughn, Alden T. *New England Frontier: Puritans and Indians, 1620-1675*. Boston, Little Brown and Company, 1965.

Warren, Winslow. "Edward Winslow." *The Mayflower Descendant* 5 (1903): 224-233.

Whitford, Kathryn. "Hannah Dustin: The Judgement of History." In *Essex Institute Historical Collections*. Salem: Essex Institute, 1972.

Wilford, John Noble. *The Mysterious History of Columbus: An Exploration of the Man, the Myth, the Legacy*. New York: Alfred A. Knopf, 1991.

Williams, Roger. *A Key Into the Language of America*. Edited by John J. Teunissen and Evelyn J. Hinz. Detroit: Wayne State University Press, 1973.

Winslow, Edward, *Good News From New England, The Story of the Pilgrim Fathers, 1606-1623 A.D.; as told by Themselves, their Friends, and their Enemies*. Edited by Edward Arber. Boston: Houghton, Mifflin and Co., 1897.

Wood, William. *New England's Prospect*. Edited by Alden T. Vaughan. Amherst: University of Massachusetts Press, 1977.

Yewell, John, Chris Dodge, and Jan DeSirey, eds. *Confronting Columbus: An Anthology*. Jefferson, North Carolina: McFarland and Co., Inc., 1992.

Index

151, 175, 180, 182, 184, 186, 188,
191, 192, 194-96, 203-5, 207-9,
211, 212, 214, 216-18, 221-23,
230, 232, 233, 235-37, 240, 241,
243-46
Haverhill, 39, 108-10, 112, 114-16,
119, 121
Hawthorne, Nathaniel, 109, 110
Hay, Daniel, 60, 61
Heritage Plantation of Sandwich, 145
Highland Light, 79
Hinckley, Governor Thomas, 177
Hobbamock, 167-69
Holland, 10, 11, 15, 38, 39, 91
Hopkins, Giles, 188
Hopkins, Joshua, 188, 192, 241, 244,
246
Hosey, 24, 152, 188, 207, 210-13,
223, 231-42, 245
Huron, 13

I

Indian Ned, 131, 133
Indian Nicholas, 178
Iroquois, 9, 13-15

J

Jacob, Jabez, 182, 184, 227
Jacob, Jacob, 228
James, Isaac, 209, 210, 216, 217, 230,
237, 240, 241
Jeems, Isaac, 131, 133, 146, 147, 209,
210, 237, 241, 245
Jeethro, 131, 211, 212, 234-36, 239,
242, 244
Jethro, Captain Joshua, 213, 233
Jethro, Sarah, 211, 212, 233
Jethrow, Joshua, 234, 244
Jones, Christopher, 11, 71-74, 76, 78,
87

K

Karlsefni, 49
Kenrick, John, 150, 216, 234
Kiehtan, 158, 160-62, 167-69

King George's War, 15, 108
King Philip's War, 173-76, 193, 225,
230
King William's War, 14, 15, 108
Knowles, Richard, 211

L

Leif the Lucky, 8, 43, 45, 48-50, 52
Lescarbot, Marc, 59, 63, 64, 67, 68
Little Robin, 178
Livermore, Charles W., 104, 106
Long Cove, 176, 180, 185, 195, 212,
223
Louisbourg, 6, 7, 15, 16, 107, 108,
123, 130, 131, 133

M

Manasses, 178, 180, 181, 226
Manatotomuske, 178, 212, 219,
224-26, 231, 232, 237
Martha's Vineyard, 151, 159, 170,
174, 178, 190
Mashpee, 23, 36, 37, 41, 158, 172-74,
181, 185-88, 213, 231
Maskuck, Sarah, 233, 239
Maskuck, alias Stephen, 211
Mather, Cotton, 88, 93, 109, 110,
180, 243
Mattaquason of Monomoyick, 6, 25,
165, 166, 177, 188, 193, 195, 233
Maushope, 36, 135, 136, 157, 158,
160-63
May, Dorothy, 90, 91
Mayflower, 8-11, 16, 17, 22, 23, 30,
31, 35, 38, 41, 43, 44, 51, 61,
69-88, 91-94, 97-99, 120, 138,
139, 143, 152, 168, 183, 188, 190,
192, 194, 199, 202, 214, 216, 218,
222, 238, 244, 246
Mayhew, Governor Thomas, 170
Meinig, D. W., 37
Mekin, Ousa, 17, 36, 39
Menekish, William, 181
Micah Rafe's Father, 228
Mohegan, 12